WITHDRAWN

day trips® from
the twin cities

help us keep this guide up to date

We would love to hear from you concerning your experiences with this guide and how you feel it could be improved and kept up to date. Please send your comments and suggestions to:

editorial@GlobePequot.com

Thanks for your input, and happy travels!

day trips® from the twin cities

first edition

 getaway ideas for the local traveler

lisa meyers mcclintick

travel

Guilford, Connecticut

All the information in this guidebook is subject to change. We recommend that you call ahead to obtain current information before traveling.

To buy books in quantity for corporate use or incentives, call **(800) 962-0973** or e-mail **premiums@GlobePequot.com**.

Editor: Kevin Sirois
Project Editors: Heather Santiago and Lauren Brancato
Layout: Joanna Beyer
Text Design: Linda R. Loiewski
Maps: Mapping Specialists Ltd. © Morris Book Publishing, LLC.
Spot photography throughout licensed by Shutterstock.com

ISBN 978-0-7627-7938-3

Printed in the United States of America
10 9 8 7 6 5 4 3 2 1

contents

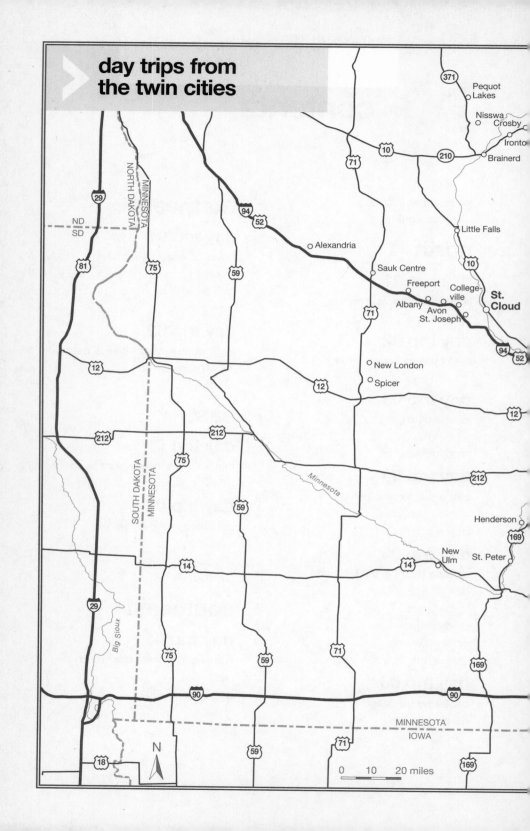

day trips from
the twin cities

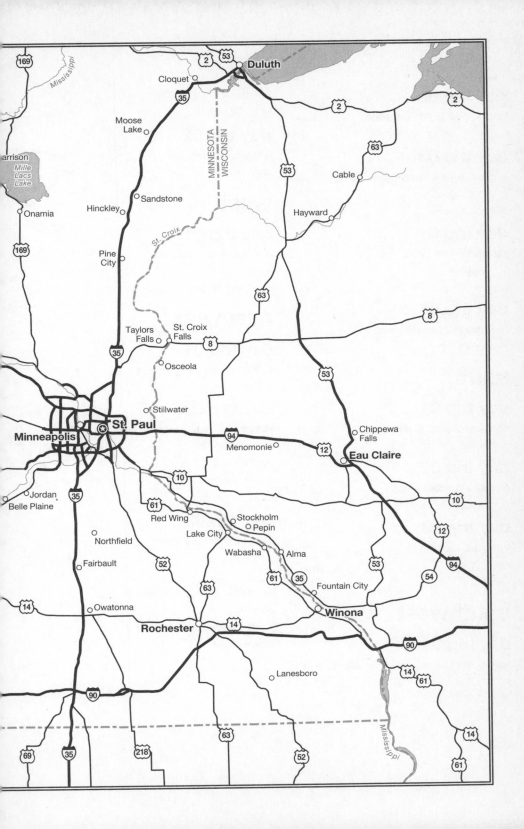

 # about the author

Award-winning writer and photographer Lisa Meyers McClintick contributes to *USA Today*'s *Go Explore* magazine, *Midwest Living,* Minneapolis *Star Tribune, AAA Living,* FamilyVacation Critic.com, and *Timber Home Living.* She wrote the latest edition of *The Dakotas Off the Beaten Path* (Globe Pequot Press, 2010) and created the first Minnesota iPhone travel app, Minnesota Lake Vacations. She also offers travel advice and features destinations throughout Minnesota, South Dakota, Wisconsin, Michigan, and Canada on her website, 10000likes.com.

A Twin Cities native and St. Cloud resident, she speaks to groups about the healing power of travel, budget and family travel, and cultural travel. Her favorite adventures include wildlife and wildflowers, local produce and products, Lake Superior, ethnic areas, hands-on learning, and skiing through the woods or camping with her husband, son, and twin daughters. As a self-confessed nature geek, she's thrilled to live near 70-plus state parks, the mighty Mississippi, and more than 10,000 lakes. See lisamcclintick.com.

 # acknowledgments

Endless gratitude goes to my husband, Bob. He was my first editor at our college newspaper and didn't falter when I left to study abroad in Germany. He's always there to welcome me home, to endure early years of rustic camping, to dream bigger and wander farther, to plunge into family adventures, and to (almost) always be willing to stop for great photos and curious places. You are my home—more than any address we've had.

Hugs, too, to our children, Jonathan, Katie, and Kylie, who gamely hit the road with Mom and offer valuable input, and to my parents, Lyn and Rik, for planting the travel bug early, always offering encouragement, and sharing the great places they discover. To the rest of our extended family and friends—especially the Quartet—know that your support and enthusiasm takes me further than a full tank of gas.

Finally, big cheers to the Minnesota and Wisconsin communities that support creative visions, local talent, and historic sites that elevate beautiful places into fantastic getaways. And thanks to Globe Pequot editor Kevin Sirois for the opportunity to write about them.

>> introduction

I've been lucky. For most of my life I've lived in Minnesota with a few stray years in Hawaii and Germany that helped me appreciate what makes my home state special.

It's really not in a Midwesterner's nature to brag—blame those Scandinavian roots—but within a 2- to 3-hour drive from the Twin Cities you can:

- Reach many of the state's 11,842 inland lakes, plus prime fishing lakes and rivers in Wisconsin.

- Follow the scenic beginnings of the world's fourth greatest river.

- Check into more than 30 state parks, as well as state and national forests and recreation areas with beaches, museums, and trails to paddle, hike, bike, ski, or snowshoe.

- Explore the world's largest freshwater lake and most inland port city.

- Taste the bounty from the farms, orchards, and wineries that grow produce developed especially for this northern climate. Think Honeycrisp apples and Frontenac grapes.

- Savor cheeses made fresh daily or carefully cave-aged.

- Look for bald eagles, deer, black bear, and elusive wolves.

The Twin Cities, which grew around the confluence of the Mississippi, Minnesota, and St. Croix Rivers, is also surrounded by many landscapes. To experience them, hit the road and listen for the hum of history. Feel the heartbeat and rhythm in Dakota and Chippewa drumming and singing. Picture oxcarts and wagons creaking and squeaking across western prairies. Hear the thunk of axes and crack of mighty pines as lumberjacks holler "Timber!" in northern Wisconsin. Touch rustic cabins where Laura Ingalls Wilder and pioneers carved out homes in the Big Woods.

The more you explore, the more the chapters of US history click together. A land of tribes and fur traders gave way to pioneers flooding in from New England, Scandinavia, Germany, and Ireland. Our ancestors were among them, establishing villages in central Wisconsin and along the Minnesota River near New Ulm.

Then came the entrepreneurs: the lumber barons and investors in railroads, shipping, and mining. They all had grand visions, leaving their mark on industry and in grand downtowns and neighborhoods.

What I find most exciting about travel is meeting the people who passionately share the best of their communities. It can be a creative way to share history, a revival of folk arts and handcrafts, or a beautifully restored mansion that welcomes bed-and-breakfast guests. Or maybe it's a heritage farm, orchard, or vineyard that nurtures the harvest or a restaurant that elevates these homegrown ingredients into exquisite meals.

Each season brings a fresh rhythm and palette to totally change even familiar day trips. The steely grays and bare trees of March in Mississippi River Bluff Country are ideal for watching bald eagles soar across the water. But there's magic to the fall when the colors blaze brightly and leaves crackle below your feet on hikes along bluffs.

So grab your keys and a map. Trade the Mall of America for vintage Main Street. Swap your car for a canoe. Wave goodbye to shiny skyscrapers and welcome the glitter of sunshine on a lake and stars in the sky.

If you don't have any lofty goals, that's okay too. Sometimes we just need to get out of Dodge. We all like scenic breathers and a break from day-to-day life. I hope these trips make it easier for you to hit the road.

Now get going and have fun!

>> using this guide

Day Trips from the Twin Cities is organized by general direction from Minneapolis and St. Paul: north, northeast, east, southeast, south, southwest, west, and northwest. It by no means tries to include every worthy destination, but instead highlights 24 trips that appeal to many travelers: families on a budget, adventurers, couples seeking romance and relaxation, girlfriends looking for fun, and history buffs. And, as this is Minnesota (with some parts of western Wisconsin included), most destinations feature lakes or rivers. Each day trip can be reached from downtown Minneapolis or St. Paul within 30 minutes to 3 hours. I have provided directions from downtown Minneapolis to the downtown of each location to start the day trip and then from one destination to the next for the following locations.

hours & prices

Hours and prices are for peak season, which generally runs from Memorial Day through Labor Day. Those times and prices fluctuate with the ebb and flow of tourists (and even the economy), so it's best to call ahead for up-to-date hours, admission, and prices. That's especially true if you are traveling during the shoulder seasons of spring and fall. They're generally great times to score a deal on lodging. And while many destinations thrive when the snow flies, a few shut down for the cold season or a month or two after Christmas.

pricing key

The price codes for accommodations and restaurants are represented as a scale of one to three dollar signs ($). You can assume all establishments listed accept major credit cards unless otherwise noted. For details, contact the locations directly.

restaurants

The price code reflects the average price of dinner entrees for two (excluding cocktails, wine, appetizers, desserts, tax, and tip). You should usually expect to pay less for lunch and/or breakfast, when applicable.

$ $10 to $20
$$ $20 to $40
$$$ more than $40

accommodations

Consider this a gauge of the average cost per night of a double-occupancy room during the peak price period (not including tax or extras). Please also note that in some areas a two-night stay (or more) is required during peak season. Prices may spike during festivals and special events as well. Always check online or call to find out if any discounts are available.

$ less than $100

$$ $100 to $175

$$$ more than $175

travel tips

General Hours of Operation: Hours for restaurants, shops, and attractions are listed for the peak summer season. Because some may close on particular holidays or change hours seasonally, it's best to call ahead before you go.

Seasonal Lodging Deals: In general, traveling Sunday to Wednesday any season is more affordable than over weekends, and shoulder seasons typically offer the best discounts with the exception of holidays. If you want summer discounts, book in early June or the last two weeks of August. Winter, too, can offer affordable escapes, except at places that thrive on skiing, snowmobiling, and ice fishing.

Remember that summer in the Midwest does not always mean hot and sunny; plan a few rainy-day options and bring warm layers of clothing just in case. For fall foliage trips, color usually peaks in northern Minnesota by the last week of September and early to mid-October for central and southern Minnesota. It varies year to year based on weather, but you can check Department of Natural Resources websites or with local visitor centers for up-to-date information.

Sales Tax: Minnesota sales tax is generally 6.5 percent, but can go up to 7.5 percent in some cities. Clothing and groceries are exempt. Wisconsin sales taxes are generally 5 to 5.5 percent.

Hotels rarely include tax or gratuities in their published rates. Such items will sometimes raise a hotel rate by more than 12 percent.

If you are near the Wisconsin border and need to tank up, Minnesota's gas prices generally run a dime cheaper per gallon.

Selected Lodging & Restaurants: Most destinations offer chain hotels and restaurants, which are generally not included in the listings in each chapter, as they operate on standards that are similar across the country. The lodging and restaurant options highlighted are typically local to the area.

driving tips

While we like to rely on GPS for navigation these days, it's unfortunately not always accurate or reliable, especially in more remote areas. I recommend that you plan your route before you head out and take along a Minnesota highway map or (even better) a detailed state atlas.

- Remember that while speed limits are up to 70 mph on rural interstates, they drop down to 55–60 mph as you near city limits.

- Law enforcement doubles the fines for speeding if you're caught in a construction zone. Check online to be prepared for detours, slowdowns, and lower speed limits. Reroute if needed.

- Thousands of accidents are caused each year by deer crossing the roads. The collisions mostly cause vehicle damage, but they can be fatal especially for motorcyclists.

- Watch carefully along roadways, especially ones marked with deer crossing signs, those in wooded areas, or roads that have forest on one side and crops on the other.

- Try to avoid driving during peak times of dawn and dusk. Watch for shadowy movements or the flash of headlights in a deer's eyes.

- Be especially vigilant in late May to early June when fawns are out and in the peak collision months of October and November when crop harvests, deer hunting, and rutting season have more deer on the move.

- If you see a deer, don't swerve! Losing control of a vehicle often leads to more damage than the collision would. Apply brakes immediately and honk your horn.

- For winter trips watch for fog, mist, drifting snow, ice, and the more nebulous black ice that forms from car exhaust at major intersections.

- Give yourself extra time to travel and allow more space between your vehicle and others in winter.

- Do not crowd snowplow crews clearing highways.

- Keep jumper cables in your trunk or ask resorts about electric battery plug-ins during winter's coldest months.

- Keep your windshield fluid reservoir filled during the slushy winter meltdown.

- Maintain good tire pressure and treads that also help during sleet storms or early summer downpours.

- Watch weather forecasts and check road conditions before heading out at www.511mn .org or www.511wi.gov.

highway designations

Major highways will be listed in this book in terms of their numbered designations, with a few secondary references used most often by residents such as Highway 61, which is known as the North Shore Scenic Byway along Lake Superior or the Great River Road south of Red Wing. Outside of the city, there are a lot of addresses with CR, which stands for County Road.

where to get more information

Day Trips attempts to cover a variety of bases and interests, but if you're looking for additional material, there is plenty out there. Most states and cities, and even some smaller towns, have their own tourism bureaus, so for most trips, you'll find them listed as a first "Where to Go" location since they are a good place to start, often offering comprehensive websites and welcoming calls, e-mails, or requests for printed visitor guides, brochures, and maps. In addition to the resources in this book, some additional sources of information include:

minnesota

Minnesota Office of Tourism

121 7th Place East
Metro Square, Ste. 100
St. Paul, MN 55101
(651) 296-5029, (800) 657-3700
www.exploreminnesota.com

Minnesota Department of Natural Resources

500 Lafayette Rd.
St. Paul, MN 55155-4040
(651) 296-6157, (888) 646-6367
www.dnr.state.mn.us

Minnesota Historical Society

345 W. Kellogg Blvd.
St. Paul, MN 55102-1906
(651) 259-3000
www.mnhs.org

Minnesota Department of Agriculture
625 Robert St. North
St. Paul, MN 55155-2538
(651) 201-6539
www.minnesotagrown.com

wisconsin

Wisconsin Department of Natural Resources
101 S. Webster St.
PO Box 7921
Madison, WI 53707-7921
(888) 936-7463, (608) 266-2621
http://dnr.wi.gov

Wisconsin Department of Tourism
201 W. Washington Ave.
PO Box 8690
Madison, WI 53708-8690
(800) 432-8747, (608) 266-2161
www.travelwisconsin.com

Wisconsin Historical Society
816 State St.
Madison, WI 53706
www.wisconsinhistory.org

north

day trip 01

north

lindbergh's hometown:
little falls, mn

little falls, mn

One of world's first megacelebrities, Charles Lindbergh, grew up in modest Little Falls, a town of about 8,500 along the Mississippi River. He watched the skies, took apart engines, and fearlessly explored the land long before making the world's first solo flight across the Atlantic Ocean in 1927. You can tour his home and hear about his unusual boyhood just south of downtown. An adjacent museum looks at Lindbergh's many (and often surprising) accomplishments.

But there's much more than Lindbergh in Little Falls. The town as a whole stands out as a dreamy destination for history buffs, lovers of classic main streets, and anyone who enjoys following the mighty Mississippi River along its wilder stretches.

The river played a key role in helping the town flourish as logging boomed and logs were floated downriver. That early success left a legacy of gracious Victorian homes on picturesque streets. Today the river thunders across a hydroelectric dam with enough power to light up Duluth.

A word of advice: If you plan a visit the second weekend in September, expect to fight a crowd but get all your holiday shopping done. The Little Falls Arts & Crafts Fair ranks among the largest in the Midwest and among the most legendary shows in Minnesota. There are more than 600 juried exhibitors, 40 vendors, and continual shuttles to get visitors from fairgrounds parking to artsy fun.

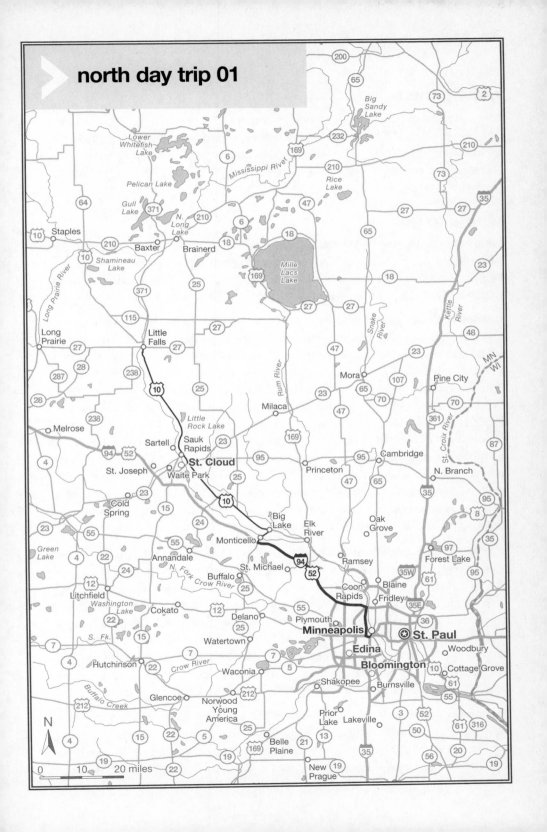

getting there

Take I-94 about 38 miles from Minneapolis to Monticello. Exit at MN 25. Go right (northeast) into town for about 3.5 miles, crossing the Mississippi River and heading to Big Lake. Go left (northwest) on US 10 for 57 miles until you reach Little Falls. Exit at MN 27/1st Avenue Northeast and turn left to reach downtown. Total trip: About 95 miles, an hour and 50 minutes.

where to go

Little Falls Convention and Visitors Bureau. 606 SE 1st St.; (320) 616-4959; www.little fallsmn.com. Grab a community guide here and get a glimpse of historic elegance in Little Falls at the 1903 Burton/Rosenmeier House built in the Classical Revival style. Guests are welcome to walk upstairs and peek into a few rooms furnished with period furniture and art.

Charles A. Lindbergh Historic Site. 1620 Lindbergh Dr. South; (320) 616-5421; www .mnhs.org/lindbergh. Walk in the footsteps of Charles Lindbergh at his boyhood home 1.4 miles south of Little Falls. Minnesota Historical Society interpreters lead seasonal tours of his home, pointing out what fueled his thirst for adventure. Even his habit of sleeping on the cold screen porch most of the year helped acclimate him to freezing altitudes when flying.

The adjacent visitor center stays open year-round with exhibits on Lindbergh's marriage to author Anne Morrow, the infamous kidnapping of their son, their joint role in mapping Pan Am routes, his controversial stance against the US entering World War II, and his groundbreaking medical inventions and work for environmental groups. Don't miss the full-size replica of his famous plane *Spirit of St. Louis*. These facilities are open Memorial Day weekend through Labor Day weekend Thurs through Sat 10 a.m. to 5 p.m. and Sun noon to 5 p.m. Prearranged group tours are available at other times. Admission: $8, adults; $7, seniors/students; $6, children 6–17; and free for kids 5 and under.

Charles A. Lindbergh State Park. 1615 Lindbergh Dr. South; (320) 616-2525; www .dnr.state.mn.us/state_parks/charles_a_lindbergh. Charles Lindbergh used to roam these woods and build bridges across Pike Creek, which flows through this 436-acre park and empties into the Mississippi River. He donated the land to the state in 1931 in memory of his father, Charles Lindbergh Sr. You can hike along the creek, watch for spring wildflowers, listen for songbirds among the oak and conifer, camp at 38 sites, enjoy the WPA picnic grounds and a playground, or seek geocaching boxes stashed throughout the park. The Lindbergh Historic Site, as well as trails along the Mississippi River, sits right across the road. Open daily. State park entrance fee: $5 per vehicle or $25 for an annual permit.

Downtown & Riverfront. Broadway Avenue and 1st Street; (320) 616-4959. Ask for a history guide at the visitor center, and then stroll through downtown. It's especially fun for families with young children. They can watch trains rumble past the Cass Gilbert train depot and explore shady pathways along the Mississippi. Downtown's brick storefronts were built in the late 1800s and house a hip restaurant, bustling bakery/cafe, boutiques, a vintage movie theater, and a bookstore.

The Minnesota Fishing Museum. 304 W. Broadway; (320) 616-2011; www.mnfishing museum.com. The wooden dock-like walkway and boat for a counter provide just a hint of the Minnesota fishing history packed into this museum. Why here in a river town? For one thing, it's only 30 minutes to the famed fishing waters of the Brainerd Lakes area, plus Little Falls was once home to Larson boat manufacturing. The museum does a surprisingly good job incorporating all aspects of Minnesota's favorite sport. Exhibits encompass motors and boats, spearfishing, ice fishing, fly fishing in southern Minnesota's trout rivers, and even the best catch from Lake Superior. Among the quirkier items: "Old Fish," a massive muskie that weighed more than 40 pounds. As a legendary catch along the Mississippi, locals would keep tossing him back until his fatal encounter with the dam. Summer hours: Tues through Sat 10 a.m. to 5 p.m., noon to 4 p.m. Sun. Call for off-season hours. Admission $4, adults; $3, students and seniors; free, age 9 and under.

Minnesota Military Museum. 15000 MN 115, Camp Ripley; (320) 616-6050; www.minne sotanationalguard.org/camp_ripley/museum. The 53,000-acre Fort Ripley has been a hub for training Minnesota's soldiers since the early days of maintaining peace on the frontier. This museum offers an intriguing glimpse of military might and soldiers' lives from those early days to the National Guard's key role in war across the globe. Outside exhibits include tanks and Jeeps, while inside exhibits display uniforms, photos, weapons, awards, and other artifacts. Open May through Sept 10 a.m. to 5 p.m. daily (except national holidays). Open 9 a.m. to 4 p.m. Thurs and Fri Oct through Apr. Admission: $5, adults; $2, children 6–16; free to military in active service.

Pine Grove Zoo. 1200 W. Broadway; (320) 616-5595; www.pinegrovezoo.com. This little zoo about 10 blocks west of the Mississippi River features a surprising number of big animals: tigers, wolves, elk, bobcat, and bears. It's especially idyllic for kids under 8, who get overwhelmed (or exhausted) by larger zoos. It takes about an hour to see this one, depending on how long you watch prairie dogs popping up and down in their holes or whether you stumble upon extra entertainment, such as wild turkeys trying to cavort with ones in captivity. Newer exhibits include expanded bear enclosures and a log cabin that displays a mount of "Lucky," a wolf from the nearby Camp Ripley pack who (despite his name) got hit by a car in 2006. Wolves are among the Minnesota species making a comeback. Don't miss the free Pine Grove picnic area and playground, which is awash in white trillium in May and always shady and fragrant beneath some of the most impressive pines you'll see. Go early or later in the day, if possible, to see zoo animals when they are most active. Open mid-Apr through mid-Oct. Admission: $5. Free for children age 3 and under.

Soo Line Recreation Trail. www.littlefallsmn.com/recreation.php. Hop onto this bike trail for a memorable trestle bridge ride high above the Blanchard Dam and Mississippi River.

The views are spectacular, especially in the fall. This former railway route runs east to west. Start at the trailhead just off US 10 and head west toward the small town of Bowlus. If you're a gonzo bicyclist, the Soo Line Trail connects with the 46-mile Lake Wobegon Trail in Holdingford. If you want a shorter ride, there are a few parking spots by the dam on either side of the river. They aren't well marked, so keep an eye open. If you take an old strainer to the east bank below the dam, you may get lucky and find a staurolite (also known as fairy stones or cross rocks) in the silt.

where to shop

Ambience@53. 302 1st St. Southeast; (320) 632-0484. This boutique's arched brick facade, blue doors, and window boxes at the edge of downtown beckon shoppers to peruse seasonal decor and housewares, from cookie cutters and fun tablecloths, to cast-iron gadgets and brightly patterned dishes. It also carries a kids' and baby section and fashionable clothes, shawls, and jewelry for women.

Bookin' It. 104B 2nd St. Southeast; (320) 632-1848; www.bookinitontheweb.com. Warm and homey, the rooms of this independent bookstore invite readers to linger over intriguing displays and recommendations. They range from seasonal home canning and regional authors to medical fiction and the most playful picture books for kids. Tin ceilings and wood floors add to its main street kind of charm. If you're on a budget, you can find some used books, too.

Great River Arts Association. 122 1st St. Southeast; (320) 632-0960; www.greatart .org. Suncatchers, playful mobiles, glass sculptures, pottery, paintings, and photography by more than 50 regional artists make this a colorful downtown stop. You also might catch a house concert here in the fall and winter or Sunday afternoons at Maple Island Park throughout the summer.

Thielen Meats. 300 NE 13th St.; (320) 632-2821; www.thielenmeatslf.com. If you're heading to lake country or home with a cooler, swing into this bustling, popular meat market for their bacon. Other goodies here include double-smoked picnic ham, Amish chickens, summer sausage and steaks, chorizo, smoked fish, turkey jerky, kraut brats, grilling glazes, and hamburger premixed with Vidalia onions, blue cheese, or wild rice.

where to eat

A.T. The Black and White. 116 SE 1st St.; (320) 632-5374; www.attheblacknwhite .com. This downtown institution built a reputation on great burgers for more than 75 years, but has added a more eclectic and tasty variety of gourmet options in the past couple of years. Think blueberry crepes and crab omelets for breakfast, almond-crusted walleye with strawberry-blueberry salsa and risotto, coconut curry noodles, and chicken roulade. Desserts range from chocolate mousse draped with ganache and strawberry sauce to specials such as bananas Foster, dramatically lit on fire. There's a great local feel with the decor: a rescued Rexall drugstore sign, massive "Airport" sign from the town's former drive-in movie theater, and vintage photos galore. It's come-as-you-are meets date night. $$

Jordie's. 105 1st Ave. South, Bowlus; (320) 584-8193. This cafe southwest of Little Falls provides a perfect stopping point for bikers on the Soo Line Trail or road-trippers on the Great River Road. Eat inside or outside in the garden. Or order a lunch to go for picnics by the Blanchard Dam. Leave room for pie. $

Pete & Joy's Bakery. 121 E. Broadway; (320) 632-6388. Little Falls's sweetest destination would be worth a stop as a bakery alone, but it ups the ante with a homey, affordable cafe. Expect to linger awhile. Temptations are everywhere: at least five kinds of brownies, homemade fudge and peanut brittle, fish-shaped cookies, dense bread made with cranberries, wild rice and walnuts, big fritters, and sticky orange blossoms. You can sense the area's Polish roots, too, with its line of blue-and-white Polish pottery, kolaches, lunch specials such as Polish sausage and dumplings, and savory soups. They even bake homemade dog treats, so no member of the family is forgotten. $

where to stay

Waller House Inn B&B. 301 3rd St. Southeast; (320) 632-2836; www.wallerhouseinn .com. This bed-and-breakfast painted don't-miss-me purple lets visitors enjoy the rich Victorian legacy of Little Falls's lumber boom and the skills of a professional baker. Choose from five guest rooms, often decorated to match stained-glass windows. Feast on breakfasts such as stuffed apricot french toast or a wedge of crispy cheesy hash brown pie flecked with locally smoked bacon and fresh herbs. $$

day trip 02

north

paul bunyan & family fun:
brainerd, mn

brainerd, mn

When Minnesotans say they're going "Up North," they're usually heading toward Brainerd. The main attraction? Close to 400 lakes that have made this area the state's top getaway for the past century. Families can easily find a resort and lake to fit their style, from a place that's small and intimate for paddling, pontoon rides, and spontaneous potlucks to sprawling resorts with waterskiing, wakeboarding, and trophy fish to catch.

It's a destination for building big family memories. Just ask any adult who experienced Paul Bunyan Land as a kid. No one forgets the shock of a 26-foot-tall lumberjack who greets everyone by name! The popular amusement park still uses the gimmick to delight new generations.

Families seeking more than a beach and a boat for entertainment can round out vacation plans with minigolf, go-karts, water parks, and full-throttle fun at the racetrack.

When winter arrives, Brainerd rolls out snowmobiling, dogsled rides, skating, hockey rinks, and the world's largest ice-fishing contest.

getting there

Take I-94 to MN 15, exiting at Monticello. Head east just over 3 miles, crossing the Mississippi and connecting with US 10 as you reach Big Lake. Follow US 10/MN 15 north for 60

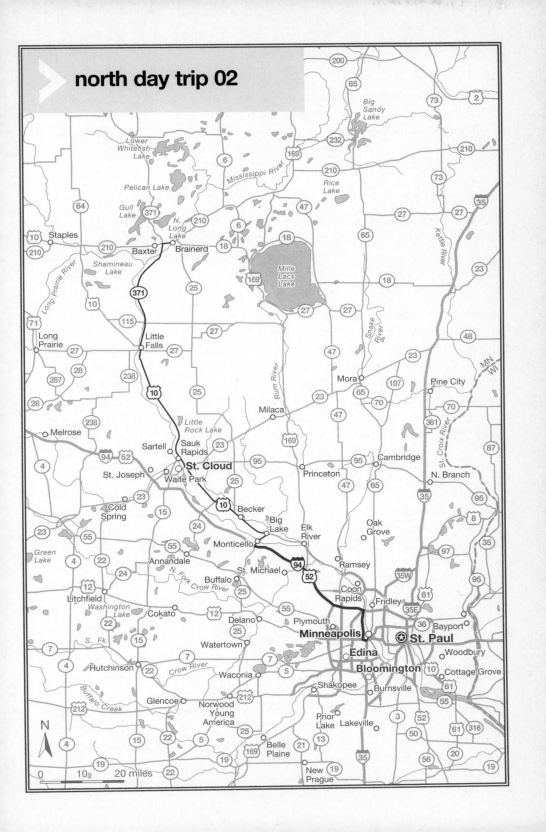

north day trip 02

miles until the highway splits. Stay right on US 10 and follow it to MN 371 to Brainerd. It blurs together with the city of Baxter on its west side.

Word of advice: Travel midweek if you can. Leave early for summer weekend get-aways or pack your patience. Cabin traffic can be heavy as Twin Citians flood north and home again on Sunday.

where to go

Brainerd Lakes Area Welcome Center. 7393 MN 371 South; (800) 450-2838; www .explorebrainerdlakes.com. With a visitor center floor that literally maps out the area's lakes, this is an ideal place to start your trip. This rest stop on an island between the lanes of the highway stays well stocked with brochures and a smattering of souvenirs. Don't forget to take a photo with Paul Bunyan out front.

Brainerd International Raceway. 5523 Birchdale Rd.; (866) 444-4455; www.brainerd raceway.com. Brainerd rumbles revs into a racing frenzy every August when it hosts the Lucas Oil NHRA Nationals. More than 100,000 people pack the raceway for the full-throttle legendary action. It's often cited as one of the favorite stops for race teams and fans alike because of on-site camping at what's affectionately called "The Zoo." The more-than-40-year-old BIR hosts events throughout the summer, including motorcycle and dragster races or the more laid-back bracket races. Bracket races are affordable amateur races with every imaginable vehicle from hot rods to snowmobiles. It's just as much fun to go behind the track and admire the vehicles up close. If you really love cars, check out BIR's driving school. Instructors give professional racing lessons or teach you how to handle your own car better to prevent accidents.

Gull Lake Recreational Area. 10867 E. Gull Lake Dr.; (218) 829-3334, www.recreation .gov. Tucked away in the woods, this federally run campground includes a public beach, fishing pier, boat launch, picnic area and grills, and the popular East Gull Lake Trail, which is paved for 7 miles. Most people don't realize it's also on the National Register of Historic Places—not for the 1912 dam, but for the 12 complete burial mounds and several partial ones that date back to the Woodland Culture and an ancient village along the lake.

Paul Bunyan Land and This Old Farm. 17553 MN 18; (218) 764-2524; www.paulbunyan land.com. If there could be one icon for generations of Brainerd-bound vacationers, award that title to this tallest-of-them-all Paul Bunyan. He greets visitors by name as they head into this amusement park that's like a summerlong county fair. You'll be lucky if your head reaches the knees of this giant. He sat for decades near the main intersection of MN 371 and MN 210 until the attraction moved to a more peaceful setting 8 miles east of Brainerd and joined with This Old Farm. You can spend half the day with bumper cars, the Ferris wheel, kiddie train, and other rides and the other half wandering the 20 historic buildings at This Old Farm Village. The astonishingly large collection features everything from pioneer

bring on winter fun

While biking, golfing, and boating rule the summer, don't overlook the exhilaration of winter fun. Stop at the Brainerd Lakes Area Welcome Center or check online for maps.

Snowmobiling

About 1,200 miles of trails radiate through the Brainerd area. For distance and a smooth ride, head across Gull Lake and catch the Paul Bunyan Trail near Nisswa. It's a 50-mile cruise to Walker and Leech Lake or about a 6-hour round-trip with lunch stop. Find more challenging loop trails through the Pillsbury State Forest. Cragun's Resort has the state's largest fleet of snowmobiles plus full gear to rent.

Cross-country Skiing

You'll find about 240 miles of Nordic ski trails throughout the area. The best-groomed trails are at Northland Arboretum. It doesn't hold the same charm as being in a state park (you'll likely hear traffic from Brainerd's nearby commercial district), but you can glide through oak and birch trees and into a heavy pine forest. Three miles are lit for nighttime skiing. Look for the beaver hut on the Potlatch Trail or choose the gentler Acorn Trail. A daily pass and parking come to $3. 14250 Conservation Dr., Baxter; (218) 829-8770; http://northlandarb.com.

You'll also need a Minnesota Ski Pass for $6/day or $20/season. Buy one online at www.dnr.state.mn.us, by phone at (888) 665-4236, or pick one up at Mills Fleet Farm, 14114 Dellwood Dr., Baxter; (218) 829-1565.

Another popular option: Pine Beach cross-country ski trails, a network of half-mile to 3.5-mile loops that cross the Legacy and Classic golf courses, circle Cragun's and Kavanaugh's properties, and stretch into Pillsbury State Forest.

Downhill Skiing

Ski Gull offers 12 runs, a terrain park, and tubing hill on the west side of Gull Lake. It's an ideal place to learn with gentle terrain and lessons from the staff at this community-run nonprofit organization. Open weekends and holidays throughout the winter. Lift tickets start at $15. 9898 CR 77, Nisswa; (218) 963-4353; www .skigull.com.

school rooms and a set piece from the movie *Iron Will* to classic cars and gas pumps. Altogether, it's a sunny dose of nostalgia and a multigenerational family pleaser. Open daily 10 a.m. to 6 p.m. Memorial Day through Labor Day. Adults admission is $12.95; kids 2–18, $14.95; seniors, $11.95.

Paul Bunyan Trail. Brainerd to Bemidji; www.paulbunyantrail.com. This close to 100-mile trail provides a biker and snowmobiler's paradise, letting them zip between 14 towns along the easy grade of this former railway line. Each year, an estimated 650,000 people use the trail as it heads through forest and along lakes. It has also been named among the top 25 of the country's 1,600 Rails-to-Trails projects. Find parking and trail access spots in Merrifield, Nisswa, Pequot Lakes, Jenkins, Pine River, Backus, Hackensack, and Walker. Need a bike? Rent one in downtown Brainerd or Nisswa. If you want to try out just one section of trail, try the 7 miles from Nisswa to Pequot Lakes. Hard-core biking warriors can connect to the Heartland Trail, as well, for an additional 49 miles.

Pirate's Cove. 17992 MN 371 North; (218) 828-9002; www.piratescove.com. This souped-up, swashbuckling minigolf course is one of 14 in the nation and the only one in Minnesota. Its holes lead players through caves (watch out for the water hazards!), across a pirate ship, over footbridges, under waterfalls, and past a battle scene where a cannon occasionally booms. It goes pretty fast, but make sure to read the pirate facts and history scattered throughout the course. This is a great family destination, but the holes are challenging—and entertaining—enough for adults. I prefer the Captain's Course to Blackbeard's Challenge, but you can get a combo deal for all 36 holes. There also are combo tickets for the adjacent Billy Bones Raceway, which continues the pirate theme. Only 3 blocks south of Brainerd International Raceway, it's tough to resist getting behind the wheel of a go-kart. Open the last week in Apr through the third week in Oct. Hours from Memorial Day through Labor Day are 10 a.m. to 11 p.m. One course: $7.50–$7.95; 36 holes: $12.95–$13.95.

where to eat

The Chocolate Ox. 25452 Main St., Nisswa; (218) 963-4443; www.thechocolateox.com. Loaded with nostalgic candy and soda pop, gourmet chocolates, jelly beans, jawbreakers, licorice, and ice cream, don't expect to get in and out of this popular stop quickly. Temptations are everywhere. Closed in the winter. $.

Ernie's On Gull. 10424 Squaw Point Rd., East Gull Lake; (218) 829-3918; www.ernieson gull.com. This restaurant and full-service marina tucked along a Gull Lake peninsula welcomes diners arriving by car, boat, or snowmobile. Look for burgers, mahimahi fish tacos, walleye po'boy, or fancier dinners such as lobster bisque and coconut shrimp with amaretto sauce. Open 11 a.m. to 10 p.m., bar until 2 a.m. $$.

Matty's Saloon. 18071 MN 371; (218) 454-1781; www.mattyssaloon.com. With a loyal local following—especially for its burgers—Matty's outgrew its original humble location on Gull Lake Road. Its new restaurant now sits along MN 371, making room for dining and its artsy decor. $$.

Prairie Bay. 15115 Edgewood Dr.; (218) 824-6444; www.prairiebay.com. For adults who love gourmet food but want a place where kids are welcome, Prairie Bay offers meals with tasty, creative twists. Even the kids' pizzas are wood-fired. Try the Big Fat Greek Pizza, smoked chicken strudel, slow-roasted duck confit with lavender aioli, braised beef short ribs, and Minnesota artisan cheese plates. If you're on a budget, the $10 lunches are the best bet, and there are 12 meals for $12 from 3 to 5:30 p.m. $$.

Zorbaz. 8105 Lost Lake Rd., Nisswa; (218) 963-4790; www.zorbaz.com. This popular up-north pizza chain sits along Gull Lake's Causeway with a steady parade of boats puttering by. They have all the expected pizzas, along with a Greek chicken pizza, one inspired by a Reuben sandwich, and a Thai-spiced creation with bacon, onions, pineapple, and banana peppers. Wash them down with one of 48 beers. If it's warm, grab a spot on the patio, join a beach volleyball game, or kick back to music provided by a DJ or band. $–$$.

where to stay

Cragun's Resort. 11000 Craguns Dr.; (800) 272-4867; www.craguns.com. Dark brown with teal alpine trim, this venerable and sprawling resort encompasses 260 units along a generous stretch of Gull Lake. Besides its history and size, the depth of year-round activities, lakeside outdoor pool and sundeck, indoor pool and play area, and lauded golf courses such as The Legacy make this resort stand out. Staff offer guided fishing, golf lessons, a summer kids' camp, waterskiing sessions, and organize welcome receptions and socials. You can also rent just about anything here: bikes, wakeboards, boats, snowmobiles, ice houses, skates, and more. Also noteworthy: lake views from the dining room and lakeside rooms with real wood fireplaces. $$–$$$.

Gull Lake Dam Campground. 10867 E. Gull Lake Dr.; (218) 829-3334; www.reserve america.com. You'll find 37 sites here, each with 30-to-50 amp electric hookups, along with flush toilets, showers, a playground, trails, and a beach open May through Sept. $.

Kavanaugh's Sylvan Lake Resort. 1685 Kavanaugh Dr., East Gull Lake; (800) 562-7061; www.kavanaughs.com. With a blend of 52 units, mostly lakeside condos and luxury cottages, this resort is big enough for tennis courts, playgrounds, and indoor and outdoor pools, but small enough not to be overwhelming. Sylvan Lake is quieter than Gull Lake. It has the area's most romantic skating rink and easy access to Nordic ski trails and golf courses. $$$.

> ## world's largest ice-fishing contest

*Put this on your bucket list: Witness or join in the world's largest charitable ice-fishing contest. The Brainerd Jaycees drill more than 10,000 holes into Gull Lake's **Hole in the Day Bay**. The pure spectacle of that many holes, huge prizes (think trucks and snowmobiles), and a festive atmosphere lures about 7,000 anglers from across the country and beyond. The annual **Brainerd Jaycees $150,000 Ice-Fishing Extravaganza** also draws about 2,000 spectators (www .icefishing.org). Dress smart and in layers. Boot- and hand-warmers help. The show goes on even with below-zero temperatures and wicked windchills.*

*In mid-February, Walker, about 60 miles north of Brainerd, hosts its annual **Eelpout Festival.** Leech Lake turns into a weekend city on ice with creative (and occasionally bawdy) ice houses, encampments, and even a bikini contest. Consider it a chilly version of spring break, meant to banish cabin fever and thumb a nose at winter (www.eelpoutfestival.com).*

Ice houses generally need to be off Minnesota lakes by the end of February, although daytime use is allowed later into the season.

The Lodge at Brainerd Lakes. 6967 Lake Forest Rd., Baxter; (218) 822-5634; www .lodgehotels.com. A Paul Bunyan–themed water park and comfy red rooms with outdoorsy names and log cabin decor make this hotel an easy family getaway. The water park features two programmable holographic slides that project illusions and sound effects onto cascades of water. Kids can slide past sharks, soothing butterflies, or through brick walls. An arcade and snack bar are on-site, but more satisfying meals are served at The Lodge Grill and Bar. Each room also has microwaves and minifridges for preparing simple meals. Specialty suites include a cinema suite, kitchen suite, and kids' suite with bunks and 3-D murals. Water park open daily June through Aug. Check the website for hours Sept through May. $.

Madden's. 11266 Pine Beach Peninsula Rd.; (218) 829-2811; www.maddens.com. Like nearby Cragun's, three-season Madden's ranks among the area's most legendary and largest resorts. Its 287 units (hotel rooms, condos, villas, and cabins) sprawl across Pine Beach Peninsula on 1,500 acres with enough to do that most guests don't bother leaving—especially if they're on the meal plan with seven eateries and restaurants. Golfers come for The Classic and three additional courses. Other activities including a summer Adventure Cove for kids, lawn bowling, croquet, tennis, trail rides, waterskiing and wakeboarding lessons, guided fishing, biking, and even seaplane certification. The newest activity, paddleboarding lessons, was added in 2011. At Madden's Spalon Montage, guests can get pedicures and manicures while gazing at the lake or settle in for massage and body treatments. Lodging ranges from 1920s hotel rooms and beachside units to luxury golf villas and supersize reunion houses. $$$.

Train Bell Resort. CR 3, Merrifield; (800) 252-2102; www.trainbellresort.com. This smaller old-fashioned family resort has been chugging along for more than a century, specializing in lighthearted themed activities throughout the summer. Think *Fear Factor* challenges, Rock 'n' Roll Week, and a Hawaiian luau, along with ongoing fun such as outdoor movies. Cabins and villas sit between the North Long Lake Beach and Paul Bunyan Bike Trails. $$$.

day trip 03

north

lakeland luxuries:
nisswa, mn; pequot lakes, mn

World-class golfing, classic cabins, luxurious resorts, funky shopping, and a cozy spa beckon vacationers to keep driving beyond Brainerd. Small towns are at their peak during summer when they hum with festivals and weekly events that lure people off the lakes. When summer crowds disperse and kids head back to school, autumn offers an ideal time for romantic escapes, man-cations, and girlfriend getaways—especially for golfers who want a swing at fall color. Winter weekends also are popular times for lodging deals, scrapbooking or craft retreats, snowy recreation, and a chance to recharge after hectic holidays.

nisswa, mn

Nisswa's concentrated downtown rules as the area's top shopping destination. It's classy enough to keep big-city shoppers happy, but down-to-earth, too. Look for Paul Bunyan on the totem pole if you've always wanted a lumberjack-themed lunchbox and Minnetonka moccasins.

You'll see turtles all over town as well in a nod to Nisswa's almost 50-year tradition of turtle races at 2 p.m. every Wednesday from mid-June through mid-August. You can bring your own turtle, pick one from a bucket, or just enjoy cheering them on for an old-fashioned afternoon.

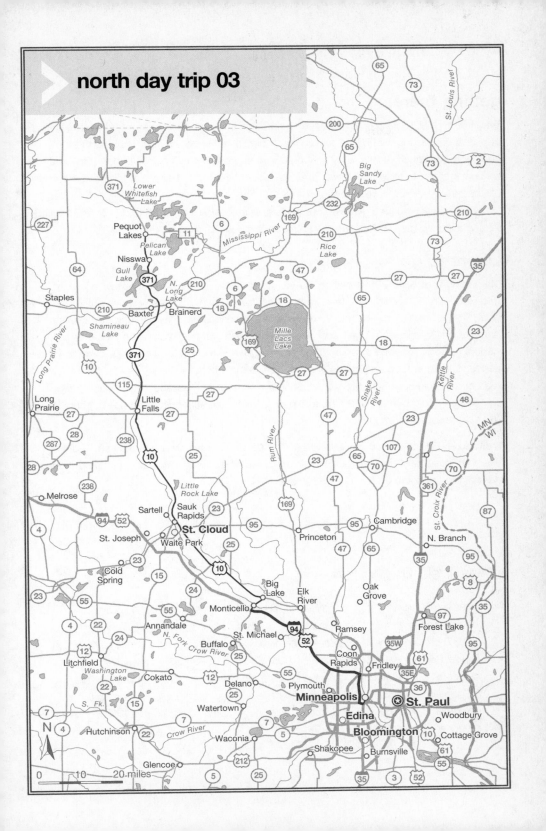

getting there

Take I-94 to MN 15, exiting at Monticello. Head east just over 3 miles, crossing the Mississippi and connecting with US 10 as you reach Big Lake. Follow US 10/MN 15 north for 60 miles until the highway splits. Stay right on US 10 and follow it to MN 371 through Brainerd continuing north to Nisswa. Nisswa is about 20 miles north of Brainerd at the intersection CR 18, which leads into downtown.

It's about 2.5 hours to Nisswa, but will take longer if you leave on a Friday or return on a Sunday during the summer when "cabin traffic" clogs US 10 and I-94.

where to go

Glacial Waters Spa. 23521 Nokomis Ave.; (218) 963-8756; www.grandviewlodge.com. This stand-alone Arts and Crafts–style spa based at Grandview Resort stays busy year-round. The classy woodwork and warm fireplaces feel especially cozy during winter. Guests can take an 85-minute fragrant soak in a private room with a fireplace and view of surrounding woods, followed by an hour-long massage. A spa cabin allows groups of up to 10 friends to bring in food and drinks and get treatments without following the hushed-voice code of the main spa. Services start at $65 for a 30-minute massage. Open Mon through Sat 8:30 a.m. to 8 p.m., Sun: 9 a.m. to 5 p.m. In winter the schedule cuts back to Thurs to Sun. Call for off-season hours.

Trailblazer Bikes. 25336 Smiley Rd.; (218) 963-0699; www.trailblazermn.com. Rent a bike right along the 112-mile Paul Bunyan Trail for a cruise to Pequot Lakes to the north or Merrifield to the south ($10/hour or $30/day).

get help finding fish

*If you're new to fishing, want to learn new techniques, or simply don't know where to go with 400-plus lakes within a 30-mile radius, a fishing guide can help. There are at least a handful in the area. One of the biggest is **Walleye Dan Guide Service** (9287 Anderson Rd., Lake Shore; 218-839-5598; www.walleye dan.com). Guides keep tabs on the local fishing scene as it fluxes throughout the four seasons and with daily weather conditions. They also supply the boat, bait, equipment, and expertise for a tasty—or trophy—catch. Rates start at $295 for a 4-hour trip and up to three people.*

where to shop

Here's a sampling of fun places in Nisswa's tightly packed, bustling downtown. Some are seasonal and close for the winter. Others open for winter weekends, and a few are steady six to seven days a week year-round. If you are visiting off-season, verify hours first.

Appaloosa Ridge. 25446 Main St.; (218) 963-7955. Look for cabin-themed home decor such as dishes, rugs, lamps, and candles, along with souvenir shirts and sweatshirts— including ones that commemorate girlfriend getaways. Open year-round.

Lundrigan's. 25521 Main St.; (218) 963-2647; www.lundrigansclothing.com. This store full of stylish, cabin-comfy men's and women's clothing has become an up-north fixture. This location includes an outlet section for off-season sale items. You'll find everything from Woolrich flannels and Norwegian wool sweaters to breezy Santiki dresses for summers on the dock. Open year-round 9:30 a.m. to 5:30 p.m. Mon through Sat and 11 a.m. to 4 p.m. Apr through Jan.

Martin's Sports Shop. 25451 Main St.; (218) 963-2341. Look for the alpine-themed building with flags, and you'll find four seasons' worth of sports equipment, along with breathable, warm clothing and gear. Rent bikes, in-line skates, tennis rackets, water skis, wakeboards, snowshoes, and cross-country skis. Open 9 a.m. to 9 p.m. Mon through Fri, 9 a.m. to 6 p.m. Sat, and 10 to 4 p.m. Sun Memorial Day through Labor Day. Shop closes earlier in the off-season and closes on Sun Jan 1 through spring.

Rebecca's. 25458 Main St.; (218) 963-0165; www.rebeccasdolls.com. This undeniably girly pink storefront brings together vintage collectibles (such as Barbies and toys), every-thing imaginable for dollhouses, purses aplenty, and pop-culture fun from *I Love Lucy* mem-orabilia to life-size cutouts of teen hotties. Open 10 a.m. to 5 p.m. Memorial Day weekend through Labor Day. Call for off-season hours. Closed Jan through Mar.

Totem Pole. 25485 Main St.; (218) 506-5244; www.totempolemn.com. If this souvenir shop feels a little old school, that's part of the appeal. It's been a mainstay in Nisswa's downtown since 1947, and there are still a few vintage automatons out front. It's the top seller of Minnetonka moccasins, slippers, and sheepskin boots with up to 10,000 pairs going out the door a year. They have an extensive selection of knives, along with everything from Paul Bunyan snow globes to chocolate-covered peanuts labeled as moose poop. Open 9 a.m. to 7 p.m. Mon through Sat, 9 a.m. to 6 p.m. Sun Memorial Day through Labor Day. Open 9 a.m. to 5 p.m. Sat and 11 a.m. to 4 p.m. Sun in the off-season.

Turtle Town Books & Gifts (formerly Rainy Days Bookstore). 2549 Main St.; (218) 963-4891. Stop in for a light lakeside novel, books on fishing techniques, guides to native flowers and trees, kids' books, and puzzles and toys. Open 9:30 a.m. to 8 p.m. Mon through Sat, 10 a.m. to 5 p.m. Sun Memorial Day through Labor Day; 10 a.m. to 5 p.m. Mon through Sat in the off-season.

golfer's paradise

It may not be sunny and warm year-round, but Minnesota has long claimed more golfers and golf courses per capita than anywhere else in the US. The Brainerd Lakes area boasts many of the best, earning endless adoration from national golf magazines, which have named it one of the best 50 golf destinations in the world. The 1990s golf boom certainly helped. The sport's top legends designed several challenging courses here that capture the beauty of northwoods forest, lakes, and wetlands.

Altogether, there are more than 20 courses within a 45-minute drive. You can find specials or stay-and-play packages at www.brainerdgolftrail.com.

Here are some of the best:

The Classic at Madden's. 11672 CR 18 Southwest, Brainerd; (800) 642-5363; www.maddens.com. This course elevated the game at Madden's, which also claims the area's first golf course, Pine Beach East, from the 1930s ($119 for The Classic).

Deacon's Lodge Golf Course. 9348 Arnold Palmer Dr., Breezy Point; (218) 562-6262; www.grandviewlodge.com. Grand View's most prestigious course was designed by Arnold Palmer to wind through pines, lakes, and wetlands ($114).

Dutch Legacy. 11000 Craguns Dr., Brainerd; (218) 825-3700. This Audubon Signature Sanctuary course is one of two Legacy courses at Cragun's Resort. Bobby's Legacy features elevated tees and lake views ($125 for each).

The Pines Golf Course. 23521 Nokomis Ave., Nisswa; (218) 963-8755; www.grandviewlodge.com. These 27 holes were carved through the forest ($104).

The Preserve. 5506 Preserve Blvd., Pequot Lakes; (218) 568-4944; www.grandview.com. It's all about the views at The Preserve with 11 of 18 holes beginning with elevated tees ($104).

Whitefish Golf Club. 7883 CR 16, Pequot Lakes; (218) 543-4900; www.whitefishgolf.com. This is the newest course at Breezy Point Resort, joining its 80-year-old course, The Traditional, which is known for tight fairways and fast greens ($64).

Zaiser's. 25424 Main St.; (218) 963-2404. This red-door boutique blends style, sass, and kitchen savvy with sections of cookware and tools, funky shoes and boots, unique jewelry, bath products, toys, gags and magic tricks, and whimsical gifts such as staplers shaped like fish or bubbling rocket lamps. Open 10 a.m. to 5 p.m. Mon through Sat and 11 a.m. to 4 p.m. Sun year-round with extended hours spring through mid-fall.

where to eat

Bar Harbor Supper Club. 8164 Interlachen Rd., Lake Shore; (218) 963-2568; www.bar harborsupperclub.com. You can't miss this supper club about 8 minutes from Nisswa on County Highway 77. Look for the lighthouse standing tall along a busy channel on Gull Lake. Its roots stretch back to the late 1930s when gambling and dancing were the focus. These days it's more surf and turf, but you can still spin around the dance floor on weekends and enjoy the lake views. Lighter, more casual fare is served on the patio. Doors open at 9 a.m. for breakfast. Early bird dinner specials offered. $$$.

Cru. 23521 Nokomis Ave.; (218) 963-8756; www.grandviewlodge.com. You can see many of Cru's 200 different wines in an illuminated wine cellar running the length of this 50-person restaurant. This trendy dining experience on the Grand View Lodge property includes a variety of small plates such as grilled lamb sliders, crab chorizo fritters, lobster rolls, and Thai corn chowder, a favorite from the former Sherwood Forest restaurant. Open 6 to 9 p.m. Tues through Sun. Call for off-season hours. $$$.

Iven's on the Bay. 19090 MN 371 North, Brainerd; (218) 829-9872; www.ivensonthebay .com. Seven miles south of Nisswa, Iven's on the Bay specializes in seafood (think Maine lobster with orange basil butter) and date-night dinners overlooking North Long Lake. It's also popular for drinks with wine flights, about 150 wines, and more than 50 martinis at its martini bar. Early bird specials run from 4 to 7 p.m. There also are $25 prix fixe specials that combine entrees such as almond-crusted walleye or cherry barbecue glazed duck breast with wine, salad, and raspberry crème brûlée. Open 4 to 9:30 p.m. for dinner from Mother's Day through mid-Sept. Open 5 to 9:30 p.m. Wed through Sat in the off-season. $$$.

Lost Lake Lodge. 7965 Lost Lake Rd., Lakeshore; (218) 963-2681; www.lostlake.com. Tucked away on a back bay, this restaurant with views of Gull Lake has built a following for home-ground grains and baked goods and breads, along with fixed-price multicourse evening meals. Dinners might include lemongrass sorbet, Brazilian seafood stew, smoked salmon with ricotta dumplings, braised beef ribs and sweet corn risotto, or Italian plum pie. More casual sandwiches and salads are also available. From Memorial Day weekend through Labor Day: Breakfast from 8 to 10 a.m. Mon to Sat, 8 to 11:30 a.m. Sun; lunch from 11 a.m. to 2 p.m. daily; dinner from 5:30 to 8:30 p.m. daily. Call for reservations and hours for May, Sept, and Oct. $$$.

Northwoods Pub at Grand View Lodge. 23521 Nokomis Ave.; (218) 963-8756; www .grandviewlodge.com. This casual pub shines during the summer when you can sit on the shaded patio of Minnesota's most picturesque historic lodge while also enjoying glimpses of Gull Lake through the trees. Try the creamy walleye chowder with sweet corn, bacon, and skin-on potatoes or the nicely spiced broiled walleye fillet with remoulade sauce on ciabatta bread. Need meat? Opt for a double-patty Paul Bunyan burger with onion rings, three cheeses, and bacon. Open 10:30 a.m. to 1 a.m. $$.

Rachel's Bakery. 25535 Main St.; (218) 963-0900. Swing into this little downtown bakery for peach scones, almond croissants, fruity turnovers, or something else sweet to start the day. They also offer daily soup or sandwich specials. Open 8 a.m. to 3:30 p.m. Tues through Fri and 8 a.m. to 3 p.m. Sat. $.

Stonehouse Coffee & Roastery. 25346 Smiley Rd.; (218) 961-2326; www.stonehouse coffee.com. You can smell the coffee roasting, not just brewing, at this artsy breakfast hot spot. The owners travel the globe to choose more than 20 varieties of beans. The bestseller: full-bodied Black Pearl, a blend of African and Indonesian beans. They also sell fresh-baked scones or muffins and their own pancake mix. Open 7 a.m. to 5:30 p.m. Mon through Fri; 7:30 to 5 p.m. Sat; 8 a.m. to 4 p.m. Sun. $.

where to stay

Beachland Cottages. 6991 CR 13, Lake Hubert; (218) 963-2417. These 10 basic, tidy cottages with 1 to 3 bedrooms sit nestled between the Paul Bunyan Trail and the sandy shore of Lake Hubert, one of the area's clearest, nicest lakes. $$.

Good Ol' Days Resort. 260050 Oak Ln.; (218) 963-2478; www.goodoldaysresort.com. Newly built luxury cottages overlook Lower Cullen Lake, while lodge rooms offer a more economical option. The lodge includes an open-hearth fireplace in the living room, a dining area, game room, and four-season porch. A 10-minute walk from Good Ol' Days via the Paul Bunyan Trail runs straight into downtown Nisswa. $$–$$$.

Grand View Lodge. 23521 Nokomis Ave.; (800) 432-3788; www.grandviewlodge.com. This imposing 1900s log lodge on a hillside above Gull Lake ranks among Minnesota's most venerable resorts. It offers 155 units that range from new hotel rooms on the lodge's second floor and cabins along Gull Lake to golf course villas, luxury homes, and reunion houses. Guests can dine at on-site restaurants, take pontoon cruises, fishing trips, go on horseback or sleigh rides or unwind at Glacial Waters Spa or the indoor pool with slides and fountains. $$–$$$.

pequot lakes, mn

This town of 1,300 residents isn't as busy as Nisswa and makes for a fun stop whether you're traveling by snowmobile, bicycle, motorcycle, or car. You know you've arrived when Pequot Lakes' red-and-white water tower—painted to be Paul Bunyan's bobber—rises into the sky. Besides paying homage to the local legend, the tower marks the start of the Paul Bunyan Scenic Byway as it loops east toward the beautiful Whitefish Chain of Lakes.

The town's population doubles in early July for its Bean Hole Days, one of the state's most unique festivals. Crews slow-cook wood-fired iron pots of beans that are buried overnight and served the next day. It's the kind of meal that would have kept early lumberjacks going as they made their way through the northwoods.

getting there

From Nisswa, continue north on MN 371 or the Paul Bunyan Trail for about 6 miles.

where to go

Pequot Lakes Welcome Center. Trailside Park (along MN 371), Pequot Lakes; (218) 568-8911; www.visitbrainerdlakes.com. Get oriented in the lobby with brochures and maps. Open 7 a.m. to 7 p.m. daily. Office hours are 9 a.m. to 4 p.m. Mon through Fri, plus Sat in the summer.

Breezy Belle Cruise. 9252 Breezy Point Dr., Breezy Point; (218) 562-7164; www.breezy pointmarina.com. Take a 2-hour guided tour of Pelican Lake 5 miles east of Pequot Lakes. This paddlewheel boat gets churning every Wednesday and Sunday night during the summer. Reservations must be made at least a day in advance ($14–$18).

Market in the Park. Downtown Pequot Lakes. This weekly summertime event each Thursday starts with yoga by the new band center and continues along the Paul Bunyan Trail, which is set up with a farmers' market and food stands. Kids can go on a bobber hunt or try bobber bowling.

Paul Bunyan Scenic Byway. Starting at CR 11 and MN 371; www.paulbunyanscenic byway.org. The legend of Paul Bunyan playfully comes to life with interpretive signs and kiosks along this 54-mile scenic drive. The first stop east of Pequot Lakes is a forest trail that leads to a former fire tower. It's worth the climb up it to see fall colors blaze across the woods. Download seven podcasts from the website above to learn more about stops along the byway. The route heads east to Breezy Point, north to Crosslake and Manhattan Beach, then west to Pine River and south to Jenkins.

where to shop

Expressions Shoe Center. 4450 Main St.; (218) 568-6690. The staff here can measure your feet with a computerized system to recommend which of the top brands will offer the best comfort. Open 9 a.m. to 5:30 p.m. Mon through Sat year-round, plus 10 a.m. to 4 p.m. Sun Memorial Day through Labor Day.

Fun Sisters At the Lake. 4522 Main St.; (218) 568-7403; www.thefunsisters.com. This is the place to go for unique purses, phone covers, accessories, jewelry, and clothes. They have stores in Nisswa and the Twin Cities, too. Open 10 a.m. to 5 p.m. Mon through Fri, 9:30 a.m. to 5:30 p.m. Sat and 11 a.m. to 4 p.m. Sun from May through Dec. Closed Tues and Wed Jan through Memorial Day.

Kendall Candles. 3506 Kendall Circle; (218) 568-5678; www.kendallcandles.com. This manufacturer of 500 candle designs with 70 fragrances has a retail store and 15-minute factory tours. Open 9 a.m. to 5 p.m. Mon through Fri, and 10 a.m. to 4 p.m. Sat May 1 through Oct 31. Sat hours 10 a.m. to 3 p.m. in the off-season.

Leslie's. 31024 CR 112; (218) 568-5981. Look for unique women's clothing in vibrant colors and textures with styles from fancy to casual. Open 9:30 a.m. to 5:30 p.m. Mon through Sat and 11 a.m. to 3 p.m. Sun.

Lonesome Cottage Furniture Company. 30671 MN 371; (218) 568-8223; www.lonesomecottage.com. It's northwoods decor to the extreme here, with rustic log tables, beds, accent furniture, and even log pool tables. Open 9 a.m. to 5 p.m. Mon through Sat year-round and 10 a.m. to 4 p.m. Sun Memorial Day through Labor Day.

where to eat

Breezy Point Resort. 9252 Breezy Point Dr., Breezy Point; (218) 562-7811; www.breezypointresort.com. This giant resort of condos, villas, hotel rooms, and unique reunion houses also boasts festive outdoor dining during warm summer nights. Have some extra cheese with your burger and watch the hip-swaying Chris Olson's *Memories of Elvis* show at the Dockside Lounge. $$.

Timberjack Smokehouse and Saloon. 4443 CR 168; (218) 568-6070; www.timberjacksmokehouse.com. With its on-site smokehouse, this restaurant along MN 371 slow-cooks pork until it falls apart and serves up "bear-size" barbecue ribs. You can get just about anything else nicely smoked, too: salmon and shrimp, chicken and Cornish game hens, and prime rib on Saturdays. This place is especially handy for snowmobilers on the Paul Bunyan Trail who can thaw over hot drinks. If you're on a budget, daily $5 hot sandwich specials fit the bill. $$.

where to stay

Black Pine Beach Resort. 10732 CR 16; (218) 543-4714; www.blackpinebeach.com. This is one of those classic family-run resorts where the kids can roam between 13 knotty-pine cottages, the beach, buy candy at the main lodge, or wander the gnome garden. Cabins sleep 6 to 10 people. $$$.

Clamshell Beach Resort. 35197 S. Clamshell Dr.; (218) 543-4731; www.clamshellbeach .com. This classic family resort on the Whitefish chain has been replacing classic stucco cabins with upscale multistory cottages. The new units feature screened porches, spacious bathrooms, and colorful woodland-themed quilts. The resort also has an outdoor pool, beach, and swimming dock. $$$.

worth more time

If you keep driving east and north on the Paul Bunyan Scenic Byway, you'll reach **Cross-lake,** another great town to explore. Look for lakeside restaurants and resorts, additional locations for many of Nisswa's top boutiques, more golfing, and a campground and beach run by the US Army Corps of Engineers.

A bonus for families: Crosslake offers Big Fun Tuesdays from late June through early August. Join in with Paul Bunyan–themed games including a pancake toss, gunnysack races, minnow races, and fish toss.

For more information, stop at the Crosslake Welcome Center at the corner of CR 3 and 66 or call (218) 692-4027.

day trip 04

north

iron ore & trading posts:
mille lacs lake, mn; crosby-ironton, mn

With famed ice-fishing villages, Native American heritage and gaming, and an iron range revamped for rugged recreation, this area due north of the Twin Cities delivers more than good fish tales.

mille lacs lake, mn

Craving a cozy luxury cabin for a unique weekend getaway? You can get one that sleeps 10, has a kitchen, and stays warm, but gets a little rustic with a port-a-potty. It's tough to get plumbing when you're in the middle of frozen 132,000-acre Mille Lacs Lake.

Minnesota's second-largest lake becomes one of the world's most famous ice-fishing destinations each winter. About two dozen resorts plow hundreds of miles of ice roads and build villages across its endless white expanse.

"On any given day there could be 3,000 to 5,000 ice houses out there," says Tina Chapman, director of the Mille Lacs Area Tourism Council.

Ice-house season starts by Christmas and wraps up by late February. With a lake this big, it helps to have a guide whether you're there in winter or on a hot summer day in search of walleye, northerns, perch, muskie, and bass.

The abundant fishing, along with wild rice harvests, hunting, and connecting rivers have drawn people to the Mille Lacs area for at least 9,000 years.

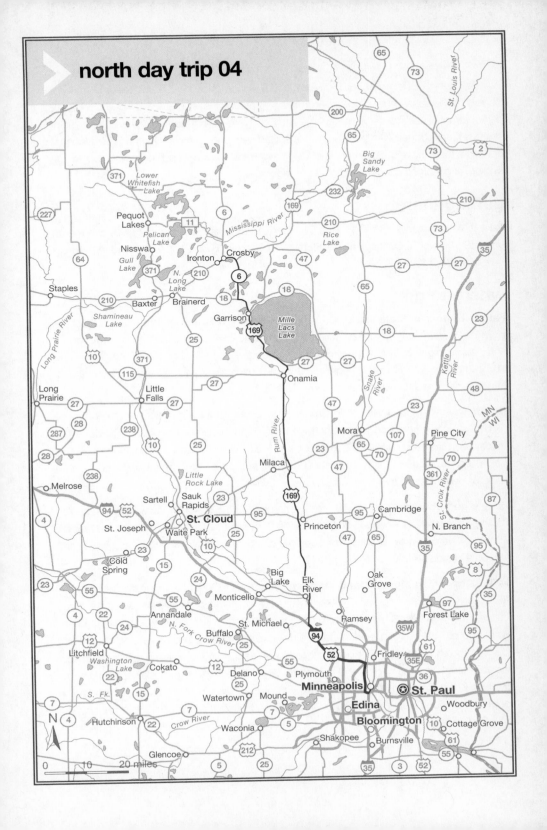

You can learn more about the Mille Lacs Band of Ojibwe at the Minnesota Historical Society's Mille Lacs Indian Museum and Trading Post. Displays, interactive videos, and craft demonstrations tell stories of their culture and long history living along Mille Lacs' 76 miles of shoreline, now dotted with the towns of Isle, Garrison, and Onamia. Don't miss the August powwow for a full appreciation of the Mille Lacs Band's vibrant traditions, with drumming, singing, jingle dress dances, and majestic regalia.

getting there

Take I-94 north about 23 miles to the Elk River/CR 101 exit. Head north 7 miles and merge onto US 169 North. Continue about 55 miles to Onamia. Follow MN 27 around the eastern side of the lake to reach Isle.

where to go

Father Hennepin State Park. 41294 Father Hennepin Park Rd., Isle; (320) 676-8763; www.dnr.state.mn.us. This 320-acre park named for a French priest and first recorded European explorer here has the largest public beach along Mille Lacs Lake. You'll also find 103 campsites, 4.5 miles of hiking trails, 2.5 miles of cross-country ski trails, 2 boat ramps, and 2 fishing piers. Daily park admission: $5.

Grand Casino Mille Lacs. 777 Grand Ave., Onamia; www.grandcasinomn.com. The 70,000-square-foot casino run by the Mille Lacs Band of Ojibwe features 1,900 video slot machines, more than 1,600 EZ Play coinless slot machines, a 280-seat bingo hall, live poker, 24 table games, and a high-limit gaming area. It's also a good venue to catch a band or performer on tour such as Bill Cosby, Lynyrd Skynyrd, Chicago, or Dierks Bentley.

Izaty's golf courses. 40005 85th Ave., Onamia; (320) 532-4574; www.izatys.com. You can play at a total of 27 holes in 2012 when the front 9 at the Sanctuary Golf Course reopen. The 6,867-yard 18-hole Black Brook course is among the 5 statewide that have been certified as a National Audubon Sanctuary.

Mille Lacs Indian Museum and Trading Post. 43411 Oodena Dr., Onamia; (320) 532-3632; www.mnhs.org/millelacs. The only state-run museum dedicated to Native American culture, the Mille Lacs Indian Museum features videos of powwow dances, intricate beadwork and basket weaving, and interactive displays to highlight Ojibwe culture. The trading post, a nod to a real one that once existed here, offers an expansive selection of beads, Indian arts and crafts, books, and souvenirs. Open 10 a.m. to 6 p.m. daily Memorial Day through Labor Day and 11 a.m. to 4 p.m. Fri through Mon in May and Sept. The trading post may be open weekends through Christmas. Admission: $7, adults; $6, senior citizens; $5, children 6–17.

Mille Lacs Kathio State Park. 15066 Kathio State Park Rd., Onamia; (320) 532-3269; www.dnr.state.mn.us. This park sprawls for 10,000 acres between the southwest corner of Mille Lacs Lake and the Rum River, which also widens to 2 inland lakes. The Rum eventually feeds into the Mississippi near Anoka and was such a convenient route and food-rich region, it has been home to ancient tribes and later the Mdewakanton Dakota and Mille Lacs Band of Ojibwe. This National Historic Landmark can be a good place to catch archaeologists in action, but most visitors key on recreation: 70 camping sites, 5 camper cabins, horseback and hiking trails, a beach, snowmobiling and cross-country ski trails, and even a sledding hill near a heated chalet. Don't miss climbing the 100-foot-tall tower—especially in the fall. Daily park admission: $5.

where to eat

Grand Casino Buffet. 777 Grand Ave., Onamia; (320) 532-7777. Typical of sprawling casino spreads, this buffet has more than 100 items. Go on Friday night if you're in the mood for seafood, Saturday or Sunday for prime rib, or Tuesday for international flair. Open 10 a.m. to 3 p.m. for brunch on Sat and Sun; 11 a.m. to 3 p.m. for weekday lunch; 4 p.m. to 8 p.m. nightly for dinner, with extended evening hours on weekends. $$.

Happy's Drive-In. 11373 Stevens Rd., Onamia; (320) 532-3336. About 1 mile north of Onamia, this is a good stop for families, especially with its play areas for running off cooped-up-in-the-car energy. They serve old-fashioned roadside food. Think soups, sloppy joes, burgers, sandwiches, and of course, ice cream. Open daily 10:30 a.m. to 9 p.m. and until 10 p.m. Fri through Sun, Apr through Oct. Open Thurs through Sun Nov through Mar. $.

Toucan's at the Wharf. 5101 Whistle Rd., Isle; (320) 676-3693; www.wharfmn.com. This restaurant at Fisherman's Wharf Resort (which also has cabins and camping) serves meals such as hearty breakfast skillets, oatmeal pancakes, seafood chowder, peel-and-eat shrimp, roasted chicken, and buckets-to-go if you want something easy to take in the boat. Open daily at 7 or 8 a.m. until 11 p.m. Open until 1 a.m. Fri and Sat. $$.

The Woodlands Steakhouse. 777 Grand Ave., Onamia; (320) 532-7777. Grand Casino's fine-dining restaurant serves walleye, mushrooms stuffed with wild rice, rib eye, king crab, steaks, and filet mignon tournedos. Look for Chef's Tour specials with custom 4-course menus. Open 5 to 9 p.m. Wed through Sun, and until 10 p.m. Fri and Sat. $$$.

where to stay

Appeldoorn's Sunset Bay Resort. 45401 Mille Lacs Pkwy., Isle; (320) 676-8834; www.sunsetbayml.com. These 18 cabins include a fireplace, kitchen, cable TV, air-conditioning, and wireless Internet. The deluxe cabins sit closest to the beach. Guests can rent Wave Runners, boats, pontoons, or snowmobiles or hire fishing guides. Ice-house rentals start at

$60 for a 12-hour stay or $300 for a weekend. Summer guests must stay 3, 4, or 7 nights. Pets allowed for an extra fee. $$.

Grand Casino Mille Lacs. 777 Grand Ave., Onamia; (800) 626-5825; www.grandcasino mn.com. If you're looking for the most modern hotel rooms on the lake, there are 494 here, including many suites with sitting areas or a Jacuzzi. The hotel includes an indoor pool, spa, and shopping. $.

Izaty's Resort. 40005 85th Ave., Onamia; (320) 532-4574; www.izatys.com. This large lakeside resort (pronounced eye-ZAY-tees) is a favorite for families with kids, golfers, and wedding parties. You can choose standard rooms in Links Lodge Hotel or larger units with kitchens in the beach villas or townhomes. Dining is open to anyone at Club XIX with pastas and seafood specials. $–$$.

McQuoid's Inn. 1325 MN 47, North Isle; (320) 676-3535; www.mcquoidsinn.com. Guests in these recently remodeled hotel rooms aren't directly on the lake, but can access it from the Thaines River as it parallels and connects with Mille Lacs. All rooms include cable TV and air-conditioning. Some have microwaves and small refrigerators or whirlpools. Guides and portable ice houses are available, as well as snowmobiles and gear for exploring 300 miles of groomed trails. $.

crosby-ironton, mn

Say "Iron Range" to most Minnesotans, and they think of Virginia, Hibbing, Chisholm, and other communities on the Mesabi Iron Range. Minnesota actually has two other iron ranges: the Vermilion Range in Ely and Cuyuna Range by Crosby and Ironton. The Cuyuna is the smallest but still produced more than 100 million tons of iron ore in the early half of the 1900s.

The open pit mines have since gone back to nature. They've transformed into one of the state's prettiest recreational areas and distinctive playgrounds. The 17 water-filled mines—some up to 500 feet deep and all crystal clear—are surrounded by wooded hillsides and a ruggedness that feels like the Boundary Waters Canoe Area without the long drive.

getting there

From Onamia, follow US 169 around the western shore of Mille Lacs Lake to Garrison. At Garrison, take MN 18 north to MN 6 north about 18 miles to Crosby. The highway will merge with MN 210 and curve west around Crosby's Serpent Lake before heading into downtown. Continue south on MN 210 into Ironton.

where to go

Croft Mine Historical Park. 101 George Spalj Dr.; (218) 546-5466. Take an elevator shaft ride into a simulated underground iron ore mine with a history lesson on the lives of miners and what it took to extract the ore that makes steel stronger. The 1924 collapse of a lake into the nearby Milford mine killed 41 men and remains one of the deadliest mining accidents in the country. Open weekends Memorial Day through Labor Day. Open 10 a.m. to 6 p.m. Memorial Day through Labor Day.

Crosby Memorial Park. Along MN 210. Kids in tow? Make a stop at one of the area's best beaches and most spacious community parks. The imaginative playground incorporates Vikings, dragons, farm animals, and ocean murals in between slides, forts, monkey bars, and tunnels. The park includes camping spots, a picnic area, a skateboard park, and the can't-miss-it giant sea serpent statue.

Cuyuna Country State Recreation Area. Follow CR 30 west from MN 210; (218) 546-5926; www.dnr.state.mn.us. Natural lakes, mine lakes, and high hills stretch across 5,000 acres, providing quiet places to kayak, hike, take beginning scuba diving lessons, go swimming, fish for trout or bass, or bike a paved path. The fun factor amped up in 2011 with about 30 miles of rugged mountain bike trails designed for both beginners and advanced adrenaline junkies who are coming from across the country to try them. Don't miss a short drive to the Portsmouth Mine scenic overlook. Bikes, skis, and kayaks can be rented through Cycle Path and Paddle (115 3rd Ave. Southwest; www.cyclepathpaddle.com).

Hallett Antique Emporium & Abbey House. 28 W. Main St., Crosby; (218) 546-5444; www.hallett-abbey.com. These dependable side-by-side antiques stores sell Blue Mountain pottery, vintage knives, military artifacts, Red Wing crocks, wooden snowshoes, furniture, and other collectibles from 40 dealers. Continue looking for treasures in a downtown considered the antiques capital of the Brainerd Lakes area. Open 9:30 a.m. to 5 p.m. in the winter, to 5:30 p.m. in the summer.

The Lakes Golf Course. 25039 Tame Fish Rd., Deerwood; (800) 450-4545; www.ruttgers .com. Minnesota native Joel Goldstrand designed this 18-hole course around 2 lakes that come into play on half of the holes. The signature 213-yard 18th hole requires a tee shot over Bass Lake. The course is part of Ruttger's resort, which also has Alec's Nine, a more leisurely executive course.

where to eat

Heartland Kitchen. 131 W. Main St., Crosby; (218) 546-5746. Grab sweet rolls or cranberry wild rice bread to go or take a seat for homey servings of hot meat sandwiches and several varieties of pie. On Sunday, they serve turkey dinner and offer an all-day buffet with unique items such as lefse layered with apples and honey. Open 7 a.m. to 3:30 p.m. $.

Louie's Bucket of Bones. 101 4th St., Ironton; (218) 545-3232. You can't miss the painted flames on this roadside joint. Line up for spice-rubbed, smoked pork ribs, Texas beef loin, juicy chicken dinners, coleslaw, homemade bread, pulled barbecue sandwiches, and pineapple upside-down cake. Open 11 a.m. to 1 p.m. and 4 p.m. to 8:30 p.m. Mon through Fri, and 4 p.m. to 9 p.m. Sat and Sun. $$.

Maucieri's Italian Bistro & Deli. 7 3rd Ave., Crosby; (218) 545-4800; maucieris.dropzite .com. Start the day with BFRs (Big Fat Rolls) and homemade biscuits slathered with Italian sausage gravy or recover from a day of biking with baked mostaccioli, meatball sandwiches, pizza, or the Italian Stallion, a sandwich heaped with Italian sausage, cheese, and sauce. Open 8 a.m. to 9 p.m. Mon through Thurs and 8 a.m. to 10 p.m. Fri and Sat. Closed Mon Oct through Feb. $$.

Ruby's Restaurant at Ruttger's Bay Lake Lodge. 25039 Tame Fish Lake Rd., Deerwood; (800) 450-4545; www.ruttgers.com. This century-old resort has more casual options, but it feels like an event to dine in the 1920s lodge with 54-foot-tall poplar logs. Entrees range from citrus-glazed scallops wrapped with bacon and grilled to grilled mint lamp chops with pear salsa or a vegetarian Thai curry. Open 7 to 10 a.m. and 6 to 8 p.m., Apr through Oct. $$$.

where to stay

Nordic Inn Medieval Brew & Bed. 210 1st Ave. Northwest, Crosby; (218) 546-8299; www.vikingvear.com. Arrive ready to channel your inner Viking, swill some beer, laugh at the bawdy interactive entertainment, and dress the part at Minnesota's most unusual B&B experience. Think dinner theater meets slumber party. Heck, you can even reserve a ship to sleep in. Just know it's hanging from the roof of this former church with colorful stained-glass windows. If you prefer your Vikings more modern than medieval, 1 of the 5 rooms ("The Locker Room") is tricked out for Vikings football fans. $$.

Ruttger's Bay Lake Lodge. 25039 Tame Fish Lake Rd., Deerwood; (800) 450-4545; www.ruttgers.com. This seasonal resort's roots go back to 1898. It has grown to be one of the largest in the Brainerd Lakes area with 200 units blending villas, condos, cottages, and lodge rooms. Many of the cabins stretch along the large beach with giant water toys. There's also a summer kids' camp, 2 golf courses, 3 restaurants, a meal plan, and a Fine Line Salon and Spa featuring Aveda products. Open Apr to Oct. $$$.

day trip 05

north

rushing rivers & thick forests:
pine city, mn; hinckley, mn;
sandstone, mn; moose lake, mn;
cloquet, mn; carlton, mn

You don't have to drive all the way to Lake Superior to enjoy rugged scenery, wild rivers, and adrenaline-pumping adventure. That all starts roughly an hour north of the Twin Cities with St. Croix State Park, the largest in Minnesota covering more than 34,000 acres.

If that's not impressive enough, consider this: the south-to-north corridor from Pine City to Carlton and east-west between I-35 and the Wisconsin border encompasses the St. Louis River, four state parks, four state forests, two rapids-rich rivers, and three state trails that stretch for hundreds of miles.

It's ideal for anyone who craves trading the urban or suburban jungle for camping, riding ATVs, bicycling, mountain biking, horseback riding, cross-country skiing, and zipping through wild woods on snowmobile.

There also are two designated Minnesota scenic byways that get you off the interstate, traveling through tunnels of pine, above deep valleys, and over to Jay Cooke State Park where a swinging bridge sways above raging rapids and ancient rocks.

If you choose quiet sports, keep your ears and eyes open for a glimpse of the black bears and wolves that make their home here.

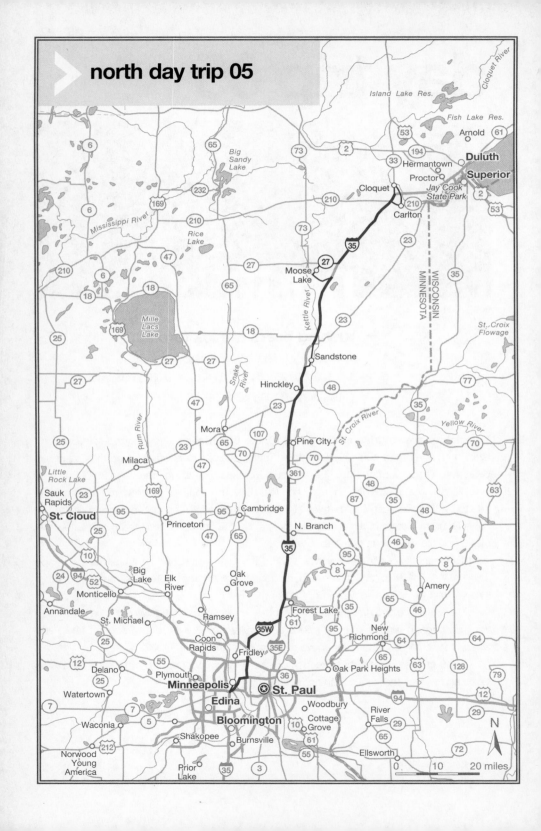

pine city, mn

More than a century before interstates and automobiles let travelers speed north to south, Pine City was an important crossroads. Native Americans, trappers, traders, and voyagers all converged here as they paddled and made their way from Lake Superior to the Mississippi and St. Croix Rivers. The town's main attraction, the Minnesota Historical Society's Northwest Company Fur Post, takes visitors back to that era with living history interpreters recreating the winter trading post from 1804–1805.

getting there

Take I-35 north of the Twin Cities about an hour and 15 minutes to reach Pine City.

where to go

Northwest Company Fur Post. 12551 Voyageur Ln.; (320) 629-6356; www.mnhs.org. This re-created winter trading post brings to life the fur trade from 1804–5. Tours and hands-on artifacts provide information about the roles of traders, trappers, voyageurs, and Native Americans in this global business. Try on a felted beaver hat, lift a typical pack the voyageurs carried, and see how much they could fit into their 24-foot canoes. This area of the state was an important crossroads as travelers moved from Lake Superior to the Mississippi and St. Croix Rivers. You can find books on voyageurs and the Ojibwe, birchbark crafts, historic toys, redware, tinware, trade silver jewelry, and reproduction goods from the fur trade era. Tours offered Memorial Day weekend through Labor Day 10 a.m. to 5 p.m., Mon and Thurs through Sat, and noon to 5 p.m. Sun. Admission: $9, adults; $7, seniors; $6, children 6–17.

where to stay

Chengwatana State Forest. www.dnr.state.mn.us. About 12 miles east of Pine City, three rivers flow through this 29,000-acre state forest with 26 sites at the Snake River Campground. $.

hinckley, mn

If there's a hub for this forested, river-rich corridor of the state, it's Hinckley. The midway point between the Twin Cities and Duluth has the most restaurants and lodging, anchored by Grand Casino.

getting there

From Pine City, it's about 14 miles to Hinckley on I-35.

where to go

Antiques America. 107 Tobies Mill Place; (320) 384-7272. More than 70 dealers sell everything from World War II collectibles and books to porcelain, toys, and furniture. Open 10 a.m. to 6 p.m. daily.

Gandy Dancer Trail. www.dnr.state.mn.us. Accessible about 18 miles east of Hinckley through St. Croix State Park, this ATV and off-road motorcycle trail starts in Danbury, Wisconsin, and runs about 31 miles, connecting with additional trails in the 42,000-acre St. Croix State Forest and 100 miles of trails in the 92,000-acre Nemadji State Forest. Off-road trucks and cars are allowed in some designated sections.

Grand Casino Hinckley. 300 Lady Luck Dr.; (320) 384-7427; www.grandcasinomn .com. Look for big-name performances here (usually country western stars), along with slot

state forest vs. state park

*The corridor between I-35 and the Wisconsin border has one of Minnesota's highest concentrations of state forests, state parks, state trails, and even national park land with what's along the St. Croix. You can find scenic biking, quiet hikes, horseback rides, and rivers to paddle, but it's even more popular for off-road vehicles: ATVs, motorcycles, and vehicles and trucks that can handle rugged forest trails. You can get campsite and trail maps through the **Minnesota Department of Natural Resources;** (888) 646-6367; www.dnr.state.mn.us.*

State forest campsites cannot be reserved, so it's good to have a backup plan if your first choice is full. The same goes for National Park Service paddle-in sites along the St. Croix River. (For comparison, St. Croix State Forest has 20 campsites versus more than 200 at St. Croix State Park.) It's also wise to check the DNR website before a trip. In addition to a state budget shutdown that closed parks and campgrounds for several weeks in July 2011, two summer windstorms damaged 95,000 acres. Cleanup was still under way several months later.

State forest campsites are generally less crowded than state parks, but they're also more rustic. You'll still have fire pits and picnic tables, but expect vault toilets and water pumps instead of flush toilets, showers, and sinks. Sites are usually $12/night versus $16–$20/night for state parks.

Plan to spend $3 to $5 for each bundle of firewood. Since outbreaks such as the emerald ash borer, no one is allowed to bring their own firewood. Only local, approved firewood vendors can be used. It's an attempt to control infestation.

machines and poker. The Mille Lacs Band of Ojibwe, which owns the complex, also has a powwow each June.

Grand National Golf Course. 300 Lady Luck Dr.; (320) 384-7427; www.grandnationalgolf .com. Joel Goldstrand designed this 18-hole course around the rolling terrain, trees, and ponds next to Grand Casino. Peak summer rates with a cart start at $53.

Hinckley Fire Museum. 106 Old Hwy. 61 South; (320) 384-7338. Heart-wrenching tales from one of Minnesota's worst natural disasters unfold at this restored 1894 St. Paul and Duluth Railroad depot. A summerlong drought, sparks from trains and small fires, too many slash piles from logging, and oppressing heat with a cold front moving in ignited the perfect storm of fires. Flames rose more than a mile high and roared across the area in 1894, devastating 6 towns, 480 square acres, and killing more than 400 people. Additional exhibits feature Native Americans, the logging era, and trains. Open 10 a.m. to 5 p.m. Tues through Sun, May to mid-Oct and Mon in July and Aug. Admission: $5, adults; $4, seniors.

St. Croix State Park. 30065 St. Croix Park Rd.; (320) 384-6591; www.dnr.state.mn.us. Minnesota's largest state park lies about 15 miles east of Pine City and Hinckley. It sprawls between the St. Croix, a National Scenic and Wild River, and the Kettle, the state's first designated Wild and Scenic River.

The park includes the state's largest trail system, 211 campground sites, remote canoe-in and backpack sites, 5 historic cabins from the 1940s ($75/night), and even 2 guesthouses that sleep 15. Climb the 100-foot fire tower on the park's west side to get a feel for the vastness of forest.

Take your pick of 127 miles of hiking trails that traverse the bluffs of the St. Croix and the rocky rapids of the Kettle. Additional trails are designated for mountain bikers, horseback riders, skiers, ATVs, and snowmobiles with extensions leading into neighboring state forests. If you like fishing, try one of the trout streams feeding into the St. Croix. Check at the park office for canoe and ski rentals.

Willard Munger Trail. Parking at intersection of County Highways 61 and 18, www.dnr .state.mn.us. This historic train route now is a 63-mile paved trail that starts a block north of the Hinckley Fire Museum. The trail runs to Duluth with a scenic trek through Jay Cooke State Park. A 37-mile segment memorializes the route the fire took from Hinckley to Barnum and how quick thinking by a train engineer helped rescue residents fleeing the flames.

where to eat

Cassidy's. 329 Fire Monument Rd.; (320) 384-6129. Like the more famous Tobies, this family restaurant has been around for decades. They also serve caramel and cinnamon rolls, but are best known for the salad bar, which includes 2 soups, 2 hot dishes (or tacos on Tuesdays), 7 homemade breads, and bread pudding in addition to salad fixings. Other all-you-can-eat options: sirloin steak on Friday or ribs on Saturdays. Open 6 a.m. to 9 p.m. weeknights year-round, and until 9:30 p.m. weekends and summer weeknights. $–$$.

Tobies. 404 Fire Monument Rd., (320) 384-6174; www.tobies.com. Many travelers consider it sacrilegious to bypass Hinckley—the halfway point between the Twin Cities and Duluth—without a stop at Tobies. The huge caramel and cinnamon rolls hog the spotlight, but this often-packed place serves meals 24 hours a day. You can order a Bavarian breakfast or cinnamon crunch french bread, splurge on steak and lobster, or try one of many salads with sides such as wild rice breadsticks or wheat-n-cranberry orange bread. Look for live entertainment Friday and Saturday nights, with karaoke on Sundays. $.

Winds Steakhouse. 777 Lady Luck Dr., Grand Casino Hinckley; (320) 384-7777. The most upscale restaurant at Grand Casino Hinckley serves crab legs, steak tournedos, braised buffalo ribs, and pistachio-crusted walleye. Opens at 5 p.m. Wed through Sun. $$$.

where to stay

Dakota Lodge. 40497 MN 48; (320) 384-6052; www.dakotalodge.com. Guests can rent a lodge with 5 bedrooms and 5 baths for groups, a 2-bedroom guesthouse with a full kitchen and fireplace, or a 3-bedroom cabin. $$.

Eagle Inn. 408 Lawler Ave. South; (320) 384-6744; www.theeagleinnbandb.webs.com. This 5-room historic guesthouse was one of the first homes built after Hinckley's big fire. Breakfast is included. $.

Grand Casino Hinckley. 777 Lady Luck Dr.; (320) 384-7777; www.grandcasinomn.com. Of the roughly 1,000 hotel rooms in Hinckley, the casino owns most of them, including a popular RV park with chalets. The main hotel, which is attached to the casino, includes 563 rooms. $.

St. Croix Haven Campground. 40756 Grace Lake Rd., Hinckley; (320) 655-7989; www.stcroixhavencampground.com. Campers here can use shuttles for St. Croix River tubing trips between Yellow River and Thayers Landing and canoe trips between Riverside and Thayers Landing. $.

sandstone, mn

With an historic sandstone quarry and the scenic Kettle River rushing through Banning State Park, this community of 1,550 residents attracts extreme athletes who tackle the rapids in the summer and climb ice formations in the winter.

getting there

Take I-35 about 11 miles north of Hinckley to Sandstone.

where to go

Audubon Center of the North Woods. 54165 Audubon Dr.; (888) 404-7743; www .audubon-center.org. This 535-acre refuge on Grindstone Lake includes 7 miles of hiking and skiing trails. While it's used as a conference center, the organization also offers several public programs including Dinner-at-the-Lake with various speakers, youth and family weekends, and women's wellness weekends. Grindstone Lake, one of the deepest lake basins in the state, is stocked with trout.

Banning State Park. 61101 Banning Park Rd.; (320) 245-2668; www.dnr.state.mn.us. The last state park along the St. Croix Scenic Byway draws gutsy adventurers for world-class whitewater kayaking on the roaring Kettle River each spring. They churn and shoot through the Blueberry Slide, Dragon's Tooth, and Hell's Gate rapids. Hikers can explore an old sandstone quarry and scenic trails along the river in this 6,000-acre park. In the winter, you may see ice-climbers here or at nearby Robinson Park, scaling their way up frozen falls. $5 daily admission.

where to stay

General Andrews State Forest. www.dnr.state.mn.us. This forest near Willow River (in between Sandstone and Moose Lake) includes a 35-site campground. Most sites are along Zalesky Lake, also known as the Willow River Flowage. The 7,700-acre forest includes a state nursery that produces 5 million forest seedlings a year. The public is welcome to tour it. $.

Waldheim Resort. 9096 Waldheim Ln., Finlayson; (320) 233-7405; www.waldheimresort .com. West of Sandstone, this traditional resort has 5 two- to three-bedroom cabins on Pine Lake and 30 seasonal RV sites. $$.

moose lake, mn

Sure, you can look for a moose in these parts, but your chances might be better looking down and trying to find a great agate. Carlton County was once the rim of Glacial Lake Duluth, making this the heart of agate country. The town hosts Agate Days each July and buries about 350 pounds of agates into four tons of rock spread across downtown. It's a good place to tap the expertise of Carlton County Gem and Mineral Club members.

getting there

Head north on I-35 again and drive about 30 miles from Sandstone to Moose Lake.

where to go

Moose Lake Chamber of Commerce. 4524 S. Arrowhead Ln.; (218) 485-4145; www .mooselakechamber.com. Use the website to register for a free agate hunting permit and maps of area quarries that allow rockhounding.

Moose Lake Depot & Fires of 1918 Museum. 900 Folz Blvd.; (218) 485-4145; www .mooselakeareahistory.com. Twenty-four years after the Great Hinckley Fire, another devastating one killed 453 people and destroyed the cities of Moose Lake and Cloquet and other communities. It was the worst single-day natural disaster in Minnesota, with the Hinckley fire close on its heels. The museum shares the details, with a 27-foot monument commemorating those who died. Open 10 a.m. to 4 p.m. Mon through Sat and noon to 3 p.m. Sun late May through mid-Oct. Admission: $2, adults; $1, children.

Moose Lake State Park. 4252 CR 137; (218) 485-5420; www.dnr.state.mn.us. Rock hounds will love this park with its impressive displays of Minnesota's official gemstone: Lake Superior agates. They are among the other polished treasures at the 4,500-square-foot Agate and Geological Interpretive Center that opened in 2003. If you're inspired to seek your own agates, ask a staff member for a map to local gravel quarries. Moose Lake Park also has a lake, beach, boat rentals, and 55 campsites. Agate exhibits are open 9 a.m. to 4 p.m. Sun through Wed, 9 a.m. to 6 p.m. on Thurs, and 9 a.m. to 9 p.m. Fri and Sat, Memorial Day through Labor Day.

Soo Line South Trail. Downtown; www.dnr.state.mn.us. This 114-mile trail starts near Superior, Wisconsin, and runs southwest to Minnesota through Moose Lake and almost to Little Falls. The Soo Line South intersects with the Willard Munger Trail in downtown Moose Lake. The Portage Trail connects both trails with Moose Lake State Park.

where to eat

Art's Café. 200 Arrowhead Ln.; (218) 485-4602. Around since the 1930s, this cafe is right on the Munger Trail and still sells a cup of coffee for 40 cents. Look for affordable big breakfasts and hearty meat sandwiches heaped with mashed potatoes and gravy. Follow up with a wedge of homemade cake or pie. Open 5:30 a.m. to 9 p.m. Mon through Sat and 7 a.m. to 9 p.m. Sun. $.

where to stay

Moose Lake City Campground. (218) 485-4761. This city campground includes a beach with lifeguards, a boat landing, tennis courts, and a playground. Open from the Friday before the fishing opener through last weekend in Sept. $.

cloquet, mn & carlton, mn

The St. Louis River rumbles and churns its way through Cloquet and nearby Carlton before spilling into Lake Superior.

getting there

Follow I-35 about 33 miles to Cloquet. The town of Carlton and Jay Cooke State Park are about 10 miles to the east along a scenic byway.

where to go

Jay Cooke State Park. 780 E. MN 210, Carlton; (218) 384-4610; www.dnr.state.mn.us. If you need a good thrill, walk across this park's iconic swinging suspension bridge at spring meltdown as water gushes beneath you and thunders between tilted jagged wedges of graywacke rock. The ancient rocks make this an especially scenic and intriguing river, along with a portage trail used by voyageurs dodging the rapids some 300 years ago. The 8,800-acre park encompasses 50 miles of hiking trails, 32 miles of easy-to-difficult cross-country skiing, 6 miles of snowmobiling with Munger Trail connections, and 13 miles of mountain biking. Look for a profusion of wildflowers each spring, head to Oldenburg Point for sweeping views of the valley and fall colors, and keep an eye open for signs of wolves. There are 79 campsites here, along with 5 camper cabins with electricity ($50/night). $5 daily permit.

Lindholm Service Station. Corner of MN 33 and Cloquet Avenue. If you're a Frank Lloyd Wright fan, this was the only gas station he ever designed. Built in 1956, it includes a copper roof, a jutting triangular canopy that points toward the St. Louis River, a second-floor waiting room, and generous windows and skylights. It cost $20,000 at a time when most service stations were built for $5,000.

Rushing Rapids and Veterans Evergreen Scenic Byways. www.minnesotascenic byways.com. Take the 9-mile scenic Rushing Rapids Scenic Byway as it parallels the St. Louis River from Carlton to Jay Cooke State Park and ends at the intersection with MN 23. Turn south on the 50-mile Veterans Evergreen Memorial Byway (a section of MN 23) for an alternative route back to I-35 and the Twin Cities.

Superior Whitewater. 950 Chestnut Ave., Carlton; (218) 384-4637; www.superiorwhite water.com. Professional guides take experienced or novice groups rafting or kayaking through St. Louis River rapids from May until Sept.

where to eat

Gordy's Hi-Hat. 415 Sunnyside Dr.; (218) 879-6125; www.gordys-hihat.com. A landmark for half a century, this popular seasonal drive-in churns out hand-pattied burgers, homemade onion rings, fries, shakes, and frothy root beer. Open 10 a.m. to 9 p.m. May through Sept. Gordy's Warming House next door serves steaming coffee drinks, ice cream, pie, soups, and sandwiches year-round from 6 or 6:30 p.m. until 10 p.m. on weekends or 9 p.m. Mon through Thurs. Open an hour longer in the summer. $.

where to stay

Black Bear Casino Resort. 1785 MN 210, Carlton; (888) 771-0777; www.blackbear casinoresort.com. This 250-room hotel run by the Fond du Lac Band of Ojibwe includes a pool, the Seven Fires Steakhouse, a buffet and deli, plus easy access to the casino with slot machines, blackjack, and bingo. Reserve early when there's a concert at the casino's Otter Creek Event Center. It brings in legendary performers such as Charlie Daniels and Glen Campbell. $.

KOA Kampground. 1381 Carlton Rd., Carlton; (218) 879-5726; www.koa.com. This is the place if you want a pool and hot tub, full hookups, and wireless access to go with your camping experience. You also can rent bikes here, join in family activities, or rent a rustic Kamping Kabin. $.

day trip 06

north

cooler by the lake:
duluth, mn

duluth, mn

Duluth knows how to make an impression. After road-tripping 3 hours north on I-35, you crest Thompson Hill and get that first breathtaking view of Lake Superior, the mouth of the St. Louis River, and the bustling harbor of the world's most inland port.

Experienced visitors know to check shipping schedules at the free Maritime Museum and be ready on the pier when boats glide beneath the 100-year-old aerial lift bridge, flocks of seagulls in their wake. If you watch from the museum or stand near it, you can usually hear a rundown of the ship—where it's from, what it carries, and how big it is.

It's easy to beeline for Canal Park by the bridge to spend a day wandering through shops and galleries and strolling the scenic lake walk. There's much more to Duluth, though, beyond its waterfront.

Duluth includes 100,000 acres of green space with 100 parks scattered among its steep hills. Many of them date back to the early part of the 1900s when the city was still booming thanks to lumber, mining, and shipping opportunities. At one point Duluth boasted more millionaires per capita than anywhere in the country. You can experience the elegance of that era while riding historic trains, sleeping in Victorian bed-and-breakfasts, or touring Glensheen Mansion or downtown's Depot.

But the grandest attraction of all is always, quite simply, the lake. It broods and drapes the city in fog or glitters like sapphires that stretch to a sky-blue horizon.

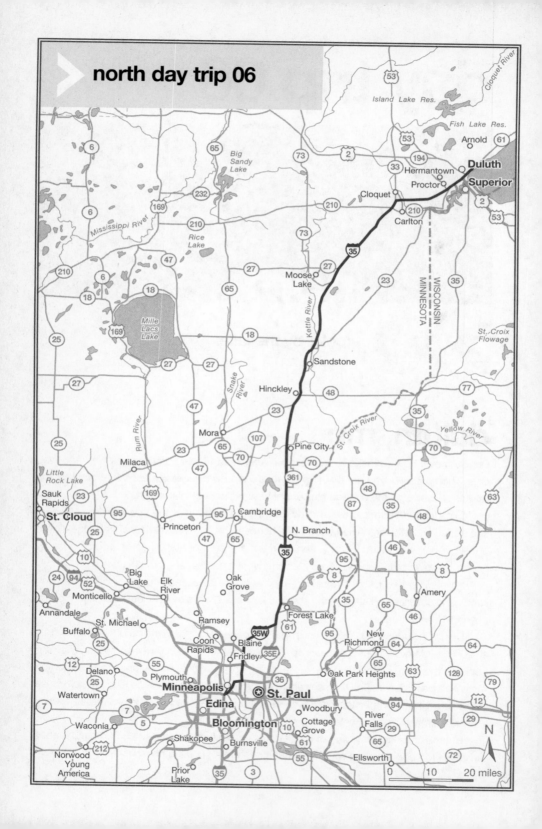

north day trip 06

getting there

Follow I-35 north from the Twin Cities for 3 hours. When you reach Duluth, exit at Boundary Avenue and go left. Go right on West Skyline Parkway to reach the Thompson Hill Information Center.

where to go

Skyline Drive. www.superiorbyways.com. Start at the Thompson Hill Information Center at 8525 Skyline Dr. West. This is the easiest place to grab maps and brochures for all of Duluth, plus it puts you on Skyline Drive as it heads north. Watch signs carefully. It can be tricky to follow through some neighborhoods. The byway takes you to Enger Tower, Hawk Ridge, and Seven Bridges Road, a favorite area for city hikes. If you're an early riser or night owl, time a Skyline visit with sunrise or moonrise. Look for a church parking lot or someplace safe to pull over.

Duluth Children's Museum. 506 W. Michigan St.; (218) 733-7543; www.duluthchildrens museum.org. Families often stumble upon this museum aimed at kids 3 to 8 years old while at the Lake Superior Railroad Museum. Both are in downtown's Depot, but the children's museum will be expanding to a historic Clyde Park location in the next few years. It's actually been around (at various locations) since 1930, making it the fifth oldest children's museum in the state. Look for exhibits such as a hands-on campsite, a music alley, and Kids Create art space. Admission: $12, adults; $6, 3–13.

Enger Park Golf Course. 1801 W. Skyline Blvd.; (218) 723-3451; www.golfinduluth.com. This 27-hole course in the hills above Duluth takes advantage of the rolling terrain and woods with views of historic Enger Tower. There's also a driving range and short game practice area ($30 for 18 holes).

Enger Tower. W. Skyline Parkway and Hank Jensen Drive; www.engertowerduluth.com. This 5-story stone tower looming 530 feet above Lake Superior was a gift from Norway in 1939, then rededicated by the king and queen of Norway in 2011. Like Enger Park itself, it's symbolic of Duluth's international ties and rich in history. Stroll through perennial and shade gardens and swing the beam that rings the peace bell in the Japanese tea garden, a gift from sister city Ohara, Japan. Visit in spring to see 4,000 daffodils. Don't miss walking out to the gazebo on the ridge overlooking the harbor. More great views can be seen from the tower. Free.

Glensheen Mansion. 3300 London Rd.; (218) 726-8910; www.d.umn.edu/glen. Consider the stats on one of the Minnesota's poshest and storied mansions: 39 rooms, 15 bedrooms, 15 fireplaces, 10 bathrooms, and 1 double murder. Just don't bring up that last bit. When the Congdon family gave the 7.6-acre lakeside estate to the University of Minnesota, it was agreed that wouldn't be part of the tour. Focus instead on craftsmanship:

intricately carved banisters, floral-themed stained glass, and a solarium that's an Arts and Crafts masterpiece. Contractors worked from 1905 to 1908 to build the mansion, gardens, gardener's cottage, boathouse, clay tennis courts, marble fountain, and stables. You can stroll the gardens and grounds for $5/person or reserve a tour, starting at $15/person with senior/student discounts. Open 9 a.m. to 5:30 p.m. daily, Memorial Day through Labor Day, and 9:30 a.m. to 3:30 p.m. on weekends the rest of the year.

Hawk Ridge Bird Observatory. 3980 E. Skyline Pkwy.; (218) 428-6209; www.hawkridge .org. You won't find a nature center or anything more permanent than a port-a-potty here, but you'll find plenty of enthusiastic birders from across the country and beyond lined up along the parkway watching close to 100,000 hawks that migrate through each fall. Migrating birds can save energy riding the warm thermals that rise from the shore of Lake Superior and high above the ridge. Most pass through between Sept 10 and 25, but naturalists with spotting scopes and field guides are usually on hand from Sept 1 through late Oct. There also are hiking trails threading Hawk Ridge's 365 acres.

Lake Superior & Mississippi Railroad. 71st Avenue West & Grand Avenue (across from Lake Superior Zoo); (218) 624-7549; www.lsmrr.org. This volunteer-run narrated excursion train operates twice a day on the weekends from June through early October. Sit in an open-air safari car or one of two 1912 passenger coaches for a trip along the St. Louis River. Admission: $10.50, adults; $6.50, ages 3 and up.

Lake Superior Railroad Museum. 506 W. Michigan St.; (218) 727-8025; www.lsrm.org. You can still hear a steam engine's whistle and the chug of a train at this attractive 1892 train depot. It's a collective hub for several Duluth arts organizations, but most fitting for the railroad museum where you can explore the Midwest's largest indoor train collection with vintage steam trains, a model railroad, and re-created turn-of-the-century downtown. Summer visitors can hop a train on the North Shore Scenic Railroad for scenic rides through the city or all the way to Two Harbors. If you've got kids along, look for family-focused rides such as weekend pizza trains, fall pumpkin patch trains, or the Polar Express over the holidays. Museum admission: $12, adults; $6, ages 3–13. Train excursions start at $14, adults; $7, children 3–13.

Lake Superior Zoo. 7210 Fremont St.; (218) 730-4900; www.lszoo.org. Tucked away in West Duluth about 10 minutes from downtown, Lake Superior Zoo takes families through outdoor exhibits for polar bear, lions, tigers, Kodiak bears, harbor seals, and monkeys. It's scenic, too, set on a wooded hillside near Kingsbury Creek. The size isn't overwhelming for kids, and they can get up close with animals in the indoor lab. Admission: $10, age 13 and older; $9, seniors; $5, children 3–12. Open 10 a.m. to 4 p.m. year-round, and until 5 p.m. during the summer.

Lester Park Golf Course.1860 Lester River Rd.; (218) 525-0830; www.golfinduluth.com. Twenty of the 27 holes here feature views of Lake Superior. Driving range and short game practice area also on-site ($30 for 18 holes).

Spirit Mountain. 9500 Spirit Mountain Place; (800) 642-6377; www.spiritmt.com. The longtime Duluth ski resort added the Timber Twister, a self-controlled alpine coaster in 2010, plus a Timber Flyer zip line and 9-hole minigolf in 2011. This variation of a traditional zip line has bench-like seats rather than a harness. It allows a parent and child to ride together. In the winter, Spirit Mountain has 22 ski runs, 700-foot vertical drops, 1 super pipe, and the largest terrain park in the Midwest. A 6-lane tubing park also debuted in 2011. The resort also has 73 campsites for $20–$32/night. Call for details on adventure park and ski prices, plus seasonal hours.

where to eat

At Sara's Table Chester Creek Café. 1902 E. 8th St.; (218) 724-6811; www.astccc.net. This college-comfy restaurant filled with shelves of books draws appreciative diners starting with breakfasts such as cranberry wild rice french toast and hippie farm breakfast. Vegetarian and global flavors influence lunch and dinner choices such as whitefish with harissa aioli and slaw on ciabatta bread, Thai tofu curry, buttermilk chicken and fresh greens salad, Peruvian steak and potato stir-fry, and a nightly hot dish special—a nod to Minnesota, moms, and church basements. Open 7 a.m. to 8 p.m. Mon through Wed, 7 a.m. to 9 p.m. Thurs through Sat, and 7:30 a.m. to 8 p.m. Sun. $$.

Clyde Ironworks. 2920 W. Michigan St.; (218) 727-1150; www.clydeparkduluth.com. Large and spacious, this converted ironworks that once built industrial cranes now stokes up huge wood-fired ovens. They use them for pizzas, crusty baguettes that accompany salads, and buns for juicy burgers and sandwiches. Even cheesecakes and apple crisp go into the wood-fired oven. Don't miss the house-smoked salmon chowder, homemade potato chips, and porketta on a hoagie. Open at 11 a.m. daily until closing. $$.

Duluth Grill. 118 S. 27th Ave. West; (218) 726-1150; www.duluthgrill.com. The humble exterior of this former Embers hides a "flexitarian" gem: a place where meat-lovers, vegetarians, vegans, and gluten-free diners can all feast on meals creatively presented and locally sourced whenever possible. Try the super-cheesy sandwich featured on *Diners, Drive-ins and Dives,* savory Scotch eggs, caprese salad, wild rice sausage, broiled Lake Superior whitefish, and a unique, tasty presentation of banana cream pie. Open daily 7 a.m. to 9 p.m. $$.

Hanabi Japanese Cuisine. 110 N. 1st Ave. West; (218) 464-4412; www.hanabimn.com. For a more sophisticated night out, head downtown for close to 80 kinds of sushi, sashimi, and a fusion mix with special rolls. Everything comes so carefully crafted, it's too bad the menu isn't all photos. You also can get other Japanese specialties: udon or soba noodles, gyoza, crispy tempura, tuna, red snapper, and other grilled seafood. Open 11 a.m. to 11 p.m. Mon through Sat, and noon to 10 p.m. Sun. $$.

Takk for Maten. 11 E. Superior St., Ste. 110; (218) 464-1260. This downtown cafe feels like Ikea meets artsy coffeehouse. Appropriately, it also taps the area's Nordic roots for great breakfasts and lunches. Look for Swedish pancakes, orange cardamom french toast with lingonberries, bacon and eggs rolled up in lefse (like a tortilla made with potatoes and milk), salmon chowder, gooseberry shakes, pizzas with lefse crust, and Swedish meatballs with cranberry wild rice bread. Open 7 a.m.to 3 p.m. Mon through Fri, 8 a.m. to 2 p.m. Sat. $.

Va Bene Berarducci's Caffé. 734 E. Superior St.; (218) 722-1518; www.vabenecaffe .com. Stroll the Lakewalk from Canal Park to here (it's just past Fitger's), and you won't feel too guilty indulging in gelato, Italian cream cake, or rich pastas. Time it right, and dine on the outdoor patio or cozy porch that faces the lake. $$.

where to stay

AG Thomsen House. 2617 E. 3rd St.; (877) 807-8077; http://thomsonhouse.biz. Owners Angie and Tim Allen have a gift for creating colorful, magazine-perfect rooms in this cheerful mansion. Four rooms in the main house include one with a balcony and another with a sunporch. Three additional rooms in the carriage house include the luxurious Superior Suite. Look for afternoon cookies and breakfast dishes such as wild rice quiche, chilled cantaloupe soup with mascarpone, lemon blueberry french toast, white chocolate craisin scones, and pistachio chocolate chunk muffins. $$–$$$.

Edgewater Resort & Waterpark. 2400 London Rd.; (218) 728-3601; www.duluthwater park.com. This hotel with more than 200 rooms and suites draws a family crowd for its 30,000-square-foot Polynesian-themed water park and complimentary minigolf, but you don't need kids to appreciate the lake-view rooms, balconies, heated outdoor pool, and availability of bikes. $$.

Firelight Inn at Oregon Creek. 2211 E. 3rd St.; (218) 724-0272; www.firelightinn.com. This 1910 brick mansion boasts a spacious front porch where you can linger with hot coffee and listen to the creek running through the ravine. Indoors, the living room draws guests in with a cozy fireplace alcove. Owners Joy and Jim Fischer leave a breakfast basket outside each room in the morning with hot coffee, a fruit, main course such as baked apple pancakes or a savory breakfast strudel, pastries such as pumpkin muffins or chocolate chip scones, and juice. There also is a room set aside for massage services. $$–$$$.

Mountain Villas. 9525 W. Skyline Pkwy.; (866) 688-4552; www.mtvillas.com. These 14 8-sided villas sleep up to 6 with 2 bedrooms, 2 baths, a full kitchen, and a living room with a pullout sofa. Some are pet-friendly. Right on Spirit Mountain with views of the lake, they're especially convenient for skiers but open year-round. $$–$$$.

Willard Munger Inn. 7408 Grand Ave.; (800) 982-2453; www.mungerinn.com. This hotel has long drawn raves for the value of its pine-sided rooms with quilts and amenities such as continental breakfast and free use of bikes or canoes. The location doesn't hurt either: it's at the foot of Spirit Mountain ski resort, 1 block from the St. Louis River, and right along the Willard Munger Trail. The trail, you may have guessed, was named for the hotel's founder, who passionately supported environmental improvements and projects including the popular trail between Hinckley and Duluth. Winter guests can hop onto the trail with Nordic skis or nab a winter downhill special. A queen room with Spirit Mountain lift tickets may be under $100 if you go on a weekday. $.

worth more time
canal park

Canal Park, Duluth's hugely popular waterfront district, stretches between downtown and the Aerial Lift Bridge. Its museums, scenery, Lakewalk, restaurants, and boutique shopping can easily fill a day—or several. The area is easy to navigate by foot, but you can also rent a bike or surrey or even a horse-drawn carriage for an alternative or more romantic way to get around.

Keep an ear out for a blast from the harbor and bells from the bridge as it rises for charter boats, ships, and gigantic ore tankers that can be up to 1,000 feet or three football fields long. You can't fathom their size until you're standing in their wake. If your timing's off and ships aren't coming in, head to the S.S. *William A. Irvin* for an in-depth look at one of Great Lakes' freshwater giants.

getting there

Take I-35 from the Thompson Hill information center into Duluth. Exit at S. Lake Avenue to reach Canal Park.

where to go

Great Lakes Aquarium. 353 Harbor Dr.; (218) 740-3474; www.glaquarium.org. Learn about the fish and wildlife that live in and around the Great Lakes through exhibits and demonstrations such as divers heading into 2-story tanks to swim among sturgeon, salmon, trout, and other freshwater fish. Even more fun: catch the river otter program when handlers bring them buckets of snow or ice filled with hidden treats such as anchovies and worms. Other live exhibits include sea horses, touch tanks with stingrays, and shorebirds. Get a little wet with a hands-on model of the Great Lakes with boats and locks. Open 10 a.m. to 6 p.m. daily. Admission: $14.50, adults; $11.50, seniors; $8.50, kids 3–16.

Lakewalk. www.duluthmn.gov/parks/lakewalk.cfm. This scenic 4.2-mile path stretches from the Duluth Entertainment Convention Center and Bayfront Park to curve around Canal Park, pass the Fitger's shopping complex, Leif Erickson Rose Garden, and end near 27th Avenue East. Along the way, enjoy the people-watching as families skip stones, teens jump off the eerie foundation of an old gravel dock in the harbor, and folks go by on the passenger train.

Maritime Museum. 600 S. Lake Ave.; (218) 720-5260; www.lsmma.com. Learn about Duluth's shipping history, shipwrecks, hear crew members and passengers tell their tales, and take the wheel in a pilothouse facing the lake. Check the front door for listings of ships coming into or leaving the harbor or go to www.duluthshippingnews.com. You can get an excellent view from the second-floor windows or out on the pier. Free admission. Open daily 10 a.m. until 4:30 p.m. (with later hours in the peak season) until shipping season stops between December and March. It's open Friday through Sunday during those months.

Park Point. Tip of Minnesota Avenue; www.duluthmn.gov/parks. Cross the aerial lift bridge and follow Minnesota Avenue onto what's considered the world's longest freshwater sandbar. It stretches for 7 miles until dead-ending at Park Point, the locals' favorite hangout with dunes, sandy beaches, picnic grounds, and a cool play structure shaped like an ore boat. It's also the least-bracing place to take a Lake Superior swim. Water can get up to 72 degrees. During windy or stormy days, Park Point may attract Great Lakes surfers. Who says you need an ocean?

S.S. *William A. Irvin* tours. 350 Harbor Dr.; (218) 722-7876; www.decc.org. Someone said "Supersize Me" when these mighty ships were built. Stand next to this one, and it's tough to fathom it was retired in 1978 because it was too small at only 610 feet long. It was launched in 1937 to haul materials to Ohio and Indiana steel mills and transport company dignitaries and guests in four luxury cabins. Climb aboard to learn about life on this "Laker"

salties vs. lakers

Duluth welcomes two kinds of ships: "Salties," which travel about 2,340 miles from the Atlantic Ocean via the St. Lawrence Seaway, and "Lakers," which stay on the Great Lakes because they're too big for the seaway. Salties have to be less than 600 feet long, while Lakers are usually 600 to 1,000 feet long.

The William A. Irvin, a retired Great Lakes flagship of US Steel, could unload 13.8 tons of ore in less than 3 hours and boasts a 2,000-horsepower engine.

Today's ships are still hauling ore and grain, as well as gigantic wind turbines that get shipped across the country.

and see the elegant rooms. You also can tour the *Lake Superior Tug* next to the *Irvin*. If you go in October, test your bravery with the *Irvin*'s Haunted Ship—a unique Minnesota scare venue. Standard tours: $10, adults; $8, students and seniors; free for kids under 10. Haunted Ship tours are $10, adults; $6 for kids 12 and under. Open 9 a.m. to 6 p.m. Memorial Day through Labor Day, 10 a.m. to 4 p.m. in the spring and fall.

Vista Fleet Sightseeing & Dining Cruises. 323 Harbor Dr.; (218) 722-6218; www.vista fleet.com. You have to get onto the water for a good overall sightseeing tour of Duluth. Vista Fleet's 2-hour cruises include Duluth history, its harbor, shipping, and the ecology of Lake Superior. They are also a chance to go beneath the aerial lift bridge. Special tours include sunset cruises, ice cream and pizza cruises, and fall color brunches. Tours run daily May through Oct with 3 a day during the peak summer season. Prices start at $16, adults; $14, seniors and military; $8, kids.

Wheel Fun Rentals. 408 Canal Park Dr.; (218) 722-1180; www.wheelfunrentals.com. Among the more distinctive ways to get down the pier, along the Lakewalk, or over to the aquarium is pedaling a single or double surrey. You also can rent kids' bikes, mountain bikes, choppers, and deuce coupes. Prices run from $6/hour to $27/hour. Open 9:30 a.m. to 9 p.m. Memorial Day through Labor Day and 11 a.m. to 7 p.m. Sat and Sun in Sept.

where to shop

Canal Park and the waterfront are full of shops, galleries, and restaurants. You can easily fill an afternoon browsing the storefronts, but you'll find additional gems tucked into the DeWitt-Seitz Building, a converted warehouse on Canal Park Drive, or Fitger's, a former brewery converted into a historic hotel with shops, restaurants, and a microbrewery. Fitger's (www.fitgers.com) is walkable from the waterfront (look for the vintage red water tower) or you can park in the ramp next to it. Call shops for hours, which vary by season. More information is available at http://visitduluth.com/shopping.

Art Dock. 394 Lake Ave. South; (218) 722-6410; www.art-dock.com. See the region through the eyes of 160 artists who create pottery, jewelry, paintings, and photographs. You can find everything from batik hangings of blueberries and agate jewelry to stained-glass snowflakes and woodblock prints.

Blue Heron Trading Company. 394 S. Lake Ave., Ste. 102; (218) 722-8799; www.the blueherontradingcompany.com. If watching the Food Network makes you drool, this is your kind of place. It's packed with gourmet ingredients, kitchen tools, a rainbow of pots and pans, playful kitchenware and textiles, and just about anything you need to be a happy host. They also sell locally roasted Alakef Coffee and offer a variety of cooking classes.

Duluth Pack. 365 Canal Park Dr.; (218) 722-1707; www.duluthpack.com. This shop sells far more than its iconic canvas bags for canoe camping. Look for stylish canvas purses and daypacks, camping supplies, heirloom paddles, hats, brand-name outerwear and active-wear, and even hiking gear for dogs like pooch packs and collapsible food bowls.

Sivertson Gallery. 361 Canal Park Dr.; (218) 723-7877; www.sivertson.com. Expect a lot of color and a good touch of humor with Liz Sivertson's dreamy twists on North Shore wildlife, Rick Allen's playful woodcuts, and Jim Brandenburg's wildlife photography. Close to 100 artists (85 percent of them local) exhibit at this gallery, which also specializes in Inuit carvings.

Waters of Superior Gallery. 395 S. Lake Ave.; (218) 786-0233; www.watersofsuperior .com. Craig Blacklock's vivid photos of Lake Superior take center stage, but you'll find much more local artistry here with wood-turned bowls, art glass birds, linoleum and wood-cut prints, and Scandinavian-influenced furniture, clothing, and accessories.

where to eat

Amazing Grace Bakery and Café. 394 Lake Ave. South; (218) 723-0075; www.amazing gracebakery.com. Life's too short to eat bad bread, and this comfy, eclectic cafe in the basement of the DeWitt-Seitz Building seeks to remedy that. The thick-sliced wide-bread sandwiches are big enough to split, leaving room for creamy soup or desserts such as lemon bars and chunky oatmeal cookies. It's one of the few places to eat breakfast in Canal Park. Look for pesto omelets, oatmeal buttermilk pancakes, quiche, and fresh muffins and scones. $.

Grandma's Restaurant & Saloon. 522 Lake Ave. South; (218) 727-4192; www.grandmas restaurants.com. Canal Park's best-known restaurant serves classic American fare in a historic building packed with antiques and local memorabilia from neon signs and a crib hanging from the ceiling to a stuffed bear that had the misfortune to crash through a hotel lobby in the 1940s. Yes, the Grandma's Marathon is named for this restaurant, which helped runners load up with pasta. The event grew so popular with close to 18,000 runners, they outgrew the restaurant, which can serve 600 people inside and on the rooftop patio. $$.

Lake Avenue Restaurant and Bar. 394 S. Lake Ave., Duluth; (218) 722-2355; http://lake avenuerestaurantandbar.com. Locavore chefs at this trendy lunch and dinner spot like to surprise diners with unusual ingredients. Think smoked bison on pizza, rabbit ravioli, and lasagna with oxtail meat. Favorite items include their "deconstructed fish and chips," and burgers are topped with pickled green tomatoes. The micro-distillery in back shakes up a creative (and potent) line of cocktails, and you can catch live music on the weekends. $$–$$$.

Little Angie's. 11 E. Buchanan St.; (218) 727-6117; www.grandmasrestaurants.com. The large patio makes this a popular hangout during balmy days. At night it's downright festive with the playful neon sign and margaritas flowing. If you're eating their fajitas, burritos, sandwiches, and salads indoors, the collection of southwestern and cowboy antiques and memorabilia gives you plenty to look at. $$.

Northern Waters Smokehaus. 394 Lake Ave. South, Ste. 106; (218) 724-7307. With locally sourced meats, you can get smoky delicious sandwiches here. Try a Pastrami Mommy with bison meat, smoked whitefish tacos, or grab salami, bacon, smoked pork, and ham for a picnic on the shore. $–$$.

where to stay

Canal Park Lodge. 250 Canal Park Dr.; (218) 279-6000. The Arts and Crafts design and colorful exterior help this hotel—the newest one in Canal Park—stand out nicely. Opened in June 2007, it features 116 rooms on 3 floors, with more than 50 of them facing the lake. There's a pool area that's popular with families, plus complimentary appetizers in the evening and hot breakfast in the morning. $$.

Fitger's Inn. 600 E. Superior St.; (218) 722-8826; www.fitgers.com. While it's not directly in Canal Park, these historic rooms built in the brewery's former bottling department have Lake Superior views and connect to Canal Park via the Lakewalk. Rooms feature the greens, blues, reds, and gold tones of the late 1920s, along with some arched windows, exposed rock walls, and high ceilings. $$.

The Inn on Lake Superior. 350 Canal Park Dr.; (888) 668-4352; www.theinnonlake superior.com. If you smell a campfire and roasting marshmallows along the Lakewalk, it's probably families in front of this 175-room inn. They have nightly storytime, campfires, and an indoor pool, plus a heated pool on the roof. Many of the luxury rooms and suites feature lake-view balconies, and all include morning breakfast. Some rooms are pet-friendly. $$–$$$.

Solglimt Bed & Breakfast. 828 S. Lake Ave.; (877) 727-0596; www.solglimt.com. With gorgeous lake views and a sandy Park Point beach out the back door, this B&B lives up to its name. It translates to "sun on the water." The home also stands out with its modern expansion, 5 artsy rooms, environmental efforts, sprawling gardens, and beautifully presented meals. The 3-course breakfasts are served on the patio or in the guest dining room facing Lake Superior. $$–$$$.

South Pier Inn on the Canal. 701 S. Lake Ave.; (800) 430-7437; www.southpierinn.com. If you love watching ships come in, South Pier's rooms facing the harbor boast the best views with ships gliding by within 100 feet of the windows. They'll even call you in the middle of the night so you don't miss one. It's also an ideal location for watching the world's largest aerial lift bridge go up and down. Rooms feature a modern look and come with binoculars, a guide to ships, and bathrobes. Breakfast included. $$.

northeast

day trip 01

northeast

lower st. croix river valley:
taylors falls, mn; st. croix falls, wi;
osceola, wi

A 200-foot-high Ice Age gorge, sculpted potholes, and funky rock formations have made the Lower St. Croix River Valley a favorite destination for more than 100 years. Travelers can explore almost 1,700 acres of state park land straddling the border between Taylors Falls, MN, and St. Croix Falls, WI.

Hikers, paddlers, campers, cliff jumpers, rock climbers, and those who prefer a laid-back paddleboat tour all come together to admire the Dalles of the St. Croix.

Surrounding towns are also a haven for food and history lovers. You can sleep in an old jail, browse for antiques, ride aboard a vintage train, sip local wines, nibble handcrafted cheese, and learn about early settlers' Swedish heritage with an easy loop drive about 45 minutes northeast of the Twin Cities.

taylors falls, mn

This favorite getaway wins raves for its dramatic scenery and outdoor recreation, but it also has fun places to eat and historic sites that preserve its early settlement by New Englanders.

If you can only pick one season to visit, choose fall. Explosions of red, gold, green, and orange carpet the valley, reflect in the river, and shimmer across the many lakes. Just be prepared for weekend crowds and a possible US 8 bottleneck as like-minded travelers converge for the spectacle.

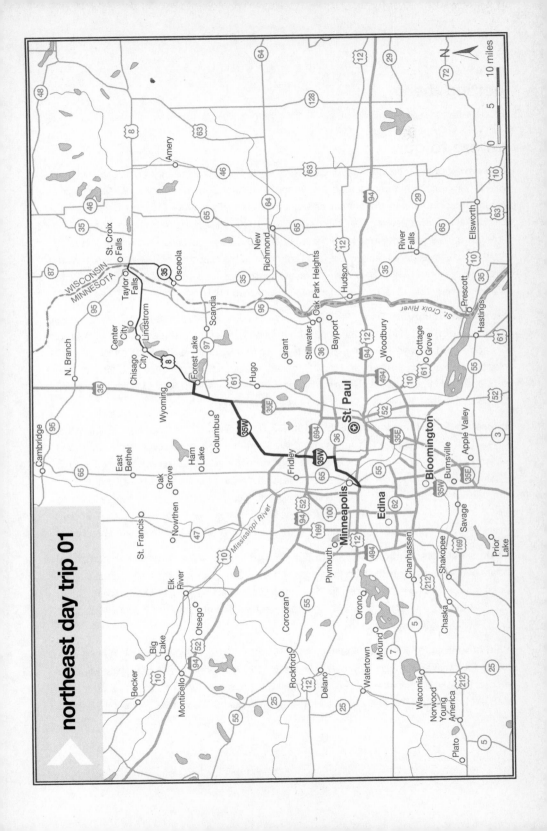

northeast day trip 01

getting there

Follow I-35 to US 8 near Forest Lake. Follow the highway east to Taylors Falls.

where to go

Folsom House. 272 Government St. West; (651) 465-3125. History buffs can tour this former lumber baron's mansion in the Angel Hill district above Taylors Falls. Most of the neighborhood's well-to-do homes reflect the community's New England heritage with Greek Revival facades. You can see the family's 1848 rosewood piano, their china gracing the walnut dining room table, Mr. Folsom's office and book collection, an upstairs nursery stocked with toys and a potty chair, and bedrooms with vintage razors, eyeglasses, a wedding dress, and a Civil War uniform. Admission: $5, adults; $1, children 6–17. Open 1 to 4:30 p.m. daily Memorial Day through mid-Oct. Closed on Tues.

Franconia Sculpture Park. 29836 St. Croix Trail, Franconia; (651) 257-6668; www .franconia.org. You can spot this fanciful attraction 3 miles before reaching Taylors Falls. Outdoors and always changing, this free 20-acre sculpture garden with more than 85 pieces ranks among the best and most imaginative places to introduce kids to art. You can see local and international artists creating works in progress from April through December. Guided tours are offered at 2 p.m. Sun May through Oct.

Interstate Park-Minnesota. US 8; (715) 465-5711; www.dnr.state.mn.us. Pull into the parking lot on the right as you near the river. There's a seasonal visitor center here and parking for hiking, rock climbing, and catching one of the tour boats down below. Take the Glacial Pothole Trail to see a unique geologic area. Melting glaciers and gravel that swirled through whirlpools carved out perfectly smooth kettles (or potholes) with names such as Lily Pond, The Squeeze, and the Bottomless Pit, which is deeper than 60 feet. The park includes 37 semi-modern campsites, 22 with electricity. A $5 daily park sticker is required.

Taylors Falls Recreation. 220 South St.; (651) 465-6315; www.wildmountain.com. Tour boats have taken visitors through the Dalles of the St. Croix for more than 100 years. Guides point out formations such as the Old Man of the Dalles, Lion's Head, or Devil's Chair. Tours from 30 to 80 minutes run daily May through mid-Oct. Tickets start at $7.50 for kids 3–12 and $11.50 for adults.

Wild Mountain. 37200 Wild Mountain Rd.; (651) 465-6315; www.wildmountain.com. This ski and snowboard area includes 26 runs across 100 acres and is one of the first Midwest resorts to open each winter and one of the last ones to close. Open 10 a.m. to 9 p.m. daily with extra hours on Fri, weekends, and holidays. Lift tickets start at $32 for youth, $42 for adults.

where to eat

The Drive In. 572 Bench St.; (651) 465-7831; www.taylorsfalls.com. Look for the giant mug of root beer above this wonderfully nostalgic and tasty summer drive-in where you'll still see carhops taking orders. It's been a landmark for more than 50 years. Get one of the juicy hand-pattied burgers, thick-cut onion rings, and a frosty mug of homemade root beer or a float. The business also includes Adventure Falls minigolf. $.

Tangled Up in Blue. 425 Bench St.; (651) 465-1000; www.tangledupinbluerestaurantin taylorsfalls.com. Named for a Bob Dylan song, this blue-hued small restaurant earns raves for its seasonal, beautifully presented dinners. Menus may include crab-stuffed salmon or

plan a picnic

On the way to Taylors Falls, you can grab a bottle of wine, gourmet cheese, or fresh produce for a picnic along the St. Croix. Here are three noteworthy stops within 10 miles of Interstate Park:

Eichten's Market and Café. 16809 310th St.; Center City; (651) 257-4752; www .theeichtensbistro.com. This specialty cheese and bison farm sells their products and serves meals inspired by them. Try the bison chili, artisan cheese board with bison sausage, fondue for two, or bison burgers, such as the Blue Mox which comes with cave-aged Minnesota Blue cheese, bacon, and a wild rice bun. You can dine outside on the patio or inside the warm contemporary cafe. Open for lunch daily, dinner on Fri and Sat, and breakfast Sat and Sun. $$.

Pleasant Valley Orchard. 17325 Pleasant Valley Rd., Shafer; (651) 257-9159; www.pleasantvalleyorchard.com. This seasonal farm 9 miles southwest of Taylors Falls opens for u-pick strawberries in June and again in September and October for u-pick apples, hayrides, apple pastries, pumpkins, and holiday gifts.

Winehaven Winery and Vineyard. 9757 292nd St., Chisago City; (651) 257-1017; www.winehaven.com. The founders of this winery about 14 miles east of Taylors Falls started in beekeeping before expanding to wine. That background, plus the area's Scandinavian heritage, led to their Stinger Honeywine (also known as mead), which became an international hit. Some other award winners from their vineyard include Deer Garden Blush, Deer Garden Red, Marechal Foch, and Riesling, plus cranberry and raspberry fruit wines. Open 10 a.m. to 5 p.m. Thurs through Sat and Mon and 11 a.m. to 5 p.m. Sun.

grilled shrimp with cauliflower puree, cilantro lime carrots, a spicy-sweet filet mignon with roasted pepper and raisin risotto, and flaming bananas Foster served over ice cream. Call for seasonal hours. $$$.

where to stay

Cottage Bed and Breakfast. 950 Fox Glen Dr.; (651) 465-3595; www.the-cottage.com. This suite overlooking the St. Croix has its own entrance and fireplace but is connected to a home inspired by 18th-century English country designs. Breakfast with fruit, bread, and quiche is delivered in the morning. $$.

Old Jail Bed & Breakfast. 349 Government St.; (651) 465-3112; www.oldjail.com. Taylors Falls' first jail was conveniently located next to the town saloon with its beer cave. The jail cottage became Minnesota's first B&B in 1981, and now you can stay in 4 suites at the former saloon, as well. Most have kitchens and views of the town below. In the Cave Suite, you can walk through a stone archway and bathe in the cave. $$.

st. croix falls, wi

The beauty of the St. Croix River Valley extends across the river from Taylors Falls to St. Croix Falls on the Wisconsin side.

getting there

Follow US 8 across the St. Croix River to St. Croix Falls.

where to go

Interstate Park-Wisconsin. WI 35; (715) 483-3747; http://dnr.wi.gov. As Wisconsin's oldest state park, this one sprawls for 1,400 acres along the river. It includes 85 campsites ($12–$20/night), 9 miles of trails, and encompasses Lake O' the Dalles with a swimming beach. The Ice Age Interpretive Center has exhibits and a film that shows three times a day. Daily park fee: $5–$7.

where to eat

Grecco's. 115 N. Washington St.; (715) 483-5003, www.greccos.com. This sumptuous menu evolves weekly to fit the season and availability of fresh ingredients. Fall choices may include Swedish meatballs with truffle sauce, pumpkin soup served in mini-pumpkins, wild rice–crusted scallops, lobster gnocchi, and duck breast with roasted spaghetti squash and honey lavender glacé. $$$.

where to stay

Wissahickon Farms Country Inn. 2263 Maple Dr.; (715) 483-3986; www.wissainn.com. This relocated country store–turned–cabin features barnwood siding, a colorful quilt and linens, a gas fireplace, and 2-person whirlpool. $$.

osceola, wi

Eclectic and small, this village on the Wisconsin side of the St. Croix River mixes art and tourism. It's best known for the train whistle that echoes through the valley during scenic tours.

getting there

Follow WI 35 south about 8 miles to Osceola.

To head back to I-35 and the Twin Cities, cross the St. Croix and head south on MN 95. Then turn west on MN 97, which passes through Scandia to reconnect with I-35.

where to go

Osceola & St. Croix Valley Railway. 114 Depot Rd.; (715) 755-3570; www.trainride .org. The train whistle echoes through the St. Croix River Valley at least three times a day as it chugs along for 50- to 90-minute scenic trips on weekends and holidays May through October. Look for dinner and pizza trains, brunch trains, and fall color and pumpkin express trains as well. Regular tickets run $12–$17, adults; $6–$8, kids; or $30–$45 per family.

St. Croix ArtBarn. 1040 Oak Ridge Dr.; (715) 294-2787; www.stcroixartbarn.com. You may be able to catch a musical, concert, or original production at this century-old dairy barn transformed into a 180-seat theater with ongoing art exhibits. In the first two weeks of August, you also can take classes in everything from making soap to playing the dulcimer through the River Valley Folk School.

where to stay

St. Croix River Inn. 305 River St.; (715) 294-4248; stcroixriverinn.com. These spacious 7 suites come with fireplaces, exposed stone walls, and hydro-massage tubs. Breakfasts, such as frittatas and french toast, are delivered to rooms, allowing guests to dine in their bathrobes or on patios overlooking the valley. $$–$$$.

worth more time

Gammelgården Museum. 20880 Olinda Trail, Scandia; (651) 433-5053; www.gammel gardenmuseum.org. Across the state line from Osceola and 9 miles south, this "Old Small Farm" open-air museum showcases a collection of authentic buildings and a church built by Minnesota's first Swedish immigrants. Look for special events during the year, such as Midsommer Dag (Midsummer Day) and sausage-making classes. Open 1 to 3 p.m. Fri through Sun, May 1 to mid-Oct, for guided tours. The Valkommen Hus and Butik (welcome house and gift shop) are open until December 23 with Scandinavian books, products, and handcrafted items for sale. Admission: $5 for tours. Free for children in elementary school or younger.

day trip 02

northeast

loggers, skiers, fat tires & fish:
hayward, wi; cable, wi

Flanked by the Upper St. Croix–Namekagon River corridor to the west and Chequa-megon National Forest to the east, the Hayward–Cable Lakes area attracts adventurers in search of something: a big fish, a thrilling mountain bike trek, a scenic paddle, an epic cross-country ski race, or serious relaxation.

hayward, wi

Hayward boasts one of the Midwest's most eclectic museum buildings and campiest photo opportunity. So go ahead. Don't be shy. Pose like human fish bait in the mouth of a four-and-a-half story muskie. This icon of Hayward, population 16,200, appropriately houses the National Freshwater Fishing Museum Hall of Fame.

During the summer, listen for the buzz of chain saws and thunk of axes during a lum-berjack show or come for the fiercely competitive International Lumberjack Olympics. Inhale the fresh sawdust and enjoy the action.

Together with Cable (17 miles to the east), the Hayward Lakes area offers close to 130 resorts, about 40 restaurants, and countless ways to get your heart pumping or find serenity among woods, rivers, and lakes.

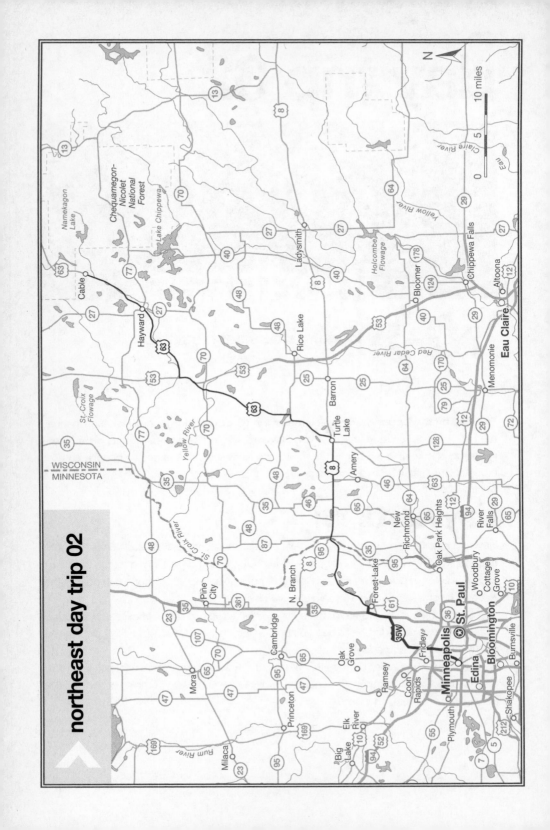

northeast day trip 02

getting there

Follow I-35 north to the US 8 exit, heading east toward Taylors Falls. Follow US 8 about 47 miles. At Turtle Lake, turn north onto US 63. It's about 60 miles to Hayward.

where to go

Hayward Lakes Visitors and Convention Bureau. 101 W. 1st St.; (715) 634-4801; www.haywardlakes.com. Open daily Memorial Day through Labor Day. Closed on winter weekends, but maps and guides can be picked up anytime.

Big Fish. 14122 W. True North Ln.; (715) 934-4770; www.bigfishgolf.com. Course designer Pete Dye sculpted hills and hazards into the forest for this 18-hole golf course named one of *Golf Digest*'s best new courses in 2005. It's a par 72 with 5 sets of tee boxes. Cost: $31 without a cart. Discounts for twilight and off-season.

Freshwater Fishing Hall of Fame and Museum. 10360 Hall Of Fame Dr.; (715) 634-4440; www.freshwater-fishing.org. Everything you wanted to know about fishing can be found in this shrine to anglers everywhere. Look for 100,000 fishing artifacts from bobbers to boats, 1,000 vintage outboard motors, and displays honoring top anglers. New in 2011: an exact replica of the Rapala family's 1950s workshop in Finland. The museum covers half a city block (about 7 acres) and includes a well-stocked pond for catch-and-release fishing during the summer.

Moccasin Bar. 15820 US 63; (715) 634-4211. Pop into this saloon to see the world's largest muskie at 5 feet long and 67 pounds. This has become an unofficial wildlife museum with quirky displays. Think taxidermy meets Dogs Playing Poker. Now picture that cult scene with bear cubs, a white rabbit, and an otter pouring a brew. If that's not bizarre enough, you'll find stuffed raccoons in a boxing ring, chipmunks having an Oktoberfest moment, and a courtroom with a wolf as the judge, a bobcat as the sheriff, and a badger in trouble for poaching. Open 11 a.m. to closing.

Namekagon Visitor Center. Intersection of US 53 and US 63, Trego; (715) 635-8346; www.nps.gov/sacn. You can learn about Namekagon River and the upper St. Croix River at this seasonal National Park Service office. A movie, exhibits, hands-on activities, and a diorama tell about the area's history and natural resources, including sturgeon—the fish that gave this 95-mile tributary of the St. Croix its name. Open 9 a.m. to 5 p.m. daily Memorial Day to Labor Day and weekends in Sept.

Scheers Lumberjack shows. 15642 County Hwy. B; (715) 634-6923; http://scheers lumberjackshow.com. There's a reason the History Channel started its *Ax Men* series and ESPN hosts the Great Outdoor Games. These lumberjacks were doing extreme sports long before the phrase was taken over by airborne boarders and bikers. So settle into "The Bowl"

> ## muskie mania
>
> *So why is the muskie (or muskellunge) so sought-after by anglers? Chalk it up to the fun and challenge of netting these huge fish that put up a good fight. A record-breaking muskie came in at 5 feet long. They have been known to eat muskrats and even ducks. You'll need all your muscles to reel one in and catch Wisconsin's state fish.*

(Hayward's 1890s holding area for logs) and watch the entertaining skills of flannel-clad competitors. They roll logs, climb poles, saw wood, and even invite kids to be part of the action. Admission: $9.95, 12 and older; $8.95, seniors; $7.95, kids 4–11.

Spider Lake Ranch. 10881W. SR 77; (715) 462-3386; http://spiderlakeranch.com. Head into the northwoods on horseback with 30-minute to 1-hour trail rides through 112 acres of meandering bridle paths. Cost: $17–$27. Children ages 2 or older can take a pony ride for $7. Winter rides are followed by a warm fire and hot chocolate.

Wilderness Walk Zoo. 9503N SR 27; (715) 634-2893; www.wildernesswalkhaywardwi .com. This family animal park includes a petting zoo, northern Wisconsin wildlife such as bears and porcupines, and exotics including a Siberian tiger and camel. The Shanty Town has an area for gold panning. Admission: $8–$11.50. Open May through Labor Day weekend.

where to eat

The Angry Minnow Restaurant & Brewery. 10440 Florida Ave.; (715) 934-3055; www .angryminnow.com. Kick back with an oatmeal stout, a River Pig pale ale, or Minnow Lite while dining on the brick terrace or inside Hayward's oldest building. They serve a variety of salads (including ones with crawfish or smoked whitefish), soups with beer bread on the side, smoked pork with plum barbecue sauce, a vegetarian wild rice and mushroom patty, and classic Friday night fish fry with Great Lakes perch or whitefish. Open 11 a.m. to 9 p.m. Tues through Thurs and 11 a.m. to 10 p.m. Fri and Sat. $$.

Famous Dave's. 9971 N. Grand Pines Ln.; (715) 462-3352; www.famousdaveshayward .com. We try to avoid chains in guidebooks, but this is your chance to visit the original Famous Dave's with American styles of barbecue, plus beans, corn, and other fixin's served on a garbage can lid. If you have room, go for bread pudding and praline sauce for dessert. Closed Mon through Wed during the winter months. Call for seasonal hours. $$.

Norske Nook. 10436 WI 27 South; (715) 634-4928; www.norskenook.com. This Norwe-gian-American hybrid wraps salmon, sandwich fillings, and even omelets in lefse. Other Nor-dic and northwoods influences: Swedish pancakes with lingonberries and stuffed cranberry wild rice french toast. This chain of four restaurants built a following with pies that have a few unusual flavors such as apple cream cheese, maple raisin, and root beer float. Open 5:30 a.m. to 7 p.m. Mon through Sat; 7 a.m. to 7 p.m. Sun. $$.

Tremblay's Sweet Shop. 10569 Main St.; (715) 634-2785; www.tremblaysweetshop .com. If you have kids or adult chocoholics, get a sweet fix at this Main Street confection-ary. They've been making fudge, turtles, truffles, chocolates, and pulled taffy since the early 1960s. Closed from Christmas through mid-Apr. $.

Turk's Inn. 11320 N. US 63; (715) 634-2597. This is the last place you'd expect a Middle Eastern restaurant, but this over-the-top Turkish dream supper club has made dinner an exotic night out since 1934. Robert and John Kennedy are among the celebrities who have dined within these red walls where archways hang with fringy tassels, rugs and beads add flair, and cozy nooks draw romantics. It's a trippy time warp. Order up ice-cream drinks such as Harem's Delight, sizzling lamb shish kebabs, baklava, and Turkish coffee. Open at 4 p.m. for happy hour, 5 p.m. for dinner Fri through Sun. $$$.

West's Hayward Dairy. 15848 2nd St.; (715) 634-2244; www.westshaywarddairy.com. It's impossible to resist a small-town dairy that's been serving homemade premium ice cream since the 1920s—especially with fun flavors like church basement lemon bar or Amazon treat with acai berry ice cream, salted cashews, and dark chocolate chunks. They serve 40 flavors from April 1 to October 31. Some others include cotton candy, black rasp-berry, coconut magic bar, and last year's addition: Mom's Favorites, a chocolate-studded red wine ice cream. You can get sandwiches and coffee here, too. Open 10 a.m. to 9 p.m. Mon through Thurs and 10 a.m. to 9:30 p.m. weekends Memorial Day through Labor Day. Call for spring and fall hours. $.

where to stay

KOA Hayward. 11544 N. US 63; (800) 562-7631; www.haywardcamping.com. This family-oriented campground rents tubes and offers shuttles for trips along the Namekagon River. There also are 2 playgrounds and a 300-foot waterslide and pool. $.

McCormick House Inn. 10634 Kansas Ave.; (715) 934-3339; www.mccormickhouseinn .com. This grand 1887 lumber baron's home offers 6 luxurious guest rooms and made-to-order breakfasts, including an option for an authentic English spread with imported bacon and sausage. Out back, guests can soak in a secluded spa or wander the formal English garden with an impressive reflecting pool. $$–$$$.

Spider Lake Lodge. 10472 W. Murphy Blvd.; (715) 462-3793; www.spiderlakelodge.com. Elegant yet rustic, this 1923 log lodge feels steeped in history. Each of the 7 rooms has unique decor and comes with breakfast, served on the huge porch overlooking the lake. Guests may also rent the cabin. $$–$$$.

Treelands on Chippewa Flowage. 9630 Treeland Rd.; (715) 462-3874; www.treeland resorts.com. This resort on the scenic Chippewa Flowage includes 10 hotel units, 27 vacation homes, a restaurant and bar, a pool, tennis courts, and a playground. $$$.

cable, wi

Cable, population 1,500, may be small, but it's huge in the hearts of world-class athletes. When the snow flies, 20,000 spectators show up to cheer on 11,000 cross-country skiers in the legendary Birkebeiner Ski Race—the largest in North America. Cable also hosted the International Paralympic competition in 2012.

In the summer, the Chequamegon National Forest hums with mountain bikers who rumble through the rugged landscape. About 2,500 competitors gather in the fall for the Chequamegon Fat Tire Festival, which includes a race along a 40-mile forest route. It's no wonder Cable has been dubbed "Trail Town USA."

getting there

From Hayward, follow US 63 east about 17 miles to Cable.

where to go

Cable Area Chamber of Commerce. 13380 County Hwy. M; (800) 533-7454; www .cable4fun.com. Stop in the visitor center between 8 a.m. and 4 p.m., Mon through Fri. Pick up maps, which especially come in handy for designated fall color routes.

American Birkebeiner Trail. (715) 634-5025; www.birkie.com. You can access the Birkie's more than 50 miles at Mosquito Brook Road, Telemark Resort, and North End Cabin in Cable. The sections near trailheads at County Highway 00 in Seeley and Hayward's Hatchery Park are lit at night. In the warm months, hikers, runners, and mountain bikers may use the trail. Parking permits are $10/day.

Cable Natural History Museum. 43570 Kavanaugh Rd.; (715) 798-3890; www.cable museum.org. If you want a full appreciation for the area's lakes, forests, and rivers, check out the displays or workshops here. You can even sign up for an eco-geo-history pontoon tour of Lake Namekagon or Lake Owen. The museum also features the work of local photographers and artists and sells fun gifts such as woodland finger puppets. Admission: $5, adults; free to kids under 18. Open 10 a.m. to 4 p.m. Tues through Sat. Free admission on Tues.

Chequamegon Area Mountain Bike Association. www.cambatrails.org. Plot your foray into the woods through this organization that creates and maintains 300 miles of marked routes through the forest. Maps also available at the Hayward Lakes or Cable visitor centers.

where to eat

The Rookery Pub. 20100 CR M; (715) 794-2060; www.cablelakenaturelodge.com. The ever-changing menu includes fresh fish specials, beef and bison steak, handmade pasta, salads, vegetarian and vegan entrees, and other dishes showcasing local, seasonal ingredients. $$.

east

day trip 01

east

minnesota's trendy grande dame:
stillwater, mn

stillwater, mn

Dubbed the birthplace of Minnesota, Stillwater gracefully reigns above the St. Croix River like a grande dame. Antiques shops and bookstores line its historic Main Street. Victorian bed-and-breakfasts beckon overnighters. Gondolas and paddleboat rides woo newlyweds and romance-seekers.

Its collective charm (and easy-to-reach location) keeps the town of 21,000 thriving with hip clothing boutiques, sophisticated dining, home and kitchen shops, galleries, and garden stores—everything that makes Main Street pure heaven for people who love to host gatherings and make houses homey.

You'll find everything from fancy armoires and funky vintage dresses to local wines and a tasting bar for extra virgin olive oil and gourmet vinegars.

Make sure you have at least a day to leisurely explore downtown. Even better: Get out on the river for a fresh look at Minnesota's first city.

getting there

Follow MN 36 east about 20 miles to Stillwater.

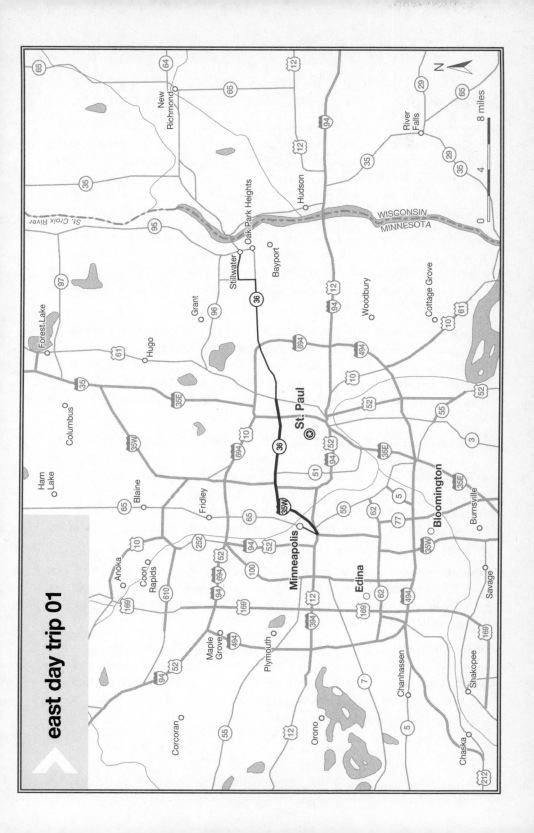

east day trip 01

where to go

Aamodt's Apple Farm. 6428 Manning Ave.; (651) 439-3127; www.aamodtsapplefarm
.com. Crowds choose their favorite bags of apples from huge bins in this historic barn. It's
loaded with temptations from pies and sugar-coated apple cider doughnuts to pumpkins
and gourmet popcorn. There are generally close to a dozen varieties, including Honeygold
and Honeycrisp, as well as fresh cider, grilled apple brats, a hay-bale maze, goats to pet,
and pedal tractors. Open 10 a.m. to 6 p.m., Aug through Dec.

Joseph Wolf Brewery Cave Tours. 402 S. Main St.; (651) 430-0560; www.lunarossa
winebar.com. Half-hour tours of these former brewery caves tell about the city's brewing
history and how the caves were used over the years. You can also see them from inside
the adjoining Luna Rossa Trattoria (and smell that distinctive whiff you get from sandstone
caves). Tours: $7, adults; $5, kids 5–11.

Northern Vineyards Winery. 223 N. Main St.; (651) 430-1032; www.northernvineyards
.com. This winery can claim one of the most scenic places to sip a glass of wine made with
locally grown grapes. Try the dry Minnesota La Crosse or elegant St. Croix Reserve wine on
a Sunday evening when there's live music on the terrace and great views of the river. Open
10 a.m. to 6 p.m. Nov through Apr; until 8 p.m. May through Oct weekdays and 9 p.m. on
weekends. Tastings, $5; tours, $10.

St. Croix Vineyards. 6428 Manning Ave.; (651) 430-3310; www.scvwines.com. You can
park among apple trees and vines during fall weekends when this place crawls with visitors.
They get a double-delight with crisp fruit and baked goods from Aamodt's Apple Farm and
this winery in a rustic barn next to it. Among its signature wines: a semisweet red wine that's
chilled for warm-weather picnics in the orchard and raspberry infusion, a sweet pairing for
chocolate and dessert. Tastings: $5. Afternoon tours offered the first Saturday of the month
May to Dec.

Stillwater Trolley. 400 Nelson St. East; (651) 430-0352; www.stillwatertrolley.com. Hop
aboard for 45-minute narrated history tours that travel downtown, along the river, and
up into the neighborhoods built by lumber barons. Runs daily May through Oct. Tickets:
$12.50, adults; $6.50, children 17 and younger.

Warden's House Museum. 602 N. Main St.; (651) 439-5956; www.wchsmn.org. As Minnesota's oldest city, it makes sense it also had the first territorial prison. Visitors can learn
more about it and see this 14-room 1853 warden's house during tours from 1 to 5 p.m.
Thurs through Sun, May to Oct. Interestingly, Stillwater is still home to the state's biggest
high-security prison. Admission: $5, adults; $1, children.

where to shop

The popularity of Stillwater means most shops are open seven days a week and often into the evening hours. Call for details. Check the Stillwater website for details on themed Ladies Night Out events during the off-season.

Alfresco Casual Living. 321 S. Main St.; (651) 439-0814; www.alfrescocasualliving.com. Bright, whimsical colors make this cheery store a refreshing place to browse for eclectic home decor, linens, pajamas, kids' clothes, accessories, toys, and cards.

The Chef's Gallery. 324 Main St.; (651) 351-2165; www.thechefsgallery.com. You'll find everything for the kitchen here from retro aprons and a rainbow of pots and pans to glassware and gadgets. It's especially good for the holidays when you need that fancy cookie press and inspiration to make Grandma's lefse. Even better: Sign up for one of their hands-on cooking and baking classes.

Darn Knit Anyway. 432 S. Main St.; (651) 342-1386; www.darnknitanyway.com. Crafters can lose themselves in an array of unique yarns (some locally made), textiles, and wool for felting. You also can find handmade gifts or take a class.

Midtown Antique Mall. 301 Main St. South; (651) 430-0808; www.midtownantiques.com. You can easily spend hours in this dizzying 3-story collection of antiques that's one of the largest in the state with more than 100 dealers. The lower levels are dense with jewelry, music, toys, textiles, and kitchenwares and tools, while the top floor is full of antique bookshelves, armoires, tables, and elegant furniture.

St. Croix Antiquarian. 232 S. Main St.; (651) 430-0732; www.booktown.com. This may be a digital age, but there's still magic in the pages of classic cookbooks, out-of-print children's classics, and art books. The shop also specializes in handpainted architectural prints and globes and maps from the 1800s.

Stillwater Art Guild Gallery. 402 N. Main St.; (651) 689-0149; www.artguildgallery.com. This cooperative sells the work of area potters, painters, photographers, sculptors, jewelers, and more. Framing offered, as well as photography and pottery classes.

Stillwater Olive Oil. 208 Main St. South; (651) 472-5789; www.stillwateroliveoil.com. Sample your way through an astonishing array of specialty oils such as grape seed or truffle; extra virgin olive oils with flavors such as basil, blood orange, or cilantro; and balsamic vinegars with flavors such as blackberry ginger, peach, and dark chocolate.

Tradewinds Spice Company. 423 S. Main St.; (651) 351-0422; www.tradewindsspice .com. Close your eyes and shop with your nose at this store filled with rich, exotic, zippy, and sweet aromas of more than 250 spices from around the world.

find a new way to get aound

Ditch your car and find a fun new way to explore the scenic St. Croix River Valley, whether you're on the river itself or dreamily drifting above it on a hot air balloon ride.

Aamodt's Hot Air Balloons. *(651) 351-0101; www.aamodtsballoons.com. Prices start at $200 per person.*

Gondola Romantica. *Nelson Street East; (651) 439-1783; www.gondola romantica.com. Striped-shirt gondoliers take couples along the river during the day or by the glow of a full moon. Prices start at $95 for a 2-person, 45-minute ride. Several packages pair a ride with dinner at the Dock Café.*

St. Croix Boat and Packet Company. *(651) 430-1234; www.stillwaterriver boats.com. Brunch, lunch, and dinner cruises let guests dine while enjoying the ever-changing scenery along the St. Croix River. Prices start at $13.95 for children and $17.65 for adults for a 2-hour lunch buffet.*

Stillwater Balloons. *135 St. Croix Trail North, Lakeland; (651) 439-1800; www .stillwaterballoons.com. Prices start at $245/person.*

where to eat

Aprille's Showers Tea Room. 120 N. Main St.; (651) 430-2004; www.aprilleshowers .com. This is the place for high tea with finger sandwiches, pumpkin curry soup, buttercream cake, tarts, and white chocolate peppermint scones at Christmas. You can have a light lunch, too, or browse the 50-plus kinds of tea sold here. Daily tea served from 10 a.m. to 4 p.m. $–$$.

Dock Café. 425 Nelson St. East; (651) 430-3770; www.dockcafe.com. This restaurant claims the best riverside view. Entrees include blackened yellowfin tuna with blue cheese sauce, grilled lamb loin with marinated cherries, curried chicken salad, and shrimp served in a Creole cream on pasta. Open 11 a.m. to 8 p.m. Mon through Thurs, 11 a.m. to 10 p.m. Fri and Sat, and until 8 p.m. Sun. $$–$$$.

Gasthaus Bavarian Hunter. 8390 Lofton Ave.; (651) 439-7128; www.gasthausbavarian hunter.com. Tucked into the woods on the edge of Stillwater, you can feast on Bavarian sausages, rouladen, smoked pork, bread dumplings, spaetzle, and potatoes and tip back a Munich brew and listen to live accordion music on Friday evenings and Sunday afternoons.

Open 11 a.m. to 9 p.m. Mon through Fri, noon to 9 p.m. Sat, and noon to 8 p.m. Sun. Sunday buffet served noon to 3 p.m. $$.

Leo's Grill and Malt Shop. 131 Main St. South; (651) 439-9294; www.leosgrill.com. This classy little diner adds a welcome dose of nostalgia to the downtown scene with its burgers, homemade skin-on fries, thick malts, and even a walk-up window for cones on a hot summer day. Open 11 a.m. to 8 p.m. daily and until 9 p.m. in the summer. $.

Luna Rossa Trattoria. 402 Main St.; (651) 430-0560; www.lunarossawinebar.com. The outdoor terrace in front of the restaurant and tucked along the bluff with caves makes this a prime place to dine while watching the action downtown. Order wood-fired pizzas, pastas, entrees, build-your-own-pasta bar for lunch, plus Italian coffee and gelato. Open 11 a.m. to 9 p.m. Mon through Fri, 10 a.m. to 10 p.m. Sat and Sun. $$$.

Marx Fusion Bistro. 241 Main St. South; (651) 439-8333; www.marxwbg.com. This vibrant wine bar serves an eclectic Asian, Caribbean, and Italian menu with walleye dumplings, shrimp tempura in red curry coconut sauce, and homemade pappardelle pasta with pistachios and a creamy parmesan basil sauce. Open 11:30 a.m. to close. $$-$$$.

where to stay

Ann Bean Mansion. 319 W. Pine St.; (651) 430-0355; www.annbeanmansion.com. This cute Victorian has 5 spacious, comfortable rooms, including one with a trap door that leads to the tower with a cozy table for two. $$$.

The Elephant Walk. 801 W. Pine St.; (651) 430-0359; www.elephantwalkbb.com. The 4 exotically decorated rooms each take inspiration from across the world with styles that reflect Singapore, Burma, and Thailand. $$$.

The Lowell Inn. 102 2nd St. North; (651) 439-1100; www.lowellinn.com. Step into the past with this inn's 35 rooms furnished in antiques and pastel fabrics. It sits a block uphill from downtown. $$.

Rivertown Inn. 306 Olive St. West; (651) 430-2955; www.rivertowninn.com. Sumptuously decorated, the lavish suites (especially one themed for Agatha Christie's Orient Express) could pass for a theatrical set. Like the sleeping chambers, all rooms are named for English poets and authors. $$$.

Water Street Inn. 101 Water St. South; (651) 439-6000; www.waterstreetinn.us. This 1890 inn can feel dark inside, but it's the best bet if you want to be right in downtown and less than a block from the riverfront. Charlie's Irish Pub has a patio overlooking the river and live Irish music Friday and Saturday nights. $$$.

day trip 02

east

the chippewa river valley:
menomonie, wi; chippewa falls, wi;
eau claire, wi

Driving east from the Twin Cities toward Menomonie, I-94 splits in two, swinging around a gorgeous stretch of hardwoods as the road dips into a valley. It's spectacular in the fall. And it's a teaser for the rolling scenery yet to come in west central Wisconsin.

Bikers and cross-country skiers come for state trails along Menomonie's Red Cedar River and the Chippewa River that runs through Chippewa Falls and Eau Claire. Approximately 20,000 University of Wisconsin students keep the area lively and youthful with campuses in Eau Claire and at Stout in Menomonie. They fuel an arts scene, live entertainment, fun coffee shops, and more than 250 restaurants.

Grab a rural road around these cities—named like alphabet soup with "OO," "E," and "H"—and the pace changes. East of Chippewa Falls in particular, you can catch the clip-clop of a Mennonite family's horse and buggy, pass fields polka-dotted with Holsteins, and taste the cheese that makes Wisconsin America's Dairyland.

menomonie, wi

Only an hour east of the Twin Cities, Menomonie ranks as a favorite among nature lovers, who bike through the shady ravines and scenery of the Red Jacket Trail. Go on a summer evening, and you may be able to wind down the day with a nostalgic Ludington Guard Band concert at Wilson Park.

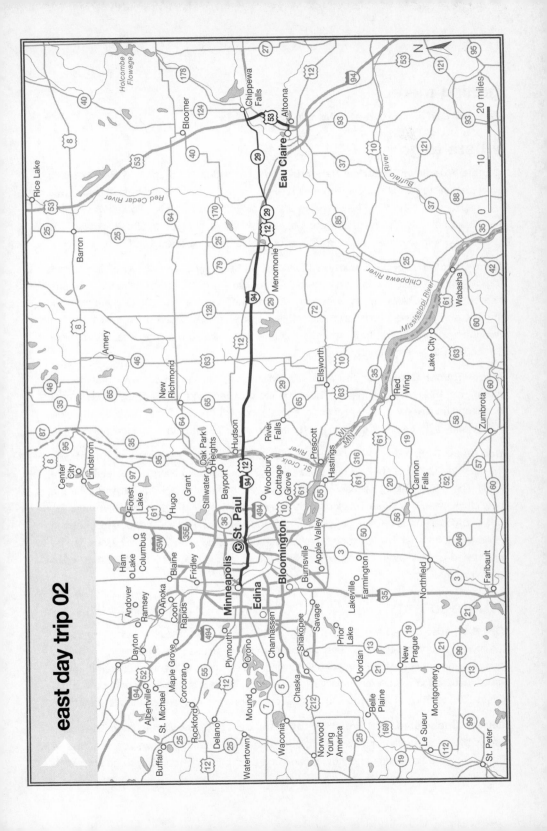

getting there

Take I-94 east about 70 miles to Menomonie.

where to go

Caddie Woodlawn Historical Park and State Wayside. WI 25 South; (715) 232-8685; www.dunnhistory.org. You can see the childhood home of Caroline Woodhouse who was the inspiration for the 1935 Newbery Award–winning children's book *Caddie Woodlawn* 9 miles south of town. Carol Brink wrote the series based on her grandmother's experiences growing up with four siblings in 1860s Wisconsin. Open spring through fall.

Dunn County Historical Society. 1820 Wakanda St.; (715) 232-8685; www.dunnhistory .org. Interactive exhibits and photos chronicle the area's history, including the Victorian era, rise of industry, golden age of American auto design, and the Kraft State Bank robbery. There's also a Caddie Woodlawn children's discovery room. Open noon to 4 p.m. Oct through Apr and 10 a.m. to 5 p.m. May through Sept. Closed Mon and Tues. Admission: $5, adults; $3, teens; $1, kids 6–12.

Mabel Tainter Center for the Arts. 205 Main St.; (715) 235-9726; www.mabeltainter .com. This 1889 Victorian theater shows off the grandeur and riches of the city's lumber boom and houses a varying array of arts, from dance performances and concerts to monthly gallery shows and tours. It's also a good place to shop for gifts made by local artists.

Red Cedar Trail. 921 Brickyard Rd.; (715) 232-1242; www.chippewavalley.net. The popular 14-mile Red Cedar State Trail has lured many with its peaceful riverside route. The highlight? The 846-foot-long railroad bridge spanning the impressive river. The trail joins the new Chippewa River State Trail forming a continuous route of 37 miles between the cities of Menomonie and Eau Claire. In winter, the Chippewa River Trail is used for snowmobiling while the Red Cedar Trail is groomed for cross-country skiing. Daily $4 trail passes can be purchased at trailheads. Bikes can be rented from Simple Sports (715-233-3493; www .simplesports.com).

where to eat

Das Bierhaus. 120 6th Ave. West; (715) 231-3230; www.dasbierhaus-wi.com. This Bavarian-style brewery sticks to the purity law German brewmasters passed back in 1516. You can hoist a cool one with flammkuchen (onions, Swiss cheese, bacon, and crème fraîche on a crust), sausage samplers, schnitzels and—since this is Wisconsin—beer cheese soup. Open Tues to Sun, 11 a.m. to 2 a.m. Ask about tours while you're there or call ahead. $.

Legacy Chocolates. 623 Broadway St.; (715) 231-2580; www.legacychocolates.com. Browse for hand-crafted, intense chocolates made with South American cocoa and Love Potion No. 9, a rich sauce of cocoa, cream, and butter. Feeling too guilty to go straight to dessert? Savor one of their soups, from sweet corn potato chowder to smoked salmon wild rice. $$.

The Raw Deal. 603 S. Broadway St.; (715) 231-3255; www.rawdeal-wi.com. Fair-trade coffee, fresh ginger lemonade, muffins, bars, and raw food items make this an artsy find—especially for vegans or anyone on a special diet. Open 6:30 a.m. to 6 p.m. Mon through Sat, 10 a.m. to 3 p.m. Sun. $$.

Sparx Restaurant. 1827 Broadway St. North; (715) 235-3000; www.sparxrestaurant.com. Kick back on the patio with a fireplace or dine indoors on truffled bison burger, sirloin, or nightly specials such as Thursday sushi, fish fry Friday, and Sunday tapas night. Open at 11 a.m. $$–$$$.

Zanzibar. 228 E. Main St.; (715) 231-9269; www.zanzibarmenomonie.com. For a trendy night out, bite into lahvosh pizza with chicken and mango, dine on pierogies and pastas, or order a round of tapas and martinis. $$$.

where to stay

Oak Lawn Inn. 423 Technology Dr. East; (715) 235-6155; www.oaklawninn.com. Once part of the Tainter family's sprawling horse farm, this historic home offers 4 spacious guest rooms and breakfasts such as stuffed french toast or creamy scrambled eggs with spinach, tomato, and basil. $$.

worth more time

Crystal Cave. W965 SR 29, Spring Valley; (800) 236-2283; www.acoolcave.com. You'll see billboards for Crystal Cave long before you hit Menomonie. It features meandering passages with stalactites, stalagmites, and rippled flowstone and is considered the longest cave in Wisconsin. Guides cover the history of the cave (discovered more than 70 years ago) and lead guests through rooms such as the Ballroom and Mother Hubbard's Cupboard. Open 9:30 a.m. to 5:30 p.m. throughout the summer, and 10 a.m. to 4:30 p.m. in Sept and Oct.

chippewa falls, wi

Chippewa Falls, population 13,500, draws visitors with its historic brick Main Street not far from the mighty Chippewa River. Coupled with natural springs, the city has long claimed some of the country's purest water. Much of it goes into making its famous Leinenkugel beer.

A dammed section of the river creates the nearby 6,300-acre Lake Wissota, a popular and scenic escape. The city also claims a key role in the technology revolution. Cray Computers, builder of the world's first supercomputer, was founded here.

getting there

From Menomonie, continue on I-94, exiting at WI 29, which leads northeast to Chippewa Falls. The cities are about 30 minutes apart.

where to go

Irvine Park & Zoo. Bridgewater Avenue and Bear Den Road; (715) 723-0051; www.irvine parkzoo.org. Kids love this spacious 318-acre historic public park that's home to tigers, bobcats, cougars, black bears, deer, bison, and a seasonal Red Barn Petting Zoo. The park is lit up with more than 100,000 lights from Thanksgiving to New Year's. Open year-round. Free admission.

Jacob Leinenkugel Brewing Company. 124 Elm St.; (715) 723-5557; www.leinie.com. Sign up at the Leinie Lodge for free tours of this popular brewery, from grain storage and mash cookers to the bottling area for everything from its Summer Shandy (with honey and lemonade) to Big Butt (a hearty cold-weather doppelbock). You'll be able to try a few samples, then shop for Leinie's and Wisconsin souvenirs at the log welcome center with its

sample a new wine

This area may be best known for its beer, but small wineries are making a come-back. They blend local fruits, cold-hardy grapes, and heritage recipes used by early German settlers.

Autumn Harvest Winery. 19947 County Hwy. J; (715) 720-1663; www .autumnharvestwinery.com. Sample fruit and grape wines, gourmet foods, and pick up fresh apples from the orchard. Signature wines include Fall Folly with black raspberries, Grandpa's Best elderberry heritage wine, and Blue Heaven, a semisweet red accented with blueberries. Open May through Oct.

O'Neil Creek Winery. 15369 82nd St., Bloomer; (715) 568-2341; www.oneil creekwinery.com. This winery specializes in fruit wines and dandelion wine. Open May through Dec.

River Bend Vineyard & Winery. 10439 33rd Ave.; (715) 720-9463; www.river bendvineyard.com. Sample wines made from cold-hardy northern grapes and fruits grown at this 8-acre vineyard. Gifts and accessories for the wine enthusiast are also available. Open May through Dec.

> ## be cheesy

You can sample a large variety of Wisconsin cheese about 20 minutes from Chippewa Falls in the small town of Cadott.

Heerde's Cheese House. *412 E. Oak St., Cadott; (715) 289-4568; www.heerdes cheesehouse.com. Look for more than 70 kinds of Wisconsin cheeses including cranberry cheddar, maple white cheddar, mild brick, morel and leek jack, and award-winning Marieke gouda. You can also find Noelchek's summer sausage, beef sticks, beef and pork jerky; jams and jellies; maple syrup; and wines from Autumn Harvest and River Bend wineries. Open 8 a.m. to 6 p.m. Mon through Sat, 10 a.m. to 5 or 6 p.m. Sun. Closed Tues Sept through Apr.*

Yellowstone Cheese. *24105 County Hwy. MM, Cadott; (715) 289-3800; www .yellowstonecheese.com. This dairy makes more than 30 flavors of cheddar, Colby, and Monterey Jack, using vegetables, olives, dill, bacon, and hot peppers for a variety of combinations. Don't miss squeaky-fresh cheese curds, plain or spiced up. The shop also sells wine, Point root beer, jams and jellies, maple syrup, take-n-bake pizzas, and meats.*

massive stone fireplace and comfy leather chairs. Open 9 a.m. to 5 p.m. Mon through Sat (8 p.m. closing on Fri) and 11 a.m. to 4 p.m. on Sun. Tours run every half an hour.

Lake Wissota State Park. 18127 County Hwy. O; (715) 382-4574; http://dnr.wi.gov. Bring your own or rent a boat, canoe, or kayak to get onto the water at this man-made lake created in 1918 by a power-and-light dam. You can camp at 116 sites in the woods (not on the water), swim at the beach, take a hike or find a scenic picnic spot. Bikers can catch the Old Abe Trail and bike 20 miles to Brunet Island State Park. Park fee required ($5–$10/day).

Loopy's Tube & Canoe Rentals. 10691 County Hwy. X; (715) 726-5667; www.723loop .com. Popular for its summer tiki bar and pizzas, Loopy's also rents canoes, kayaks, and inner tubes and provides a shuttle service up the Chippewa River. The approximately 2.5-hour downriver floats and paddles end at Loopy's Saloon & Grill. Open at 9 a.m. during the summer, 10 a.m. in the off-season.

Mason Shoe Outlet Store. 301 N. Bridge St.; (715) 723-4323; www.masoncompanies inc.com. Chippewa Falls is home to Mason Shoe's catalog company, giving local shoppers access to 15,000 pairs of shoes. The choices are dizzying: sturdy Keen hiking boots, Sorel winter boots, Puma athletic shoes, Born and Tommy Hilfiger dress shoes, glitzy high heels, and hard-to-find sizes and widths. A newer addition to the business is a women's clothing line. Open at 9 a.m. to 5:30 or 6 p.m. Mon through Sat, 11 a.m. to 4 p.m. Sun.

where to eat

Bake & Brew Café and Coffee Shop. 17255 County Hwy. X; (715) 720-2360; www .bakenbrewcafe.com. Close to Lake Wissota, this cafe offers a sweet way to start the day with gooey cinnamon and pecan rolls or heartier fare such as omelets, breakfast burritos, or fruity crepes. Lunch items include soup, sandwiches, burgers, pies, and cheesecake. $.

High Shores Supper Club. 17985 County Hwy. X; (715) 723-9854; www.highshores .com. This sturdy log restaurant overlooks the scenic wooded shore on the south end of Lake Wissota. It's known for its Friday fish fry, along with steak, pasta, and a salad bar with soup. Summer diners can opt for a pontoon ride afterward or soak in the sun on the outdoor patio. $$–$$$.

Olson's Ice Cream Parlor and Deli. 611 N. Bridge St.; (715) 723-4331; www.olsons icecream.com. Grab a croissant, sub, or hot sandwich and chicken dumpling soup at this downtown landmark, then stop kidding yourself. You know you're there for the ice cream with 28 "homaid" flavors from chocolate monster and caramel cashew to seasonal tiramisu or black licorice. Call for seasonal hours. $.

where to stay

Pleasantview Bed and Breakfast. 16649 96th Ave.; (715) 382-4401; www.pleasantview bb.com. This lakeside B&B takes advantage of Lake Wissota views with a private patio or deck access for some of its 5 rooms. Breakfast may include from-scratch doughnuts, bacon waffles, or french toast with fruit. $$.

eau claire, wi

Named for the "clear water" at the junction of the Chippewa and Eau Claire Rivers, this city of more than 65,000 residents has grown from a bustling lumber town to a commercial center for the area's farmers and an educational hub with more than 10,000 students.

getting there

From Chippewa Falls, take US 53 south about 15 miles to Eau Claire.

where to go

Action City. 5150 Fairview Dr.; (888) 861-6001; www.metropolisresort.com. This 55,000-square-foot play area blends an outdoor maze, indoor go-karts, minigolf, bowling, a climbing wall, batting cages, arcade, and laser tag. Most play packages start at $25/person. Call for seasonal hours.

Carson Park. 1040 Forest St.; (715) 839-5032; www.eauclairewi.gov. If you can go one place in Eau Claire, head to this 134-acre peninsula nestled inside horseshoe-shaped Half Moon Lake. It's the hub for the city's key family attractions and museums.

Children's Museum of Eau Claire. 220 S. Barstow St.; (715) 832-5437; www.cmec.cc. There aren't many places where you can crawl through a mouth, down a digestive track, and exit into a toilet bowl, but it's part of the learn-through-play approach to exhibits about the human body, small towns, show business, construction sites, and waterworks. Admission: $5. Open 9 a.m. to 5 p.m. Tues through Sat (7 p.m. on Thurs) and noon to 5 p.m. Sun Memorial Day through Labor Day weekend. Call for off-season hours. Admission: $5.

Chippewa Valley Museum. 1204 Carson Park Dr.; (715) 834-7871. This year-round museum makes use of the park's historic buildings to recreate parts of the past, Ojibwe exhibits, a Swedish log home, one-room schoolhouse, 21-room dollhouse, and a 1950s ice-cream parlor. You can visit the parlor without admission. Open 10 a.m. to 5 p.m. Mon to Sat in the summer and 1 to 5 p.m. Sun. Closed Mon during the school year. Call for details. Admission: $5, adults; $2, students 5–17.

Chippewa Valley Railroad. 101 Carson Park Dr.; (715) 831-0900; www.chippewavalley railroad.com. Tour Carson Park and see Half Moon Lake while riding in a miniature quarter-size working railroad car powered by steam and gasoline. Open noon to 5 p.m. Memorial Day weekend through Labor Day. Admission: $3, adults; $2, children.

Paul Bunyan Logging Camp. 1110 Carson Park Dr.; (715) 835-6200; www.paulbunyan camp.org. Paul Bunyan and Babe, his faithful blue ox, loom large in front of this multibuilding museum dedicated to the area's logging history and its 1890s boom. Tours begin in the Strand Interpretive Center and continue to a cook shanty, bunkhouse, equipment shed, blacksmith shop, and barn. Open daily May through Sept from 10 a.m. to 4:30 p.m. Admission: $4, adults, $2, children 4–17.

Riverside Bike & Skate. 902 Menomonie St.; (715) 835-0088; www.riversidebikeskate .com. Rent bicycles, in-line skates, or ice skates to take on the Chippewa Valley Trails or take out a canoe and kayaks for 1- to 4-hour trips on the Eau Claire or Chippewa Rivers.

where to eat

Fanny Hill Victorian Inn and Dinner Theatre. 3919 Crescent Ave.; (715) 836-8184; www .fannyhill.com. Fanny Hill is a threefold attraction with lighthearted shows such as "Church Basement Ladies," a dinner restaurant and Sunday brunch overlooking the Chippewa River Valley, and bed-and-breakfast rooms. Not everyone likes the floral decor, dolls, or teddy bears, but this local attraction is on its third decade. Dinner is served from 4 to 9 p.m. and Sunday brunch from 9:30 a.m. to 2 p.m. Rooms $–$$.

Mona Lisa's. 428 Water St.; (715) 839-8969; www.monalisas.biz. Kick back on the patio or inside this exposed brick and contemporary restaurant downtown. The Italian and Mediterranean pastas, salads, thin-crust pizzas, and seafood and steak choices change frequently with seasonal fare. $$.

Northwoods Brewpub. 3560 Oakwood Mall Dr.; (715) 552-0510; www.northwoodsbrew pub.com. They've got burgers and pizza and even pie, lefse, and hearty breakfasts from the Norske Nook at this all-day restaurant. What makes it stand out, though, are the microbrew beers. Look for Floppin' Crappie, Mouthy Muskie, and Whitetail Wheat among more than a dozen brews ranging from pale ale and red lager to porter and stout. They also brew Walter's, a long-ago Eau Claire pilsner that's back in a bottle. Open at 7 a.m. Mon through Sat and 8 a.m. Sun. Food served until 10 p.m. Mon through Thurs, 11 p.m. Fri and Sat, and 8 p.m. Sun. $$.

Obsession Chocolate Café and Lounge. 18 S. Barstow St.; (715) 830-8301; www .obsessionchocolates.com. With a newly expanded location, this downtown cafe serves decadent breakfasts of beignets and espresso, omelets, and lunches with sandwiches on home-baked hearth breads and salads. Follow up with gourmet chocolates. Look for weekly hands-on classes such as making truffles and artisan breads. Open 8 a.m. to 7 p.m. Mon through Sat, 8 a.m. to 4 p.m. Sun. $.

where to stay

Metropolis Resort. 5150 Fairview Dr.; (888) 861-6001; www.metropolisresort.com. Modern and funky, this resort caters to both kids, with its water park and outdoor entertainment, and adults, with sophisticated suites themed like Milan, New York City, Miami, or Vegas getaways. A locker room suite sleeps 20 with arcade games between bunks. Room rates include breakfast. Water park passes come with a package rate. $–$$.

southeast

day trip 01

southeast

wisconsin's great river road:
stockholm, wi; pepin, wi; alma, wi;
fountain city, wi

Colorful small towns dot the Wisconsin side of the Great River Road as it winds its way south of the Twin Cities and around Lake Pepin. Historic villages sit tucked between steep, wooded coulees, the Mississippi, and backwaters strewn with water lilies through which herons stoically stalk their prey.

It's a perfect laid-back road trip whether you're goofing off with girlfriends or hugging the curves with a motorcycle rumbling beneath you. Keep an eye out for eagles as you soak up some of the best scenery by following the shore of 28-mile Lake Pepin. Technically a widening in the Mississippi where the Chippewa River joins it, this stretch includes Stockholm, Pepin, and Alma with a short drive to Fountain City.

Together they serve up memorable meals, unique lodging, and a nostalgic dose of history with the birthplace of Laura Ingalls Wilder.

stockholm, wi

The population clocks in at fewer than 100 residents, but this small but mighty village pulls in a steady flow of visitors. Chalk it up to the inherent historic charm of a river town matched with the fresh energy of more than 20 artsy shops, galleries, cafes, and unique places to stay. They roll out a gracious welcome with blue bikes for visitors to borrow and blue water bowls for canine guests.

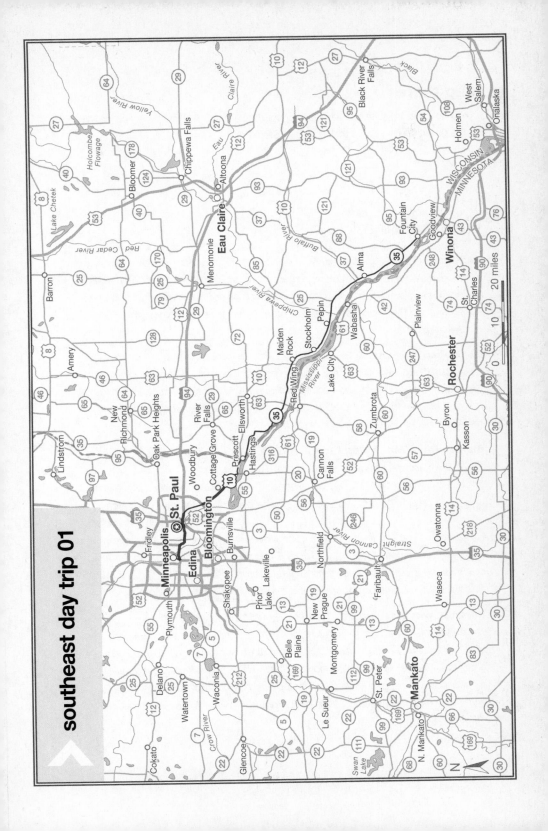

southeast day trip 01

getting there

Follow I-94 to meet up with US 61 heading southeast from St. Paul. Veer left on WI 35 to access the Great River Road and follow into Stockholm.

> ## great river wines

Orchards and vineyards can thrive along bluffs and embankments of river valleys, which keep them above cold temperatures that creep in during spring and fall. Here are a few places that are part of the Great River Road Wine Trail and near Lake Pepin on the Wisconsin side. For more information, go to www.greatriver roadwinetrail.org.

Danzinger Vineyards & Winery. *S2015 Grapeview Rd., Alma; (608) 685-6000; www.danzingervineyards.com. Among their many award winners are Crescent Moon with a citrus finish and LaCrescent grapes, Mississippi Mist and White Velvet, both sweet white wines, and a raspberry table wine. The tasting room opened in 2010. Hours are 10 a.m. to 5 p.m.*

Maiden Rock Winery and Cidery. *W12266 King Ln., Stockholm; (715) 448-3502; www.maidenrockwinerycidery.com. This winery makes three apple wines (including a Dolgo crab apple) and expanded with a cidery in 2008. There is no charge to sample hard ciders such as Honeycrisp Hard, Scrumpy, and Bitter Love.*

In the fall, you get the best deal: hard ciders and wines, fresh apples from the Maiden Rock Orchard (open 10 a.m. to 6 p.m., Wed through Sun), and stunning colors along the bluffs. Winery and Cidery open 10 a.m. to 6 p.m. Wed through Sun April 1 through December 31, and 4 to 7 p.m. Tues May through Oct.

Seven Hawks Vineyards. *17 North St., Fountain City; (866) 946-3741; www .sevenhawksvineyards.com. These more than a dozen wines all feature northern grape varietals. Their signature blends of northern white grapes (Smiling Moon) and reds (Hunter's Blend) have both won awards. Look for special reserves, a crisp apple wine, and Fountain City Ruby and Gold, their port-style red and white dessert wines. Open daily in the summer. Closed Mon and Tues in the off-season.*

where to go

Abode Gallery. N2030 Spring St. #3; (715) 442-2266; www.abodegallery.com. Admire handmade furniture, rugs, pottery, sculpture, paintings, and colorful accessories meant to make your house more homey.

Ingebretsen's av Stockholm Scandinavian Gifts. 12092 WI 35; (715) 442-2220; www .ingebretsens.com. This offshoot of the popular Minneapolis store sells imported tableware, textiles, and foods, along with bakery goods on the weekends.

The Palate. W12102 WI 35; (715) 442-6400; www.thepalate.net. This gourmet kitchen store features a little of everything hostesses love: fun linens, stylish aprons, great glassware, colorful kitchen pots and pans, gourmet foods, and inspiration for seasonal gatherings. Usually open 9 a.m. to 5 p.m. Tues through Sat and from 10 a.m. to 5 p.m. Sun.

Rush River Produce. W4098 200th Ave., Maiden Rock; (715) 594-3648; www.rushriver produce.com. If you visit in summer, have a cooler handy for the produce of this farm about 6 miles north of Stockholm and 3 miles inland from the river. Look for asparagus in May; red, white, and black currants and gooseberries from July through early August; plus fall raspberries and autumn apples. The biggest attraction: 9 acres with 14 varieties of u-pick blueberries, including some that grow on vines. Call before visiting to check what's ripe and available.

where to eat

Bogus Creek Café & Bakery. N2049 Spring St.; (715) 442-5017. Start the day with a Scandinavian treat: Swedish pancakes with lingonberries or a Swedish doughnut. You can go more traditional with hash and french toast, salads, pastas, sandwiches on artisan breads, ice cream, and espresso. Call for seasonal hours. $$.

Stockholm Pie Company. N2030 Spring St. #1; (715) 442-5505; www.stockholmpie company.com. As you can guess, this cafe with sandwiches on homemade bread and quiches has built its reputation on pie. Look for double lemon, caramel apple crunch, and blackberry pear. Get it warm, topped with a scoop of Timm's ice cream. $$.

where to stay

Journey Inn. W3671 200th Ave., Maiden Rock; (715) 448-2424; www.journeyinn.net. This eco-retreat tucked into a coulee north of Stockholm features 4 rooms named for the elements and a 1-bedroom cottage. Amenities include organic fabrics, green practices, balconies or patio, and a seasonal organic breakfast with fair-trade coffee and tea. Watch for retreats featuring massage, meditation, and life coaching. $$$.

quick tip: take earplugs

If you're staying the night along either side of the Mississippi River and consider yourself a light sleeper, take earplugs to muffle the sound of train whistles.

The River Road Inn. W12360 Great River Rd.; (612) 306-2100; www.riverroadinn.com. This new inn features 3 modern, spacious rooms including a Jade Room with Asian decor and another with a nautical theme. The fourth unit is the carriage house, which offers a little more privacy. All have their own decks overlooking Lake Pepin. $$$$.

pepin, wi

Pepin is known worldwide thanks to the popularity of Laura Ingalls Wilder, who wrote about her early years here in *Little House in the Big Woods*. You can sit back and ponder those simpler times while eating a sophisticated meal, sipping a local wine, gazing across the marina, or getting onto the lake.

getting there

Continue on WI 35, driving 6.5 miles south of Stockholm to reach Pepin.

where to go

BNOX Gold & Iron. 404 1st St.; (715) 442-2201; www.bnoxgold.com. This gallery features the work of several jewelry artists who craft custom rings, pendants, and earrings with stones such as fire agate, freshwater pearls, and opals. Open Thurs through Mon in the summer. Call for off-season hours.

Laura Ingalls Wilder Museum. 306 3rd St.; (715) 442-2142; www.lauraingallspepin.com. This small but endearing museum shares artifacts from the pioneer days and stories about the famous author who was born by Lake Pepin. If you want to see a replica of her cabin, drive 7 miles through farmland to the Little House Wayside on CR CC. Pepin also marks the beginning of the Laura Ingalls Wilder Historic Highway, which links the places where she lived, including sites in Minnesota and South Dakota. Museum open 10 a.m. to 5 p.m. May 15 through October 15.

Nelson Cheese Factory. S237 SR 35; (715) 673-4725; www.nelsoncheese.com. A cheese shop and dairy since the mid-1800s, this shop has evolved into a sophisticated place with gourmet and imported foods, a restaurant, a cheese store, and an ice-cream stop. Grab a savory soup, sandwich, or pizza for indoors or out on the patio. Or pull together your own picnic basket with a wide selection of wine, meats, cheese, and crackers for a favorite spot along the river.

Sail Pepin. 400 1st St.; (715) 442-4424; www.sailpepin.com. The crew for this 31-foot sloop takes groups on 2-hour Lake Pepin sails in the afternoon, at sunset, or by starlight. Tours run May 15 through Oct. Price: $50, adults; $40, kids; or $195, a couple.

Smith Brothers Landing. 200 E. Marina Dr.; (715) 442-2248; www.pepinsmith.com. Look for whimsical and creative metal and glass sculptures for homes and gardens, as well as select perennials for sale. Open daily Mar through Oct.

where to eat

Harborview Café. 314 1st St.; (715) 442-3893; www.harborviewpepin.com. Consider this restaurant the granddaddy of the Great River Road culinary scene. Its seasonal opening in March sparks road trips for foodies across the Twin Cities. They come for succulent local lamb, buffalo, sirloin, and pork beautifully plated with seasonal vegetables and served with soups, salads, and artisan breads. Bring your cash or checkbook and patience. They don't take reservations. Open mid-March through the Sunday before Thanksgiving, 11 a.m. to 2:30 p.m. for lunch and 5 to 9 p.m. for dinner. Closed Tues and Wed. $$$.

where to stay

Harbor Hill Inn. 310 2nd St.; (715) 442-2324; www.harborhillinn.net. Pick 1 of 3 rooms in this Victorian home with a tower or rent the guest room for a kitchen and space for 2 couples or a family. An English breakfast is served in the morning. $$.

A Summer Place. 106 Main St.; (877) 442-2132; http://summerplace.net. With white walls and wicker furniture, this B&B with 3 guest rooms aims for the feel of a New England cottage. Appetizers and wine served from 4 to 6 p.m., with pastries and quiche in the morning. $$$.

alma, wi

Like Stockholm, this small river town (pop. 948) is drawing a growing number of creative residents inspired by the setting that first drew Swiss settlers. If you're a history buff, look for self-guided walking tours that highlight the best of Alma's 200 buildings on the National Register of Historic Places.

getting there

Continue on WI 35 22 miles to Alma.

where to go

Art and Soul. 303 N. Main St.; (715) 448-2049; www.art-soul.org. This is one of several historic Main Street stores selling original work. You'll find paintings and jewelry, as well as stylish mission-based imports. Nearby shops specialize in leather, fiber arts, and other media.

Buena Vista Park. Buena Vista Road; www.almawisconsin.com. Enjoy one of the best views in the area with this overlook 540 feet above the Mississippi. You'll be able to see islands, sandbars, and barges heading through Lock Dam No. 4. You can drive here along Highway E or hike up from a trailhead at 2nd Street and Elm by the Wings Over Alma Nature & Art Center.

pizza farms

Yep, that's right. Pizza. Farm. What is it? A delicious trend unique to this area. Owners of three working farms stoke fires in brick ovens during the warm sea-son. The savory aroma of bubbling cheese, crisp crust, spicy meats, basil, and roasted tomatoes wafts across fresh-cut fields and a happy lineup of customers who find their way into the coulees, up in the bluffs, and down gravel roads.

Prices typically run $16 to $24 per pizza. Most pizza farms only take cash, and you may have to wait a few hours for your food. Fortunately, the experience is about more than just eating: it's about paying homage to the local harvest, say-ing hello to the livestock, listening to music (either planned or spontaneous), and celebrating the countryside and camaraderie. Most of all, it's a chance to let pas-sionate farmers and bakers work their magic.

A to Z Bakery—The Pizza Farm. *N2956 Anker Ln., Stockholm; (715) 448-4802; www.atozproduceandbakery.com. Decorative lights and pots of herbs add to the atmosphere here where everything comes from their farm, including the sausage, bacon and pepperoni, grains, and a rainbow of heirloom vegetables from eggplants to exotic peppers. They've been serving pizza and baking sour-dough bread here for more than a decade, letting what's ripe dictate the weekly menu. Bring your own blanket or table and chairs, utensils and napkins, and drinks. All garbage (including the pizza box) must go with when you leave. Open 4:30 to 8 p.m. Tues mid-Mar through Thanksgiving.*

Castlerock Museum. 402 S. 2nd St.; (608) 685-4231; www.castlerockmuseum.com. It may be far from Europe, but this museum that opened in 2010 features collections of arms and armor from Dark Age warriors, the Vikings, the Norman invasion of England in 1066, the Crusades, Feudal Age knights in chain mail, and foot soldiers of the 1400s and 1500s to the armored cavalry of the 1700s.

Mississippi River Pearl Jewelry Company. 125 N. Main St.; (651) 301-1204; www .mspearlco.com. Artist Nadine Leo makes jewelry from increasingly rare freshwater pearls and creates oil paintings often depicting Native Americans.

Rieck's Lake Park & Observation Deck. Highway 35; (608) 685-3330. About 3 miles north of Alma, this is the best place to see tundra swans as they linger and rest while migrating between mid-October through freeze-up. You can get swan watch updates by calling the above number. The park also has a dozen first-come, first-served campsites.

The Stone Barn. *S685 CR KK, Nelson; (715) 673-4478; www.nelsonstonebarn .com. A few miles south of Pepin, this vintage stone barn welcomes customers with creative pizzas such as the Muffaletta (Canadian bacon, olives, and pepperoncini), Alaskan (smoked salmon, capers, and dill), and Modena (marinated chicken, feta cheese, mushrooms, and snap peas). Open Fri through Sun, mid-May through early Oct with seating inside the well-lit, airy barn hung with artwork.*

Suncrest Gardens. *S2257 Yaeger Valley Rd., Cochrane; (608) 626-2122; www .suncrestgardensfarm.com. Experienced customers bring their own chairs, tables, stemware, and even candles to the lawn by this weathered wood barn 10 miles from Alma. You don't have to go that fancy, but you do need to bring your own utensils, drinks, and at least a blanket. You can admire the gardens and say hello to the chickens, llamas, and other livestock while you wait for pizzas vibrant with vegetables and heirloom tomatoes. Open Thurs in May, Thurs and Fri June through Aug, and Fri in Sept.*

Vino in the Valley. *W3826 450th Ave., Maiden Rock; (715) 639-6677; http://vinoin thevalley.com. With 5 acres of northern grapes planted, this farm will eventually produce local wine. For now, it's more like a pizza farm with extras. It opens on Thursday and Saturday nights with pizzas, pastas, Italian nachos, meats, and cheeses plus wines and Wisconsin beers. It's also open for a Sunday buffet ($9–$19) from noon to 7 p.m. May through Sept.*

Wings Over Alma Nature & Art Center. 118 N. Main St.; (608) 685-3303; www.wings overalma.org. This nonprofit center offers a great overview of the community with historic photos, local art, and exhibits on the area's wildlife—including what's migrating through. There's a 50-foot viewing platform with binoculars and a spotting scope to look for eagles and other birds. Open daily 10 a.m. to 5 p.m.

where to eat

Great Alma Fishing Float. On the river; (608) 685-3786. There's a small dock across the tracks by the foot of Pine Street where you can lift a board and signal you want a $5 shuttle ride to the Great Alma Fishing Float. Obviously popular with anglers, it's also a unique place for breakfast starting at 7 a.m. until the cafe closes at 4 p.m. Ask for The Mess, a pile of eggs, bacon, ham, sausage, potatoes, cheese, and tomatoes. Sauerkraut's optional. Open mid-Mar through Oct. $.

Kate and Gracie's. 215 N. Main St.; (608) 685-4505; www.kateandgracies.com. You can get everything from tasty sandwiches to rib eye in Alma's oldest building, dating back to 1861. Open for lunch and dinner Wed through Mon with breakfast on Sat and Sun. $$.

Pier 4 Café and Smokehouse. 600 N. Main St.; (608) 685-4964; www.pier4cafe.com. Grab a seat on the screened porch overlooking the lock and dam, then dig into their pulled pork, beef brisket, or beer-battered perch. They're also known for German pancakes for breakfast. Open 6 a.m. to 2 p.m. Closed Tues. $.

where to stay

Hotel de Ville. 305 N. Main St.; (612) 423-3653; www.hoteldevillealma.com. With its courtyard and formal gardens, this place oozes elegance and charm, drawing raves from guests who compare it to a European getaway. There are 4 suites (some with full kitchens), 3 economical rooms with shared baths, and a cottage. Fire & Ice on the first level serves coffee drinks and Chocolate Shoppe ice cream. $$.

fountain city, wi

You can enjoy quirky folk art, a sprawling collection of cars and toys, and a family-friendly farm stay experience in this small town of 983 residents. Fountain City was settled by Germans, Swiss, and Norwegians in the late 1830s, but the Scandinavian influence inspires Lefse Time as a mighty sweet destination.

getting there

Follow WI 35 about 17 miles south from Alma to Fountain City.

where to go

Elmer's Auto and Toy Museum. W903 Elmers Rd.; (608) 687-7221; www.elmersautoand toymuseum.com. Head up Eagle Bluff to tour 5 buildings packed with hundreds of antique cars, vintage Indian and Harley Davidson motorcycles, high-wheel bicycles, and one of the country's largest collections of pedal cars. There also are thousands of dolls and cast-iron, pressed steel, tin wind-up, and battery-operated toys dating back to the 1800s. Open 9 a.m. to 5 p.m. most weekends May through mid-Oct. Call to check before traveling. Admission: $7, adults; $3, kids.

Lefse Time. 115 North Shore; (608) 687-4299; www.lefsetime.com. For anyone who loves these tortilla-thin potato rounds usually rolled with butter and sugar or lingonberries, this is the place to get them, learn about them, and to buy the tools to make iconic Scandinavian specialties at home, including aebleskiver, krumkage, rosettes, sandbakkels, and glogg. Open Thurs through Sun.

Prairie Moon Museum & Sculpture Garden. S2921 CR G; (608) 685-6290; www.kohler foundation.org. What started out as a hobby for retired farmer Herman Rusche in 1952 became a full-blown folk art experience about 8 miles north of Fountain City. Rusche created close to 40 concrete sculptures such as dinosaurs, a woodsman fighting a bear, a rocket, a huge arched border, and two-story turret. They're embellished with paint, seashells, broken glass, mirrors, and pottery shards. The site, now managed by the Kohler Foundation, includes a museum with Fred Schlosstein's rock art modeled after local buildings. He also put trolls in the hillsides to scare hikers. Garden open during daylight hours, while the museum's open Sunday afternoons May through Oct. Free.

where to stay

Hawk's View Lodges & Cottages. 320 Hill St.; (866) 293-0803; www.hawksview.net. If you want someplace a little roomy and luxurious, these hillside cottages make the most of the river valley scenery. You can hike up to them from the Seven Hawks Vineyards. $$$.

Merrick State Park. S2965 WI 35; (608) 687-4936; www.dnr.state.wi.us. Camp at one of 65 sites in this 322-acre state park that encompasses Mississippi backwaters about 2 miles north of Fountain City. Join the anglers or look for herons, egrets, muskrat, and even otters. The park rents canoes for scenic paddles, or you can hike and snowshoe along 2 miles of trails. $5–$10 daily pass. $.

Room to Roam. W656 Veraguth Dr.; (608) 687-8575. The Veraguth family rents out a neighboring farm house for a family-friendly hay-cation or farm stay. Guests are welcome to help feed calves, gather eggs, raid the garden, pick apples and berries, and enjoy the old-fashioned fun of roaming through barns, taking a hayride, and listening to the cows moo. The house feels frozen in a previous generation, but includes air-conditioning and a full kitchen. $$.

day trip 02

southeast

boots, pottery & romance:
red wing, mn

red wing, mn

More than any other Minnesota town, Red Wing shows pride in its history, craftsmanship, and products. You can feel it walking the floors of the Red Wing Boot factory or posing next to a size 638½ boot downtown. You can sense it in sturdy Red Wing pottery that draws a few thousand collectors for an annual convention and steady visitors to its year-round showroom.

Still even without those products and the stories behind them, Red Wing offers a memorable getaway. Romantics can have the most fun. Stroll the quaint downtown sitting nestled between bluffs and the Mississippi River, take a cruise on the Mississippi, drive through neighborhoods of Victorian homes, and watch for Minnesota's last passenger train—Amtrak's Empire Builder—as it stops at the depot twice a day.

If it's too hard to leave, you can slip beneath the quilts at the St. James, Minnesota's oldest hotel, or a variety of bed-and-breakfasts.

getting there

The easiest-to-follow route is taking US 61 from I-494 at the southeastern edge of the Twin Cities then following WI 35 into Red Wing.

You can take the scenic Empire Builder train from St. Paul to Red Wing, as well (www .amtrak.com). Ideally, it arrives early to mid-morning, but weather, flooding, and any number of delays can throw off the schedule. The westbound return train is more punctual.

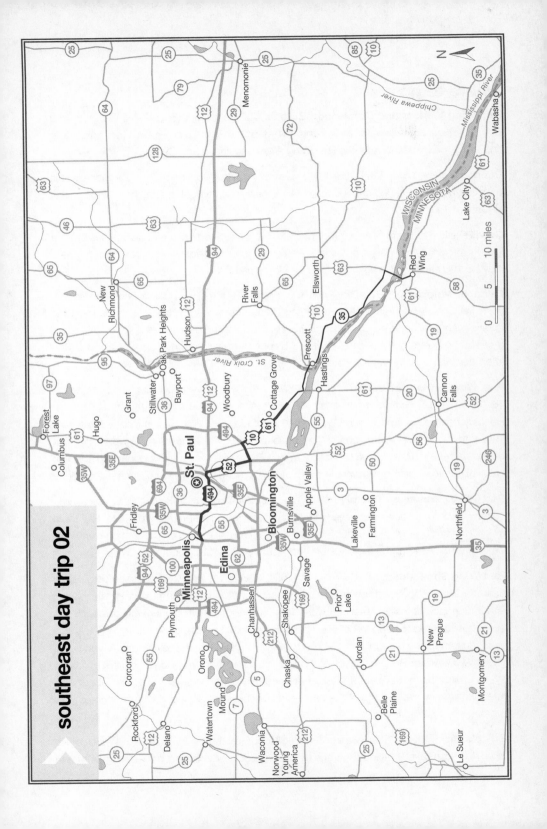

southeast day trip 02

where to go

Red Wing Visitors and Convention Bureau. 420 Levee St.; (800) 498-3444; www.red wing.org. Housed in the historic working train depot, you can pick up a visitors guide here and enjoy rotating exhibits at the Red Wing Arts Association and Gallery.

Cannon Valley Trail. (507) 263-0508; www.cannonvalleytrail.com. You can access this popular trail for biking and cross-country skiing near the riverfront. It stretches 19 miles east to Cannon Falls.

Colvill Park. 515 Nymphara Ln.; (651) 385-3674; www.ci.red-wing.mn.us. Besides being a lovely park along the Mississippi, this is a local hot spot for eagle watching in March. There may be 100 eagles roosting in the trees or along the bluffs.

Falconer Vineyards. 3572 Old Tyler Rd.; (651) 388-8849; www.falconervineyards.com. John Falconer, who brought the Red Wing Pottery company back to life, turned to wine in retirement. Tastings are $3 for up to 5 wines, including Frontenac, a dry red; St. Pepin, a semidry white; slightly sweeter St. Urho blends; and a rich port. Open Fri through Sun afternoons late Apr through Christmas.

Red Wing Pottery Museum. 2000 Old West Main St.; www.rwpotteryplace.com. In the 1860s, a German immigrant harvested the local clay for durable stoneware with salt glazes. He fashioned bowls, crocks, and jugs for the state's pioneers. With mechanization in the early 1900s, the company became one of the biggest pottery manufacturers in the world. The self-guided museum on the second floor of the Pottery Place Mall shows its evolution from utilitarian kraut crocks to elegant dinnerware in the company's mid-century heyday. Open daily. Free.

Red Wing Stoneware Factory. 4909 Moundsview Dr.; (651) 388-4610; www.redwing stoneware.com. If you want to see Red Wing pottery being made, there are 3 factory tours a day Mon through Fri. They last 15 to 25 minutes. You also can see production work from viewing windows near the factory store. Admission: $3, adults; $2, ages 12–17.

Red Wing Shoe Museum. 314 Main St.; (651) 388-8211; www.redwingshoe.com. Head past the 2-story boot and upstairs to this museum with an intriguing look at the evolution and importance of the all-American work boot. For more than 100 years the company has built boots tailored to each trade. They have helped build skyscrapers, drill for oil, clear forests, run farms, and hunt for food. The company also made the first ski boots. A high point: World War II, when Red Wing provided boots in 200 sizes for America's soldiers. Kids can try on costumes for several trades and pretend to walk on a skyscraper. Ask about narrated weekday walking tours of the off-site factory between May and October to see how the boots are made. Free.

Rusty's River Rides. East Avenue & Levee Road; (612) 859-6655; www.rustysriverrides .com. You can take 90-minute cruises on a 37-passenger boat mid-April through October for an up close look at herons, eagles, barges, and other river sights. There's a longer lock-and-dam cruise, as well. Fare: $12, adults; $10, seniors; $5, kids ages 5–14. If you're spending the night, some hotels/B&Bs have package discounts.

where to shop

Much of Red Wing's shopping is concentrated downtown near Main Street or in the lower levels of 4-story historic **Pottery Place Mall** (2000 Old West Main St.; 612-822-0367; www .rwpotteryplace.com). It's open 10 a.m. to 6 p.m. Mon through Sat and 11 a.m. to 5 p.m. Sun. The shopping expands outside May through October with outdoor flea markets the first and third weekends of the month.

Hobgoblin Music and Stoney End Harps. 920 MN 19; (877) 866-3936; www.stoneyend .com. This quaint barn in rural Red Wing houses a music store with mandolins and pennywhistles, plus a variety of Stoney End harps, mountain dulcimers, and bodhrans that are made here. Watch for folk concerts in the Music Loft or outdoors during balmy weather.

Hush Puppies Outlet Store. 2000 Old West Main St.; (651) 388-4670. Red Wing Boots aren't the only footwear in town. This shop brings together more than 10,000 pairs of casual, comfortable shoes and boots from Merrell, CAT, and Wolverine among the many brands it carries.

Moments on Main. 329 Main St.; (651) 388-2343; http://momentsonmain.com. Always festively and seasonally decorated, this downtown store blends home decor, lamps, mirrors, gifts, glasses and kitchenwares, garden flags, and textiles.

Pete's Kitchen Corner. 2000 Old West Main St.; (651) 385-9008. Shop for utensils, dishes, gadgets, or a new pan for the kitchen, including those made by Minnesota's Nordicware, creator of the Bundt pan.

Pottery Place Antiques. 2000 Old West Main St.; (651) 388-7765; www.potteryplace antiques.com. With about 50 dealers, this sprawling collection of Red Wing collectible pieces and aisles dense with floral juice glasses, Watts ware, rare bottles, vintage hats and aprons, rare toys, beer glasses, old books, and colorful quilts can be nirvana for antique lovers.

Red Wing Pottery Salesroom and Shops. 1920 W. Main St.; (800) 228-0174. Next door to Pottery Place Mall, this strip of shops sells Red Wing Pottery's full line of crocks and wares, and you can often catch potters handcrafting the sturdy pieces in a demo area. You can find the iconic Red Wing design on coffee mugs, lamp bases, French butter dishes, and more. There also are bread bakers that work well with another local favorite: Sturdiwheat bread or buckwheat pancake mixes. This shop also is the nation's No. 1 retailer of Fiestaware and boasts an extensive selection of kitchenware and decor. Connecting shops sell playful birdbaths, women's clothing, candy, and Minnesota souvenirs.

Red Wing Shoe Store. 314 Main St.; (651) 388-8211; www.redwingshoe.com. While the upstairs is dedicated to the company's history, the main floor shows off Red Wing's fashionable lifestyle shoes that are hot items overseas, the sporty Vasque line of hiking boots and shoes, motorcycle boots, and classic, hardworking boots with optional steel toes, Kevlar, or antistatic soles.

Uff-Da Shop. 202 Bush St.; (651) 388-8436; http://uffdashoponline.com. Browse a lovely assortment of Scandinavian imports such as silver jewelry and charms, Finnish linens and glassware, cookware, and holiday ornaments such as woven straw stars and colorful gnomes.

where to eat

Harbor Restaurant, Bar & Marina. N673 825th St., Hager City; (715) 792-2417; www .harborbar.net. Right across the river channel from Red Wing, this casual eatery rocks with summer music festivals, authentic Jamaican jerk seasonings, and great Mississippi views. Get a swamp burger with Cajun seasonings or try red snapper, tiger shrimp, and chicken with jerk seasoning and a side of Jamaican rice and beans with a kick of coconut. Concerts include a Parrot Head Party and reggae festival. $$.

The Port Restaurant. 406 Main St.; (800) 252-1875; www.st-james-hotel.com. Cozy up to the see-through fireplace, check out vintage steamboat photos on the brick walls, and settle into this basement restaurant for high-end cuisine. First courses may be rabbit strudel, beet salad, or a wild rice soup with smoked pheasant, cranberries, and wild mushrooms in a clear broth. Main courses may include locally raised chicken, braised lamb shank with dense farro risotto, or North Dakota bison rib eye. Open 5 to 9 p.m. Tues through Sat. $$$.

Sarah's (formerly Norton's). 307 Main St.; (651) 388-2711; www.sarahsinredwing.com. This creative, spacious restaurant specializes in small plates, tempting diners to try Vietnamese meatballs, Cuban roast pork, Spanish-style grilled chicken, and scallops with a spicy orange-mint penne pasta. Open for dinner Tues through Thurs, and lunch and dinner Fri and Sat. $$$.

Smokey Row Café & Jenny Lind Bakery. 1926 Old West Main; (651) 388-6025; www .jennylindbakery.net. Close to Pottery Place shopping, this is a popular stop for breakfast and lunch with creative soups and chowders, panini with pesto, flaky quiche, and sandwiches on a variety of breads such as cranberry walnut or sunflower whole wheat. Leave room for pastries and desserts such as cardamom rolls, caramel cashew bars, chocolate-dipped cardamom shortbread cookies, and lemon-raspberry cake. $.

The Veranda. 406 Main St.; (800) 252-1875; www.st-james-hotel.com. With views of the river and the option to eat outside, the Veranda is popular for breakfast and lunch with waffles, pastries, salads, and sandwiches. Try the local Sturdiwheat pancakes with a warm vanilla butter sauce, a California salad with chicken, fruit, and banana dressing. Open 6:30 a.m. to 3 p.m. Mon through Sat with a 7:30 a.m. opening on Sun. If you want someplace within the hotel for dinner but more casual than The Port, there's a manly Brit-style pub called Jimmy's on the St. James's fifth floor. $$.

where to stay

Candlelight Inn. 818 W. 3rd St.; (800) 254-9194; www.candlelightinn-redwing.com. Three blocks from downtown, this more than 130-year-old Victorian B&B features 5 rooms, afternoon appetizers and wine, and 3-course breakfasts. $$$.

The Golden Lantern Inn. 721 East Ave.; (888) 288-3315; www.goldenlantern.com. While this spacious Arts and Crafts home 3.5 blocks from downtown grabs attention, it's the secluded gardens that wow guests—especially with a roaring fire on any of its 3 patios. There are 5 bedrooms and the option for a sit-down or private breakfast. $$$.

Moondance Inn. 1105 W. 4th St.; (866) 388-8145; www.moondanceinn.com. This stone 1875 home with purple trim offers 5 spacious rooms and a guesthouse next door for groups. Guests can enjoy wine and appetizers Friday and Saturday nights, afternoon cookies, and huge breakfasts with warm pastries. Among its quirks: two Puli dogs, a Hungarian breed that loves to twirl and sports a coat like delicate dreadlocks. Gathering places range from a formal dining room with Tiffany chandeliers and rich woodwork to a cozy area on the third floor with a round window. Downtown and the river are a few blocks away. $$$.

Round Barn Farm B&B. 28650 Wildwood Ln.; (866) 763-2276; www.roundbarnfarm .com. Call this place a B&B&B&B—bed, breakfast, bread, and barn—or just call it charming. The property has always drawn attention with its distinctive round barn south of Red Wing, and guests get to take home loaves of fresh-baked buttermilk bread shaped like the barn and to make their own loaf of brick-oven bread. The owners built a new farmhouse from scratch, but you would never guess thanks to reclaimed pine flooring and woodwork and an authentic 1800s home plan. They've filled it with enough antiques—especially bread-related items—to make it worthy of a magazine cover. There are 5 rooms, including the spacious Willow Suite with a twig swing facing the fireplace and an alcove bed positioned to catch moonlight. $$$.

St. James Hotel. 406 Main St.; (651) 388-2846; www.st-james-hotel.com. This 1875 hotel retains the elegance of an earlier century with spacious accommodations, Amish quilts, rooms named for riverboats, and hallways built wide enough to allow ladies socializing in hoop skirts. Each room is different, and you can request a river view. Don't miss the cozy library and organ pipes in the original lobby. Look for holiday decor and special events such as wine tastings, performances at the elegantly restored Sheldon Theater, and eagle-watching or other seasonal packages. $$.

day trip 03

southeast

eagles, toys & grumpy old men:
lake city, mn; wabasha, mn

Downriver from Red Wing, the Great River Road makes its way along steep embankments, below scenic bluffs, and through towns full of treasures. You'll find everything from a national eagle museum and world-class bird watching to a hand-carved carousel and opportunities to get onto the Mississippi River.

Lake Pepin, a widening of the Mississippi River which stays open during the winter, ranks as one of the best places to see eagles, especially in March when trees are still bare and eagles migrating north join those who never left the state. They rest along the Mississippi, feasting on fish and small game and roosting along bluffs and in wooded lowlands.

It isn't hard to spot their white heads perched on bare branches. But if you do have difficulty, you can rely on the experts. Five resident eagles at Wabasha's National Eagle Center drop their calm, watchful demeanors and shriek indignantly as wild eagles come into view far across the river. They make it abundantly clear how the term "eagle eye" came to be.

lake city, mn

This town was the birthplace of waterskiing and still hums with the happy energy of people heading out for a day on the water. You can camp along Lake Pepin, stroll its 2.5-mile walkway, count the sailboats and barges, and catch a beautiful sunset along the waterfront marina.

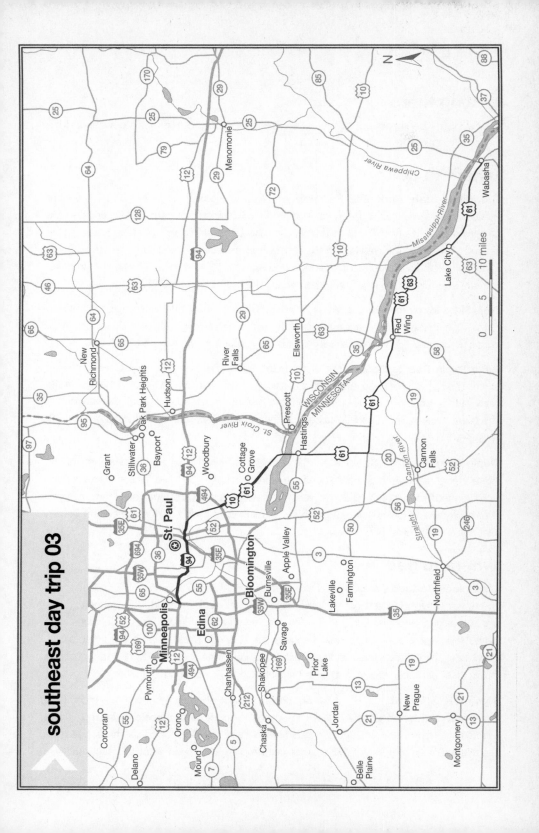

getting there

Follow US 61 southeast out of the Twin Cities. It's about 70 miles from downtown Minneapolis to Lake City.

where to go

Frontenac State Park. 29223 County 28 Blvd., Frontenac; (651) 345-3401; www.dnr .state.mn.us. More than a dozen miles of hiking trails thread along the bluffs leading to the Mississippi. Be warned: If you hike down, you have a memorable but steep hike up. The reward? Immersing yourself into Mississippi bottomlands and finding surprises such as yellow lady's slippers in bloom. The campground includes 58 sites, plus 6 rustic walk-in ones. In the winter, close to 5 miles are groomed for skiing. Entrance fee: $5.

Hok-Si-La Municipal Park. 2500 N. US 61; (651) 345-3855; http://lakecitymn.govoffice2 .com. This 252-acre city park sprawls along the river, offering visitors a riverside beach, picnic areas, and 38 campsites ($30/night in peak season). Open Apr through Oct.

Lake Pepin Paddle Boat. 100 Central Point Rd.; (651) 345-5188; www.pearlofthelake .com. The *Pearl of the Lake,* a replica of Mississippi riverboats which traveled the river in the early 1900s, goes out for 90-minute narrated cruises Wednesday through Sunday during the peak season. Board early for a seat on the popular upper deck. Cost: $15, adults; $8, kids 6–13; $20 for live music cruises.

Pepin Heights. 1753 S. US 61; (651) 345-2305; www.pepinheights.com. One of the state's most recognized orchards opens seasonally in Lake City to sell its line of fresh ciders and blended juices, sparkling apple juice, and snappy fresh apples such as Honeycrisp and the much-desired SweeTango, a University of Minnesota hybrid of Honeycrisp and Zestar. Open seasonally 9 a.m. to 5 p.m.

where to eat

Chickadee Cottage Café. 317 N. Lakeshore Dr.; (651) 345-5155; www.chickadeecottage .com. It's easy to feel at home in this early 1900s lodging surrounded by gardens. They serve breakfast and lunch daily and dinner on Friday and Saturday. Look for choices such as a Mexican breakfast wrap with mango salsa, wild rice sausage and cheesy potatoes, a caramel apple french toast sandwich, an apple and tuna salad sandwich, pork ribs with apple cider barbecue sauce, and grilled shrimp. Open Apr through Oct. $$.

Nosh. 310 S. Washington St.; (651) 565-2277; www.noshrestaurant.com. The menu here constantly changes as chefs present in-season produce and ingredients served with a western Mediterranean influence. A guaranteed item: the colorful paella that's been the most popular entree. They have a small plate menu, too, if you want to nosh your way through a variety of beautifully plated foods. Breads, sausages, and ice cream are all home-made daily. Open 4 to 9 p.m. Wed through Sat and 3 to 8 p.m. Sun. $$$.

where to stay

John Hall's Alaska Lodge. 1127 N. Lakeshore Dr.; (800) 325-2270. This log-lodge-style hotel offers lake-view suites with a cabin feel. All have a microwave and minifridge or a full kitchen. $$.

Villas on Pepin. 1215 N. Lakeshore Dr.; (651) 345-5188; www.villasonpepin.com. These luxury 1- and 2-bedroom condos include balconies and kitchens, with many facing the lake. There's a rooftop patio and access to the 2.5-mile Lake Walk that follows Lake Pepin. $$$.

Willows on the River. 100 Central Point Rd.; (651) 345-9900; www.willowsontheriver .com. Each of these condo units offers sweeping river views with floor-to-ceiling corner windows and a fireplace, plus full kitchens and balconies. $$$.

wabasha, mn

Wabasha (population 2,800) provides a playful family getaway with hands-on exhibits at the National Eagle Center and LARK Toys, which is like Santa's workshop and a free antique toy museum rolled together. LARK's whimsical hand-carved carousel alone is worth a stop.

This also is the famed setting for the *Grumpy Old Men* movies with Jack Lemmon and Walter Matthau. While the movie wasn't actually filmed here, you can dine at Slippery's (as mentioned in the film) or time a visit with their annual Grumpy Old Men Festival in late February for an ice-fishing contest and hot dish luncheon.

getting there

It's about 14 miles from Lake City to Wabasha, following US 61 Great River Scenic Byway.

where to go

Wabasha-Kellogg Area Chamber of Commerce. 137 Main St.; (800) 565-4158; www .wabashamn.org. You can download maps online for walking tours of downtown with 50 buildings on the National Register of Historic Places.

Big River Adventures. 1110 Hiawatha Dr. East; (507) 951-5286; www.bigriveradventures .com. Pack binoculars and a camera for 90-minute ecotours of the Mississippi backwaters and isolated areas, showcasing remote beaches, great bird watching, wildlife, plant life, and the area's scenic beauty. Seasonal tours offered daily. Cost: $39/person.

Coffee Mill Golf. 180 Coffee Mill Dr.; (651) 565-4332; www.coffeemillgolf.com. These 18 holes are built along the bluffs above the river valley. $28 to play on weekends.

Coffee Mill Ski & Snowboard Resort. 99 Coulee Way; (651) 565-2777; www.coffeemill ski.com. Less crowded than Twin Cities ski hills and more affordable than most, these runs feature 425 feet of vertical drop and 3 terrain parks. Open Wed through Sun. Weekend lift tickets: $30, adults; $26, kids 6–12.

Jewels on the River. 257 W. Main St.; (651) 565-4776; www.jewelsontheriver.com. While the focus is on jewelry with semiprecious stones, sterling silver, and Mississippi pearls, this shop also features local artwork.

LARK Toys. 171 Lark Ln., Kellogg; (507) 767-3387; www.larktoys.com. You can get happily lost for hours in America's largest independent toy shop 6 miles south of Wabasha. You don't even a need a child in tow. The impressive Memory Lane exhibits coax the kid out of every generation with Howdy Doody dolls, metal robots and Erector sets, Barbies, and pedal cars. In the various shops, you'll find magic tricks and gags, wind-up toys, musical instruments, tea sets, wooden pull toys, fuzzy puppets, and puzzles galore. There is a snack cafe, bookstore, and even outdoor minigolf, but the biggest "Wow!" factor goes to the carousel. Line up early to nab a seat with your favorite character. Among the 19 that whirl around every half hour, you'll see an otter, a flamingo, a cat with a fish, a hairy troll, a wizard riding a dragon, and a reindeer. All that's missing are elves, but maybe they're in the back. Carousel: $2.

National Eagle Center. 50 Pembroke Ave. South; (651) 565-4989; www.nationaleagle center.org. The National Eagle Center, which opened in its current location in 2007, includes two airy floors of exhibits and artwork that explain the lives of eagles, their habitat, and their

eagles make a comeback

With a stern look, keen eyesight, majestic flying, and fierce, fish-shredding legs, the bald eagle has long been America's national symbol of strength. They're also one of the country's best comeback stories.

Consider this: In 1953, there were 1,000 eagle pairs in the lower 48 states. A decade later, they were down to 450 pairs after the farm chemical DDT thinned their eggshells, causing eaglets to be crushed to death. Between 1968 and 1972, there was a single nesting pair left along a 260-mile stretch of the river. The chemical was banned, and eagles slowly made their comeback.

Now there are close to 40 nesting pairs along Lake Pepin and side rivers such as the Chippewa, which flows into Wisconsin. Together, Minnesota and Wisconsin are home to more than 2,400 pairs of eagles.

cultural significance, especially to Native Americans. One exhibit is dedicated to Old Abe, an eagle that followed soldiers into 37 Civil War battles. Kids can do crayon rubbings, scavenger hunts in the museum, color pictures of birds, and participate in hands-on activities like one that lets them feel the weight difference between a cat and an eagle. Each weekend in March the center offers Soar with the Eagles special events that include speakers and demonstrations, along with family activities. Year-round daily programs give visitors an up close look at the rescued and rehabilitated resident eagles. There's even a chance to pose nose-to-beak for photos. Among the resident eagles, Harriet is the most famous. She has been on the *Today Show,* the *Tonight Show,* and is featured on license plates (with a little airbrushing to take care of an eagle's version of a permanently bad hair day). Leave time to stroll the riverfront with a fountain and sculpture of Chief Wapasha.

Open 10 a.m. to 5 p.m. Sun through Thurs and 9 a.m. to 6 p.m. Fri and Sat. Eagle programs are presented at 11 a.m. and 1 and 3 p.m. daily. Admission: $8, adults; $6, seniors; $5, children 4–17.

Troy's Bait Bucket & Kayak/Canoe Rental. 406 W. Grant Blvd.; (651) 565-4895. You can rent kayaks, pontoons, and canoes here or get what you need to go fishing on the Mississippi.

Wind Whisper West. 128 Main St.; (651) 565-2002; www.windwhisperwest.com. Utterly unexpected, this Japanese textile and art gallery showcases the rich colors of handpainted and embroidered silk kimonos. It's the biggest seller of wedding kimonos in the US. Open 10 a.m. to 4 p.m. and noon to 4 p.m. weekends.

where to eat

Chocolate Escape. 152 W. Main St.; (651) 565-0035; www.chocolateescape.com. If you truly need an extra nudge to duck into this chocolate shop, tell yourself it's educational with a 70-foot-long mural that shows the history of chocolate and how it's made. The shop also sells ice cream and beverages. Open daily 7 a.m. to 8 p.m. $.

Flour Mill Pizzeria. 146 W. Main St.; (651) 560-4170. Sit inside or on the deck overlooking the river only a block from the National Eagle Center. They have pizzas from 7 inches to 18 inches. Look for expected flavors and more unusual ones such as "Fennel, fig and the pig" with a white sauce. Pizzas can be ordered between 11:30 a.m. and 7 or 8 p.m. Closed Tues and Wed. $$.

Slippery's Bar & Restaurant. 10 Church Ave.; (651) 565-4748; www.slipperys.com. Being part of the *Grumpy Old Men* mystique makes this a busy tourist stop for burgers and American fare, but it also has an idyllic location with decks right on the river. Open 11 a.m. to closing Mon through Fri and 8 a.m. to closing Sat and Sun. $$.

where to stay

AmericInn Wabasha. 150 Commerce St.; (651) 565-5366; www.americinn.com/hotels/ MN/Wabasha. Don't let the chain ownership of this hotel throw you off. This is no ordinary AmericInn thanks to the efforts of local businesses and artists who designed 14 themed suites that represent Wabasha. The Cat Suite is dedicated to town's former Anderson House Hotel that would offer you a live cat with your room. The Carousel, inspired by LARK Toys, includes a hand-carved headboard with an otter, an Asian-themed suite has kimono art from Wind Whisper West, and the Fisherman's Suite includes decor from the Loon Lake Decoy Company. Some of the hotel's 64 rooms have kitchenettes, and all include hot breakfast. $$.

day trip 04

southeast

stained glass, shakespeare & spice:
winona, mn

winona, mn

Winona calls itself the Island City, given its location on a massive sandbar wedged between the Mississippi River and Winona Lake. Both give it beauty, especially with spacious Lake Park and a backdrop of bluffs.

To truly appreciate the city's landscape and the full scale of the river valley, head up the 530-foot-high Garvin Heights bluff for sweeping views.

You'll be able to spot the Winona State University campus, which along with St. Mary's University, brings in 2,200 students and adds to the city's culture with dance, theater, music, and art programs. WSU hosts the annual Great River Shakespeare Festival which has become a popular summer tradition.

You also can see downtown. Like Duluth to the north, Winona's prosperity exploded in the late 1800s thanks to its strategic location for getting lumber and materials to a booming nation. Millionaires showered their wealth on homes and the state's biggest Victorian commercial district.

For an intriguing (and even funny) look at how culture has changed since Victorian times, pop into the Watkins Heritage Museum to see how apothecary and personal care products have evolved over more than 140 years, from hair cream to tooth powder. An early product for the world's oldest direct-selling company was "Watkins Female Tonic," promised to be a "boon to womanhood" by stimulating nutrition and acting "as a sedative on the

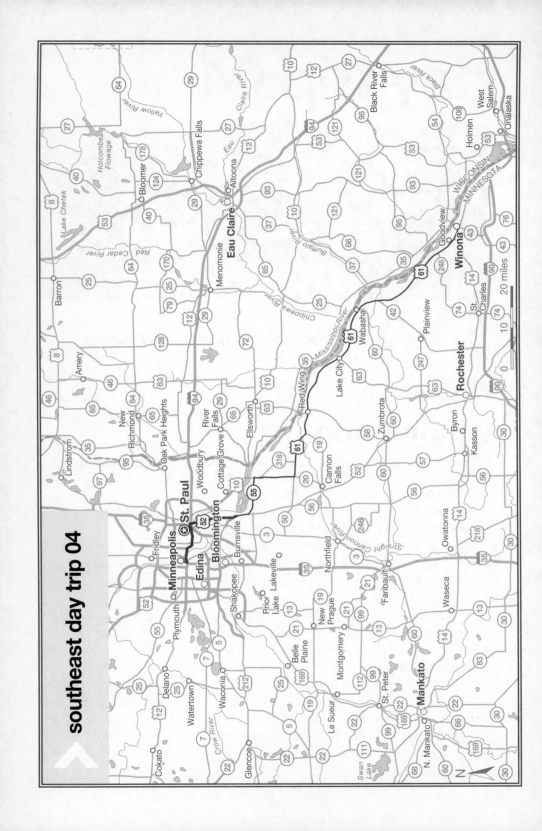

southeast day trip 04

pelvic organs." Some items have stayed just the same, including a camphor and spruce oil liniment for aching athletes and its well-known line of vanilla extracts and spices.

getting there

Take US 61 southeast out of the Twin Cities. Winona is about 40 minutes south of Wabasha. You also can take Amtrak's Empire Builder train from the Twin Cities or Red Wing.

where to go

Visit Winona Visitor Center. 924 Huff St.; (800) 657-4972; www.visitwinona.com. Get oriented with brochures here, including walking maps for Winona's historic downtown. You also can log onto www.winonamntours.org with a smartphone and get a free "Stories in Structure" architecture tour. Open daily Apr 1 through October 31. Call for off-season hours.

> ## winona's stained-glass legacy
>
> *Winona is known as Minnesota's stained-glass capital. Part of that is due to its many Victorian buildings, but the city also grew to be a hub for producing stained glass. Here are a few places to enjoy the opulence and rich colors:*
>
> ***Merchant's Bank.*** *102 E. 3rd St.; (507) 457-1100. This ranks among Minnesota's prettiest banks—and a nod to the talent of Louis Sullivan and Prairie School influences. You have to step inside to fully appreciate it with a mural of the river valley and Sugar Loaf bluff on one wall and a glowing, colorful display of art glass on the other. Open 9 a.m. to 4 p.m. Mon through Fri.*
>
> ***Watkins Administration Building.*** *150 Liberty St.; (507) 457-6095; www.jrwatkins .com. This George Maher–designed landmark was built in 1913 for more than a million dollars. It features a beautiful dome, art glass windows depicting Winona's Sugar Loaf bluff, plus Italian marble, mahogany, and mosaic accents and trim. Open 10 a.m. to 4 p.m. Mon through Fri.*
>
> ***Winona State Bank.*** *204 Main St.; (507) 454-4320. George Maher of Chicago also designed this 1874 bank with ornate metalwork, white marble staircases, green marble accents, and ornate art glass windows from the Tiffany Studio in New York. There's also a safari museum with the taxidermy trophies of the first bank president. The exterior is Egyptian Revival with granite columns while the inside has a Prairie School feel. Open Mon through Fri 8:30 a.m. to 5 p.m.*

Garvin Heights Vineyards. 2255 Garvin Heights Rd.; (507) 474-9463; www.ghvwine .com. This scenic winery sells a variety of wines made from northern varietals such as Minnesota's Frontenac or Sabrevois red from southern Quebec. Look for St. Urho and Bluff Country blends, a few fruit wines, and dessert wines. Open 10 a.m. to 6 p.m. May through Oct, plus 1 to 5 p.m. weekends in Apr, Nov, and Dec.

Great River Bluff State Park. 43605 Kipp Dr.; (507) 643-6849; www.dnr.state.mn.us. With gorgeous wooded bluffs overlooking the Mississippi River 12 miles south of Winona, this 3,067-acre park is especially popular for hikers and campers. There are 31 campsites, so you'll have to reserve early for the peak fall weekends when the maple-basswood and oak forests are ablaze. Winter visitors can use the sliding hill or cross-country ski trails, while spring and summer visitors can look for wildflowers, watch for migrating birds, and learn about the so-called goat prairie on steep bluffs. Daily fee: $5.

Great River Shakespeare Festival. 79 E. 3rd St.; (507) 474-7900; www.grsf.org. This professional theater festival runs about 6 weeks from late June to early August, using Winona State University's 435-seat theater to perform favorite dramas and comedies from William Shakespeare.

Minnesota Marine Art Museum. 800 Riverview Dr.; (507) 474-6626; www.minnesota marineart.org. This impressive and surprising riverfront museum devotes itself to paintings, photography, and sculptures that reflect life on the water. Offerings range from historic and impressionist paintings of ships and oceans (including a Van Gogh) to special exhibits on canoes and the art of fishing lures. There is also a display of more than 400 folk art pieces created by locals Leo and Marilyn Smith. Open 10 a.m. to 5 p.m. Tues through Sat, Nov through Feb, and until 6 p.m. Mar through Oct. Leave time to stroll the waterfront and enjoy the museum's lovely setting. Admission: $6, adults; $3, children ages 5 and up.

princess wenonah

Many of Winona's grandest mansions surround historic Windom Park, which is anchored by a statue of Princess Wenonah. Local legends say she chose to leap to her death off Maiden Rock bluff rather than marry an Indian brave she did not choose.

The name "Wenonah" can also be seen on the sides of canoes that have been manufactured in Winona for more than four decades. Family-owned Wenonah Canoe has 40 designs, including high-performance canoes and kayaks that are paddled around the world.

Polish Cultural Institute of Winona. 102 Liberty St.; (507) 454-3431; www.polish museumwinona.org. This museum celebrates Winona's Polish roots, which started with a flood of immigrants who came for the booming lumber work in the 1870s. They could earn $1 a day (or $1.25 if they could sharpen a saw). Exhibits include a variety of books, photos, Polish-language newspapers, and Kaszubian folk costumes and embroidery. Open 10 a.m. to 3 p.m. Mon through Sat May through Oct, and 10 a.m. to 3 p.m. Thurs through Sat in the off-season. Admission: $2.

Watkins Heritage Museum. 150 Liberty St.; (507) 457-6095; www.jrwatkins.com. At the turn of the twentieth century, this company with its line of spices, extracts, health tonics, and cosmetics was bigger than Proctor & Gamble is today. It started in 1868 and became the country's first direct-selling company. (If you haven't seen the touching movie *Door to Door* with William H. Macy starring as Bill Porter, check it out before a visit.) Open 10 a.m. to 4 p.m. Mon through Fri and 10 a.m. to 2 p.m. Sat. It's free, but you'll likely want a tin of cinnamon, a bottle of vanilla, or minty lip balm.

Winona County History Center. 160 Johnson St.; (507) 454-2723; www.winonahistory .org. The stained-glass windows in this converted 1915 armory tell the stories of Winona's past. The upper-floor Winona County time-line exhibit follows the armory's former exercise track. Downstairs you'll find a replicated Main Street and hands-on exhibits for kids, who can crawl into a cave, a tepee, and a riverboat pilothouse. There's also a much-lauded modern addition that opened in 2010. Admission: $5, adults; $3, children. Open 9 a.m. to 5 p.m. Mon through Fri, noon to 4 p.m. Sat and Sun. Closed weekends in Jan and Feb.

where to eat

The Acoustic Café. 77 Lafayette St.; (507) 453-0394; www.theacoustic.com. This afford-able cafe serves soups and sandwiches on home-baked breads and authentic pitas, plus coffee roasted on-site. Bands play live music on the weekends. Open 7:30 a.m. to 10 p.m. Mon to Thurs, 7:30 a.m. to 11 p.m. Fri, 9:30 a.m. to 11 p.m. Sat, and 9:30 a.m. to 9 p.m. Sun. $.

Bloedow Bakery. 451 E. Broadway; (507) 452-3682. The Saturday line might snake out the door at this timeless 1924 corner bakery. It's tough to resist that sugary, yeasty aroma and the cases packed with doughnuts, rolls, maple long johns, and every variation of Bis-marcks, including a strawberry-filled one with peanut-butter frosting. Gooey goodness. You can get breads and cookies, too. Open 6 a.m. to 5:30 p.m. Mon through Fri and 7:30 a.m. to 3 p.m. Sat. $.

Blue Heron Coffeehouse. 162 W. 2nd St.; (507) 452-7020; www.blueheroncoffeehouse .com. Creative, local ingredients and an attached bookstore make this cafe a favorite gathering place. For breakfast, look for quiche or egg strata with homemade sausage; moist, sweetly glazed cardamom scones; granola with ginger; chai-spiced oatmeal; and whole wheat buttermilk pancakes with maple syrup and blackberry sauce. Vegetarians and vegans will find several lunch options, including curried lentil soup; spring minestrone; and Nepalese egg salad with toasted black mustard and cumin seeds on pita bread. You can relax on the outdoor patio or stroll to the Mississippi riverfront 2 blocks away. Open 7 a.m. to 6 p.m. Mon through Fri (open until 8 p.m. on Thurs) and 8 a.m. to 5 p.m. Sat and Sun. $.

Lakeview Drive Inn. 610 E. Sarnia; (507) 454-3723; www.lakeviewdriveinn.com. Take a trip into the past on Wednesday nights mid-June through mid-September when classic cars gather at this nostalgic eatery. $.

where to stay

Alexander Mansion B&B. 274 E. Broadway; (507) 474-4224; www.alexandermansionbb .com. Lush and opulent, this Victorian mansion boasts incredible woodwork and a sprawling porch that's perfect for balmy days. There are 4 guest rooms with historic decor and the local Watkins body care products. The D.C. Alexander Suite also has an antique fireplace, original soaking tub, a window seat overlooking the gardens, and a private sunroom. A multicourse formal breakfast in the dining room include pastries, fresh fruit, a savory egg frittata or quiche, and a sweet dessert. $$$.

Carriage House B&B. 420 Main St.; (507) 452-8256; www.chbb.com. The Salyards opened this B&B in 1986, creating 4 guest rooms in a huge 3-story carriage house. They will pick up guests arriving by train or river and have complimentary bikes for them to use. $$.

Village House Inn. 72 College Rd.; (507) 454-4322. There are 4 pleasant guest rooms in this renovated brick farmhouse from the 1870s. Breakfast is help-yourself continental-style. $$.

day trip 05

southeast

bluff country americana:
lanesboro, mn

lanesboro, mn

No matter what the season, it's breathtaking to dip into the town of Lanesboro.

In winter, snowflakes swirl over a 300-foot limestone bluff and gently fall onto the historic brick downtown. By spring, there's a haze of bright-green buds and the rush of the Root River as it parallels the main street and curves around the bend. Summer's burst of flowers decorates restaurants and Victorian homes, while brilliant fall colors sweep through the bluffs and into the surrounding Richard Dorer State Forest.

Inspiring scenery helps infuse Lanesboro (population 788) with creative residents who run memorable B&Bs, contribute to galleries, and support a thriving local theater company. It's outdoorsy, too, with paddlers on the river and bikers and skiers gliding by on the immensely popular Root River Valley Trail.

Most of all, there's a tangible feeling of Americana, of a small-town pace that lets you downshift from city life. Crave even more simplicity? Slip into the past at Historic Forestville, a living history site, or join one of a handful of tour companies that take you into the countryside to visit Amish farms.

Don't worry if you're suddenly craving a front-porch swing and lemonade. It happens a lot.

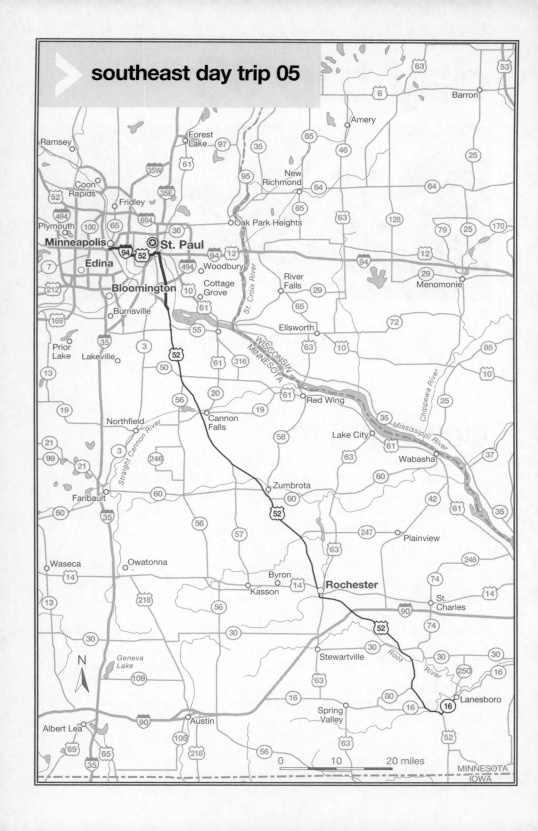

getting there

Follow US 52 from the southeast Twin Cities toward Rochester. It's about 130 miles to Lanesboro. Exit at MN 16 East and continue about 6 miles to downtown.

where to go

Lanesboro Area Chamber of Commerce. 100 Milwaukee Rd.; (507) 467-2696; www .lanesboro.com. Most businesses stay open daily through the summer, but restaurants often cut back to Thurs through Sun in the winter. Verify hours online or ask the chamber for details.

Amish Tours by R&M. 105 Coffee St. (Little River Store); (507) 467-2128; www.rmamish .com. The area's longest-running Amish tours take trips to see farms and workshops with quilts, furniture, baskets, rugs, and baked goods. Tours are south of Lanesboro to the Harmony and Canton areas or north of Lanesboro to farms in St. Charles and Utica. Tours run three times a day and last up to 3 hours with 5 stops. Rates: $25, adults; $15, teens; $10, kids 6–12. Tickets include a complimentary 2-hour bike rental.

Bluffscape Amish Tours. 102 E. Beacon St.; (507) 467-3070; www.bluffscape.com. These 3-hour tours by van or minibus include stops at Amish farms and the chance to buy crafts, furniture, and baked goods. Tours also include a stop at Austin's Mohair Goat Farm and Gift Shop in Harmony and the 1856 Lenora Stone Church. Tours depart from the Feed Mill in downtown Lanesboro. Rates: $30, adults; $20, teens; $10, kids 6–12. Tours offered Mar through mid-Nov.

Commonweal Theatre Company. 208 Parkway Ave. North; (800) 657-7025; www .commonwealtheatre.org. This professional company has entertained audiences with family-friendly comedies and musicals for more than 20 years. In the winter, the tone switches to brooding dramas for its acclaimed Henrik Ibsen Festival. Even if you don't have time for a show, pop inside to admire how they've transformed a former cheese factory into a 192-seat thrust stage with funky lobby art. Be sure to look up at the upside-down chairs hanging from the ceiling and decorated thematically. Interior wood- and stonework was salvaged from barns, with dioramas tucked into the walls. Even the bathrooms are fun with farm-tool handles on the stalls.

Historic Forestville. 21899 County 118 Rd., Preston; (507) 765-2785; www.mnhs.org/ places/sites/hf. An 11-mile drive from Lanesboro will plunge you more than a century back in time. Historic Forestville, a forgotten town that died out when the railroad bypassed it, comes to life each summer with costumed interpreters portraying its residents from 1899. Chickens squawk and scurry as visitors cross the historic Carnegie steel bridge to tour the barns, browse the historic inventory at the Meighen store, inhale aromas of fresh bread or stew in the kitchen next door, learn about the wheat boom and crash, and watch the gardener at work. It's a toss-up on what's more intriguing: the lost-world Brigadoon feel of the place or the shop with its quirky assortment of Turkish worm cure and tonics, tools, and tiny ladies' boots, plus corsets and union suits. Have a good map for navigating these back roads. Open 10 a.m. to 5 p.m. Thurs through Sat, Memorial Day through Labor Day. Rates: $6, adults; $5, seniors; $4, kids 6–17.

Lanesboro Art Center. 103 Parkway Ave. North; (507) 467-2446; www.lanesboroarts .org. Browse through a classy collection of regional artwork, from funky mosaics and smooth spherical ceramic fountains to silk scarves, jewelry, and paintings inspired by the rolling countryside. Open Tues through Sun in the off-season with expanded summer hours.

Lanesboro Farmer's Market. Sylvan Park; (507) 467-2358. Look for grass-fed beef and pork, rhubarb soap, perennials, fresh produce, pies, jams, jellies, lefse, and Amish cashew crunch made with butter, sugar, and cashews. Open 9 a.m. to noon May through Oct, plus 3 to 6 p.m. Wed June through Sept. Great time to visit: During the Rhubarb Festival in early June.

Little River General Store. 105 Coffee St.; (507) 467-2943; www.lrgeneralstore.net. Conveniently located along the Root River Valley Trail, this shop offers an impressive array of bikes from tandems and recumbents to 4-seat surreys for rent. They have a shuttle service if you don't want to backtrack and canoes and kayaks if you'd rather paddle than pedal.

Root River Outfitters. 109 Parkway Ave. South; (507) 467-3400; www.riversideontheroot .com. You can tube down the Root River starting at $10/tube or try your hand at paddling kayaks or canoes (starting at $30). The river is generally gentle and undeveloped, dwindling through the Richard J. Dorer Memorial Hardwood Forest. They also rent bikes for the Root River Valley Trail, starting at $10/hour.

Root River Valley Trail. Trailhead in downtown Lanesboro; (800) 944-2670; www.root rivertrail.org. The 42-mile trail runs parallel to the river, connecting small towns such as Whalan, Peterson, and Rushford. It's a gentle route. If you crave a better workout with hills, connect to the 12-mile Harmony-Preston Trail.

Scenic Valley Winery. 101 Coffee St. West; (888) 965-0250; www.scenicvalleywinery .com. This winery focuses on locally harvested fruits for mostly sweet wines such as a crisp rhubarb and cranberry, which they promote for holiday dinners. Tastings are complimentary. Look for onion, garlic, and green pepper cooking wines, too. Open 10 a.m. to 4:30 p.m. Mon through Fri, until 5 p.m. Sat; and noon to 4 p.m. Sun. Closed in Jan. Expanded hours in peak season.

where to eat

Aroma Pie Shop. 618 Main St., Whalan; (507) 467-2623. This is the best incentive for a 4.7-mile bike ride from Lanesboro to Whalan. The town's so tiny, it has a standstill parade

underground wonderlands

Southeast Minnesota's Bluff County claims some of the state's best scenery, but there's another side to it. To appreciate it, you have to head underground.

Filmore County has about 400 known cave systems. It's part of what's called karst topography. The glaciers missed this area, and it's filled with sinkholes, natural springs, and streams that dip underground and disappear.

You can see some of this landscape at Forestville/Mystery Cave State Park. One-hour seasonal tours give visitors a sample of the glossy flowstone and stalactites found throughout its 13 miles and finds such as a prehistoric squid fossil. You can gaze into dark shallow "aquariums" along a rock shelf and admire an otherworldly underground pool. The cave closes in the off-season when thousands of bats winter here.

If you head about 16 miles south of Lanesboro, you can take 1-hour tours into Niagara Cave, a trendy and quirky place to get married in the late 1930s and 1940s. There were more than 400 weddings at its underground chapel.

Modern visitors head down 250 steps past a 60-foot waterfall and onto a tour that includes stalactites, undulating rock draperies, delicate soda straws hanging from the ceiling, and an intriguing echo chamber. A highlight includes walking through the mazelike limestone canyon with walls as high as 100 feet.

Mystery Cave. *21071 County Hwy. 118, Preston; (507) 352-5111; www.dnr .state.mn.us. Open weekends mid-Apr through Oct with daily tours Memorial Day through Labor Day. There are 3 options for seeing the cave: 1-hour tours ($6–$10), a more in-depth 2-hour flashlight tour ($10–$15), and a rigorous 4-hour wild caving tour ($55 per person).*

Niagara Cave. *29842 CR 30, Harmony; (507) 886-6606; www.niagaracave.com. Open weekends Mar through Oct, with daily tours May through Sept. Call for seasonal tour times. Tickets: $7–$12.*

each year, but there's a steady flow of visitors to this homey cafe that goes through 50 to 100 cream and fruit pies a day. It also offers sandwiches, wild rice brats, wraps, and soups such as tomato basil, but pie's the real allure. Get the rhubarb custard, then sit back to watch the jeweled buzz of the hummingbirds that hover around to the multiple feeders outside. Open 10 a.m. to 5 p.m. Thurs through Sun and 10 a.m. to 3 p.m. Mon. $.

Lanesboro Pastry Shoppe. 202 Parkway Ave. North; (507) 467-2867. Locals heartily recommend this as a favorite breakfast spot. Tell them what you want, and they'll whip it up.

Lunch specials could be roast beef with morel mushrooms or tomato pesto soups, quiche, or a plate of biscuits and gravy. They always have a salad, too, with salmon or shrimp, plus monster-size cookies and sticky buns. $$.

Old Village Hall. 111 Coffee St.; (507) 467-2962; www.oldvillagehall.com. This Lanesboro mainstay has crafted a small menu with creative local and seasonal ingredients for close to two decades. On an early May visit, menu choices included locally foraged morel mushrooms, which were served in a soup with chopped sirloin and on flatbread with beef tenderloin, tomatoes, and Manchego cheese. Another choice was curry-seasoned black cod on a bed of morels with sorrel pearl pasta and teriyaki sauce. You can eat outdoors or in the second-floor dining room. $$$.

Pedal Pusher's Café. 121 Parkway Ave. North; (507) 467-1050; www.pedalpusherscafe .com. Look for the family-friendly and fun cafe for beef, eggs, cream, and many other ingredients coming from local farms, and kids can go to the prize chest for eating all their vegetables. They roast their own coffee to go with breakfasts such as flaxseed pancakes and homemade pies. Dinners include burgers and specials such as beef ribs with grilled asparagus. $$.

Riverside on the Root & the Dirty Martini Bar. 109 Parkway Ave. South; (507) 467-3663; www.riversideontheroot.com. You can order wood-fired pizzas (including one inspired by a Reuben), peel-and-eat shrimp simmered in Cajun-spiced ale, a Greek lamb burger, raspberry chipotle pork, and peanut butter chocolate mousse at this lunch and dinner spot. They also pour 14 signature martinis, including white chocolate, chai, and a key lime martini with graham crackers on the rim. Look for live music on Wednesday and Sunday evenings on the patio overlooking the river. Call for seasonal hours. $$.

where to stay

Berwood Inn. 22139 Hickory Rd.; (800) 803-6748; www.berwood.com. With a 200-acre hilltop location and whimsical gardens, this 1870 farmhouse makes it easy to stay put and relax. There are so many things tucked into the gardens—cherubs, a giant rooster, statues, farm equipment, and frogs—that you could play I Spy all day and into the evening with gentle lighting. There are 2 rooms on the second floor, a spacious owl-themed suite in the attic, and a budget-friendly rustic Garden Cottage for warm-weather overnights. Look for breakfasts such as yogurt topped with fruit and granola, crème brûlée french toast, a potato–green pepper hash with Canadian bacon, a brie quiche with hollandaise sauce, and rhubarb crunch for dessert. $$–$$$.

Brewster's Red Hotel. 106 Parkway Ave. South; (507) 467-2999; www.brewstersredhotel .com. Built into the hillside, this downtown hotel stands out with its wraparound balcony, affordable sleeping rooms with patchwork quilts, the option for an apartment with kitchenette, and its location almost right on the bike trail. $–$$.

Habberstad House B&B. 706 Fillmore Ave. South; (507) 467-3560; www.habberstad house.com. Each of the 5 rooms in this historic home has its own personality, from traditional quilts in the upper-level Amish Suite to a nicely themed Scandinavian Suite. There's also a spacious and modern Carriage House with a huge whirlpool tub, walk-in shower, ceramic fountain, and full kitchen. Breakfast specialties include baked Dutch apple pancakes with local bacon on the side and chocolate-drizzled crepes made with orange liqueur and filled with a cheese mixture. $$–$$$.

Historic Scanlan House B&B Inn. 708 Parkway Ave. South; (507) 467-2158; www .scanlanhouse.com. This is one of Minnesota's most venerable B&Bs, approaching almost three decades of welcoming guests to its 1889 Queen Anne Victorian built by Lanesboro's founder. It's filled with antiques, stained glass, elaborate woodwork, alcoves, and balconies, with a few of its 7 rooms located in the grand turret. $$.

south

day trip 01

south

chic boutiques & antiques:
rochester, mn

rochester, mn

The more recent phrase "medical tourism" gets thrown around like it's a new trend as people head out of the country for cheaper health care. Rochester, though, has medical tourism down to a science (and an art) as patients from across the globe have come for the Mayo Clinic's cutting-edge research and care and a team approach to getting well for more than a century.

What does that have to do with someone just wanting a good day trip or weekend escape? Consider this: Rochester draws about 760,000 patients and their families a year— even presidents and royalty. The city of 100,000 residents (and home to IBM) knows how to discreetly roll out the red carpet and offer a classy array of escapism through downtown boutiques, sophisticated galleries, and delicious dining.

Prefer antique to chic? Rochester's three-times-a-year Gold Rush ranks among the nation's largest antiques shows. You can find dealers and intriguing shops throughout the city, which sells an estimated $80 million a year in antiques.

If you're spending the night in one of Rochester's 5,000 hotel rooms, deals may pop up on Friday and Saturday as clinic traffic ebbs. Like all downtowns, it can be quiet on Sunday, but you can while away a day with a big brunch, strolling along the Zumbro River, exploring Quarry Hill with its fossils and caves, or watching the city's famed (and rather vocal) population of Canada geese at Silver Lake.

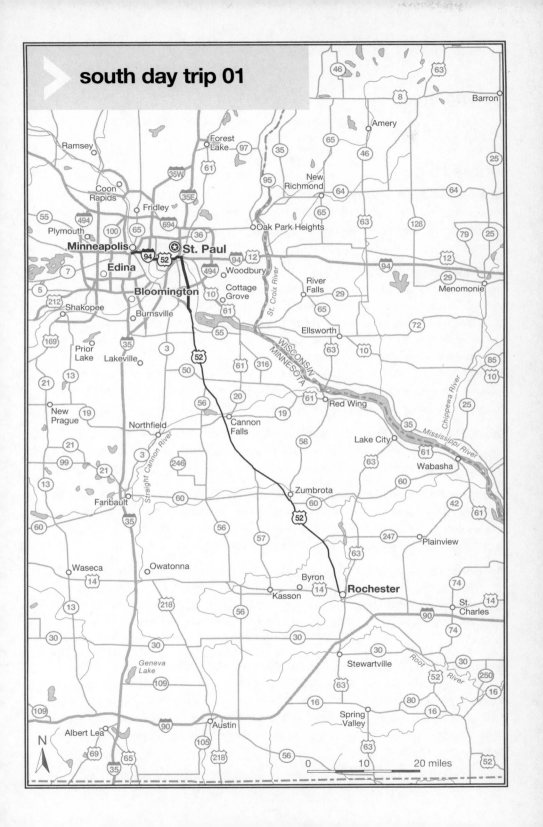

south day trip 01

getting there

From I-94 on the southeast side of the Twin Cities, exit at US 52. Follow it about 90 minutes to Rochester.

where to go

All American Segway tours. 11 4th St. Southeast; (507) 206-0958; www.allamerican segway.com. You can glide through Quarry Hill Park, the Soldier's Field Memorial, and other historic sites on these 3-hour weekday Segway tours offered Apr through Oct, running $65/ per person.

Mayowood Mansion. 3720 Mayowood Rd.; (507) 282-9447; www.olmstedhistory.com. The best time to see Charlie Mayo's 100-year-old, 38-room country home is during the summer when extensive gardens bloom or during the holidays when lavish Christmas decorations and lights make it shimmer and twinkle. The regular spring through fall tours cover highlights of Dr. Charlie's career, touch on famous houseguests, and showcase the property itself overlooking the Zumbro River Valley. There are extensive limestone terraces and walls, ponds, a long pergola and teahouse, and once were innovations such as a hydroelectric dam and man-made lake on what used to be a 3,000-acre estate. Call for hours and days of tours, which can vary. Tickets are $12 for adults and $5 for children.

Quarry Hill Nature Center. 701 Silver Creek Rd.; (507) 328-3950; www.qhnc.org. This is one of the top family attractions with a 2-acre fishing pond and a chance to look for ancient sea fossils, tour sandstone caves, or head for a hike or bike in this 320-acre park.

Rochester Art Center. 40 Civic Center Dr. Southeast; (507) 282-8629; www.rochesterart center.org. This modern museum has a gorgeous riverside location and fun museum shop an easy walk from downtown. Exhibits change monthly. Open Wed through Sun. Admission $5, adults. Free to Olmsted County visitors and military personnel.

Rochester Trolley & Tour Company. Info kiosk at Peace Plaza downtown; (507) 421-0573; www.rochestermntours.com. This company is best known for 2-hour trolley tours of the city, but it also offers shuttles to bike trails and special tours that may include bald eagle watching or guided fly-fishing trips. There are 700 miles of trout streams in this section of the state.

Silver Lake Park. 700 W. Silver Lake Dr. Northeast; (507) 328-2525; www.ci.rochester .mn.us. This widening of the Zumbro River ranks among the prettiest places in the city and stays ice-free throughout the winter with warm water discharging from the power plant. That open water has drawn more than 35,000 geese each winter (and helped nurture the bird's comeback decades ago). In the summer, get out on the water or bike or jog the pretty pathways through this huge park.

a closer look: the mayo clinic

Mayo Clinic's daily weekday clinic and art tours are open to patients and their families, but you can easily pop into its gorgeous, modern Gonda Building (200 1st St. Southwest) to admire a huge Chihuly sculpture and other renowned artworks, not to mention the building's interior design. You might even catch an impromptu concert if someone steps up to the baby grand piano in the atrium. Ask at the info desk for self-guided brochures of its impressive art collection.

Permanent history displays also tell about Mayo's beginnings, which were sparked by a devastating 1883 tornado that left the Franciscan sisters scrambling to care for the injured. They asked Dr. William Mayo to lead what became the cutting-edge St. Mary's Hospital in 1889. Their efforts expanded to a world-class medical system with top surgery techniques, research to support new medicines, and a unique philosophy of team care.

You can find historical displays in these locations:

Mayo Clinic Heritage Hall. *Mathews Grand Lobby of the Mayo Building.*

Mayo Historical Suite *and preserved offices of Drs. William J. and Charles H. Mayo in the Plummer Building. You can't miss this ornate 1928 building that rises above downtown with gargoyles and a 56-bell carillon. The office suite includes the Mayo brothers' degrees, honors, and photos of presidents and dignitaries, but also examples of how crude early surgical instruments were.*

Main lobby, St. Mary's Hospital, *1216 2nd St. Southwest. The lobby gleams with green marble that surrounds a central courtyard with gardens. Ask for directions to its beautiful cathedral.*

Silver Lake Boat and Bike Rental. 700 W. Silver Lake Dr. Northeast; (507) 261-9049; www.silverlakefun.com. Rent canoes, kayaks, rowboats, and paddleboats at Silver Lake Park.

where to shop

About Face. 112 1st Ave. Southwest; (507) 292-0922; http://aboutfacerochester.com. This is the place for a full makeover with NYC-worthy, trendy cosmetics and body care from brands such as Smashbox, Gucci, Prada, Fusion Beauty, Juicy Couture, and The Art of Shaving.

oldies are goodies

Rochester sells an estimated $80 million in antiques each year thanks to a global audience, a number of shops, and its Gold Rush weekends that bring together about 1,500 dealers a few times a year. Here are a few places to troll for treasures. Call for exact hours.

Blondell Antiques. *1406 2nd St. Southwest; (507) 282-1872; www.blondell .com. This motel across from St. Mary's Hospital specializes in Scandinavian antiques and folk art such as carved and painted furniture and cupboards, immigrant trunks, textiles, clocks, beds, and folk costumes.*

John Kruesel's General Merchandise. *22 3rd St. Southwest; (507) 289-8049; www.kruesel.com. This shop on historic 3rd Street specializes in vintage lighting from whale oil table lamps to sconces to Art Deco and Mission-style fixtures. It also sells a variety of American antiques, estate jewelry, and historical documents.*

Kismet. *600 block of North Broadway; (507) 424-2636. This trio of shops sells vintage and used furniture, housewares, and fashion from hats and dresses to kitchen tables and tea sets.*

Baby Clementine. 14 1st St. Southwest; (507) 282-0430. Brighten a cloudy or midwinter day by breezing into this adorable, whimsical, and Technicolor collection of baby and toddler shoes, clothes, and toys.

Barnes & Noble. 15 1st St. Southwest; (507) 288-3848; www.barnesandnoble.com. The 636-bulb vintage sunburst marquee clues you in that this isn't your typical Barnes & Noble. It's housed in the 2-story 1927 Chateau Theatre with a domed starry midnight-blue ceiling and mock French village that feels like a children's theater set. Duck under turret cutouts, and you've got Minnesota's most memorable entrance into a fiction section.

Counterpoint. 111 S. Broadway; (507) 280-6419; www.counterpointhome.com. Browse 2 stories of classy, colorful, and just plain fun home furnishings, kitchenware, clothing, kids' stuff, purses, funky shoes, and Marimekko designs.

The Nordic Shop. 111 S. Broadway; (507) 285-9143; www.thenordicshop.net. Rochester's Scandinavian roots show at this convergence of warm Norwegian sweaters, Helly Hansen sport clothing, Royal Copenhagen dinnerware, and Kosta Boda crystal.

SEMVA Art Gallery. 16 1st St. Southwest; (507) 281-4920; www.semva.com. Southeastern Minnesota Visual Artists sell the best of their work here, including paintings, photography, metalwork and jewelry, blown glass, sculpture, and fiber arts from vivid hand-dyed scarves to boiled wool gnomes and hats. The area's hardwood forests and Nordic folk roots also assure plenty of handcrafted pieces that make the most of swirling wood grains and luminous colors for vases, decorative bowls, rosemaled plates, and ornaments.

Tangerine. 110 1st Ave. Southwest; (507) 252-8119. Wildly colorful and a bit wacky, this is the kind of place girlfriends can spend an hour at, laughing at everything from funky stockings and sunglasses worthy of Elton John to floss that tastes like frosting and pens that say things like "Nudist Camp" so no one will swipe them from you. Open 9:30 a.m. to 7 p.m. Mon through Fri, 10 a.m. to 6 p.m. Sat.

where to eat

The Canadian Honker. 1203 2nd St. Southwest; (507) 282-6572; www.canadianhonker .com. This is a home-cooked, home-food kind of place, run by two generations for the past 20 years. Think apple cinnamon pork chops, 4-hour slow-cooked ribs, or hot beef sandwich. There's outdoor seating and live music on the weekends, plus a nice little bar that serves a cream-style martini rimmed with icing and inspired by their most beloved dessert: Bunnie's coconut cake. I can't vouch for the martini, but the cake is fantastic. $$.

Chester's Kitchen and Bar. 111 S. Broadway; (507) 424-1211; www.chesterskb.com. Hip and stylish, this University Square restaurant deservedly draws steady diners with a wood-fired oven, creative twists on traditional meals, and outdoor seating on the Peace Plaza. Menu favorites include crispy, beer-battered walleye on ciabatta bread, wood-fired rotisserie chicken, grilled barbecue salmon, slow-roasted prime rib, and a salad with pulled chicken, sweet corn, bacon, apples, homemade croutons, and vinaigrette. Try the made-to-order banana cream pie on a walnut-almond crust for dessert. Open at 11 a.m. for lunch Mon through Sat, closing at 11 p.m. Fri and Sat (when you can catch live jazz music) and 10 p.m. other nights. Sunday brunch runs from 10 a.m. to 2 p.m. $$–$$$.

Jasper's Alsatian Bistro & Wine Bar. 14 3rd St. Southwest; (507) 280-6446; www .daubesbakery.com. This historic brick restaurant a few blocks from the Mayo Clinic serves thin-crust pizzas, pan-crusted walleye with wild rice risotto cakes, savory soups and crusty breads, and Alsatian specialties such as tart flambé, which merges German and French influences. The bistro is part of Daube's Bakery, so expect a wide array of sumptuous desserts such as dense carrot cake and kolaches, pear almond tarts, and raspberry-filled Linzer torte. $$.

Mac's Café. 20 1st St. Southwest; (507) 289-4219. This homey cafe on the Peace Plaza has been serving Greek specialties and American comfort foods since 1951. Look for shish kebabs, quinoa, gyros, salads with fig and honey dressing, lemon ricotta pancakes, lamb and orzo, and spanakopita. $.

Newt's. 216½ 1st Ave. Southwest; (507) 289-0577; www.live2dine.com/newts.htm. Grab a lot of napkins before you dig into the city's award-winning burgers made from fresh coarse-ground, hand-pattied beef. Look for gut-busting specials such as Jucy Lucy that oozes with cheese inside, a burger topped with peanut butter and bacon, and the famous Fatty Melt: a burger, onion rings, and bacon wrapped in two grilled cheese sandwiches. They come with an over-the-top full pound of fries and free unlimited popcorn while you wait. You can reach Newt's via an outdoor fire escape or up the indoor stairs from City Café Seafood Grille and Bar. Open 11 a.m. to 11 p.m. daily except Sun when it closes at 10 p.m. $$.

Roscoe's Barbecue. 603 4th St. Southeast; (507) 285-0501; www.roscoesbbq.com. Roscoe's has a year-round location at 3456 E. Circle Dr. Northeast, but head to this nostalgic drive-in during the warm months. They serve a sweet, tangy barbecue, thin-sliced Jo-Jos instead of traditional fries, and brew their own root beer. If you prefer a more vinegary, savory barbecue, try John Hardy's on the city's south side. $.

where to stay

Doubletree Hotel. 150 S. Broadway; (507) 281-8000; http://rochesterdowntown.doubletree.com. There are countless choices (and every chain you can imagine and more) for lodging in Rochester. This one stands out for its colorful, modern lobby and 212 guest rooms within a block of shops at University Square and close to the river downtown. Another bonus: Pescara (www.pescarafresh.com) on the lobby level serves a big Sunday brunch plus weekday breakfasts including spinach and mushroom frittata, oatmeal pancakes, beef rib hash, and smoked gouda hash browns. It's best known for its seafood focus at lunch and dinner: crab cake and scallop sliders, Hawaiian fish, lobster bisque, wild mushroom risotto, wasabi mashed potatoes, Nawlins jambalaya, and cioppino. Cool lighting and sparkly red counters add to the chic atmosphere. $$.

Kahler Hotel. 20 2nd Ave. Southwest; (507) 280-6200; www.kahler.com. Rochester's grande dame started in 1921 when the Mayo brothers needed a classy hotel to cater to global visitors. It's the place to go for visiting presidents and royalty, too, with its exclusive International Hotel within the Kahler. There are more than 660 rooms in the general hotel with a large indoor swimming pool beneath a rooftop dome and indoor access to the Grand Shops of Kahler and Marriott Hotels and University Square and the Peace Plaza outside the front door. $$.

day trip 02

south

outlaws & academics:
northfield, mn

northfield, mn

Northfield, population 19,800, has always dreamed big and known how to a make an impression. Chalk it up to smarts with two of the nation's top liberal arts colleges. Or maybe it's the chutzpah that led the community to kill two bank robbers and chase the Jesse James gang out of town in 1876.

John Wesley North started the community in 1855 after sizing up the Cannon River. He harnessed its hydropower to run a sawmill and gristmill, and that legacy lives on with the Malt-O-Meal Company wafting the aroma of wheat cereal across the outskirts.

A decade after its founding, Northfield welcomed its first college. Today, Carleton College and St. Olaf draw 5,000 students who keep the town vibrant, youthful, and cultured with plays, concerts, and art shows throughout the year. The St. Olaf Christmas Festival is broadcast around the world. Visit in September to see the campuses burst into fall colors and hear the thunder of hooves and blast of guns as folks reenact the defeat of Jesse James.

getting there

Follow I-35 about 30 miles south of the Twin Cities. Exit at MN 19.

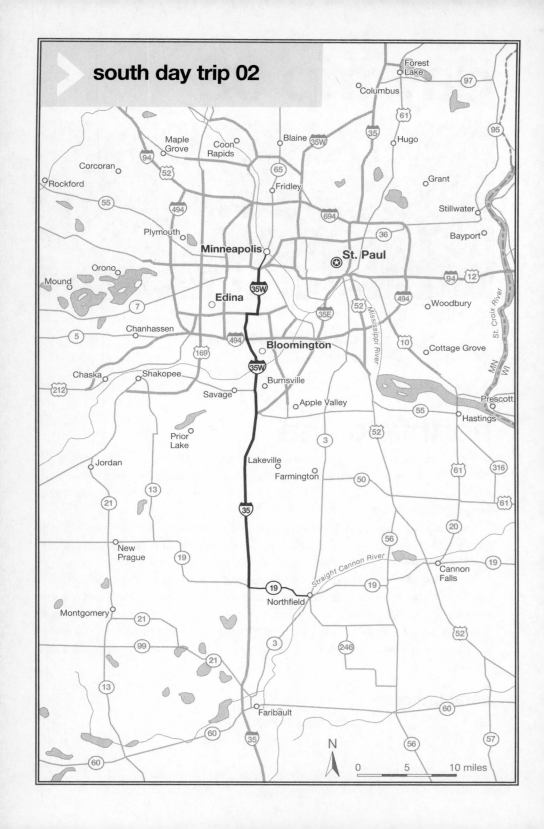

south day trip 02

where to go

Carleton College Cowling Arboretum. 1 College St.; (507) 222-5413; www.carleton
.edu. Enjoy the picturesque campus by strolling the Garden of Quiet Listening with its
Japanese design and the 880-acre Cowling Arboretum with views of the Cannon River. The
arboretum ranks among the top places in the state to go for a run.

Nerstrand Big Wood State Park. 9700 170th St. East; (507) 333-4840; www.dnr.state
.mn.us. This 3,000-acre remnant of original Big Woods forest sits about 7 miles from Northfield on the way to Faribault and offers one the state's best places to see spring wildflowers
and enjoy fall colors. There are 13 miles of hiking, 8 miles of paths for cross-country skiing,
and 5 miles for snowmobiling.

Northfield Historical Society Museum. 408 Division St.; (507) 645-9268; www.northfield
history.org. Get the details on why the James Gang came all the way from Missouri and
why this robbery was considered by some to be the last battle of the Civil War. The outlaws
were apparently after bank funds belonging to two despised carpetbaggers. It's also a good
place to catch a video showing the annual reenactment and to grab maps and brochures for
historic buildings downtown, the home of Norwegian-born author O. E. Rölvaag, and other
James Gang sites on the Outlaw Trail as it heads through Minnesota.

Riverwalk Market Fair. Between 2nd and 5th Streets along the Cannon River; (507)
786-9700; www.riverwalkmarketfair.org. The best place to hang out on a Saturday morning is downtown by the river from early June through mid-October. You'll find a little bit of
everything from flowers and local organic produce to paintings and pottery, pastries and
artisan bread.

Willingers Golf Club. 6900 Canby Trail; (952) 652-2500; www.willingersgc.com. This
6,809-yard course was built along a 40-acre forest and among 60 acres of open water and
wetlands, achieving Audubon Cooperative Sanctuary status. It's been recognized as one of
Minnesota's top courses in *Golf Digest* and is easy to reach at 1.5 miles from I-35. It boasts
a 74.4 course rating. Weekend peak season rate: $48.

where to shop

You'll find plenty of quirky, artsy, and even thrifty shops concentrated along Division Street.
Most are open seven days a week, but call for details on hours.

Glass Garden Beads. 413 Division St.; (507) 645-0301; www.glassgardenbeads.com.
Browse through thousands of beads, findings, handcrafted jewelry and decorations, and
trendy bottle cap art. A sampling of hands-on classes include glass-fusing, wire wrapping,
bead weaving, precious metal clay, felted beads, lampworking, and metal stamping.

Monarch Gift Shop. 405 Division St.; (507) 663-7720; www.monarchgiftshop.com. Besides its line of new age crystals and mind-body books, you'll find handblown glass energy balls, wedding bowls, playful and fragrant bath and body products, candles, and gifts.

Northfield Yarn. 314 Division St.; (507) 645-1330; www.northfieldyard.com. Whether you shop by color or texture, this shop is filled with temptations from sturdy wools and soft alpaca to funky buttons for experienced knitters or wannabes. Look for a how-to and special project classes or open-knit nights.

The Rare Pair. 401 Division St.; (507) 645-4257; www.rarepair.com. This cornerstone of downtown has been in business more than 30 years, selling comfortable shoes from Birkenstocks to UGGs, along with casual clothes and accessories for men and women.

The Sketchy Artist. 300 Division St. South; (507) 645-2811; www.thesketchyartist.com. With its vibrant decor, playful merchandise, and inviting store (a chalkboard keeps little kids busy), this is one of Northfield's best shopping surprises. Search for the perfect journal, a groovy new pen, stationery and cards, art supplies, and creative gifts.

Swag. 423 Division St.; (507) 663-8870. Whether you want a laugh-out-loud greeting card or funky piece of art for your home, they've got it. Here's a fun twist on hunters' mounted trophy heads: bison, deer, and moose heads made from recycled farm equipment.

where to eat

Chapati. 214 Division St. South; (507) 645-2462; http://1001solutionsllc.com. Grab a seat on the front porch of the Archer House or indoors for this popular lunch buffet or made-to-order dinners with tandoori chicken, warm naan, pakora, and curries. Open 11:30 a.m. to 2 p.m. and 5 p.m. to 9 p.m. Tues through Sat. $$.

The Contented Cow. 302B Division St.; (507) 663-1351; www.contentedcow.com. You can get English pub foods such as shepherd's pie or spinach and artichoke dip for a light afternoon nosh, but it's the atmosphere more than the food that keeps people coming to this 1876 riverside restaurant—especially when balmy days make its patio and deck the place to be. It promises "no lame beer." The conversation isn't too shabby either with its "Politics and a Pint" discussions. Live music ranges from a Beatles tribute and Norwegian bands to honky-tonk country. Open 3 p.m. to midnight Mon through Thurs, until 1 a.m. Sat and 11 a.m. to 11 p.m. Sun. $$.

The HideAway Coffeehouse and Wine Bar. 421 Division St. South; (507) 664-0400; www.hideawaycoffeehouseandwinebar.com. You can get an affordable and creative sandwich with their fresh ciabatta bread or wraps and salads. Open 6 a.m. to 10 p.m. Mon through Fri and 7 a.m. to 10 p.m. Sat and Sun. $.

Just Food Co-op. 516 Water St. South; (507) 650-0106; www.justfood.coop. Stop here for ready-made salads, sandwiches, or organic soups that you can grab to go or pack up for a state park picnic. The co-op was a leader in the statewide trend to support local farmers and producers. $.

Tavern of Northfield. 212 Division St. South; (507) 663-0342; www.tavernofnorthfield .com. Located within the Archer House, this restaurant opens early and stays up late, inviting diners to linger and soak up the historic feel with limestone walls, stained glass, and pub-cozy woodwork. The extensive menu features granola whole wheat pancakes, Cajun beef tips on fettuccine, roast duck with orange sauce, vegetarian lasagna, tavern burritos, and Thai salad. Open at 6:30 a.m. daily, closing at 10 p.m. Sun through Thurs and 11 p.m. Fri and Sat. $$.

where to stay

Archer House River Inn. 212 Division St.; (507) 645-5661; www.archerhouse.com. You can't miss this striking red French Second Empire inn in the center of downtown. It features 36 modernized, individually decorated rooms with touches of its rich history in four-poster beds, quilts, and some claw-foot tubs. $$.

Froggy Bottoms Suites. 309 S. Water St.; (507) 650-0039; www.froggybottoms.com. On the river side of the Froggy Bottoms Pub you'll find 4 suites that perch above the river. Most sleep up to 6 guests. $$.

Magic Door B&B. 818 Division St. South; (507) 581-0445; www.magicdoorbb.com. This 3-story blue Victorian offers 3 rooms within walking distance of downtown. Besides a large breakfast, guests can enjoy an evening drink, snacks, and a bottomless cookie jar. $$.

day trip 03

south

nature & nurture:
faribault, mn; owatonna, mn

If you keep driving past the Northfield exit on I-35, you'll reach Faribault and Owatonna. Each of these towns was settled early along the Cannon and Straight Rivers. That led to sturdy downtowns, grand neighborhoods, and an intriguing legacy of state schools.

Faribault's Minnesota State Academy for the Deaf opened in 1863 and is still going strong on its historic 40-acre campus. Shattuck St. Mary's, an Episcopal boarding school, opened in 1858—the year Minnesota became a state. It draws more than 400 students from 37 states and 20 countries to its 250-acre campus.

Owatonna was home to Minnesota's State School for Dependent and Neglected Children from 1886 to 1945. It was, in simpler terms, an orphanage. Any museum in the state can offer tales of hard times, from grasshopper plagues and starvation to war and natural disasters. There's an extra poignancy, though, to the Orphanage Museum with its photos of the kids who grew up in these historic cottages. If you call ahead, you can arrange a personal tour or take a self-guided walk around the campus.

faribault, mn

The name "Faribault" (aka "Faribo") is known across the country for its woolen blankets. They keep beds toasty in winter, laps warm during fall football games, commemorate events such as the Olympics, and re-create vintage stripes of fur-trade blankets.

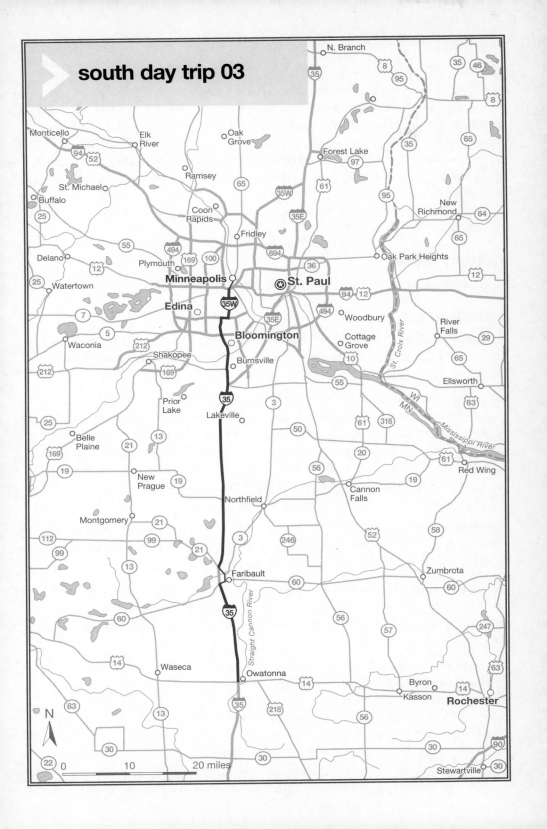

Faribault Woolen Mills—the last wool-to-blanket mill in America—had closed and was rescued in 2011. Looms are once again chugging and weaving. Faribault (population 23,000) is also known for making people joyously dizzy. The carnival ride Tilt-A-Whirl was created here.

Visit in the summer, and you may see the distinctive canning trucks hauling fresh peas, green beans, and sweet corn for Butter Kernel canned vegetables, which keeps the town's agricultural roots running deep.

Don't miss a trip to the historic downtown, which doubled as Wabasha in the movie *Grumpy Old Men*.

getting there

From Northfield, follow MN 3 about 13 miles south to Faribault.

where to go

Faribault Chamber of Commerce. 530 Wilson Ave.; (507) 334-4381; www.visitfaribault .com. Grab maps at the chamber, which is within a half mile of the Sakatah Singing Hills State Trail.

Donahue's Greenhouse. 420 10th St. Southwest; (507) 334-7156; www.donahues clematis.com. If you're passionate about gardening, don't miss these explosively colorful greenhouses. While they have a variety of plants (especially geraniums and hanging baskets), they're known for the staggering variety of clematis vines they sell wholesale to garden centers across the country. You can choose from about 50 varieties when they open for spring sales in April. They open again in mid-November, when greenhouses are awash in the red, pink, and creamy tones of 20,000 poinsettias.

The Faribault Woolen Mill Co. 1500 NW 2nd Ave.; (507) 412-5520; http://faribaultmill .com. Because of new owners reopening the mill in 2011, you'll need to check the website or call for details on its outlet store and possible summer tours.

Paradise Center for the Arts. 321 Central Ave. North; (507) 332-7372; www.paradise centerforthearts.org. Look for gifts made by regional artists, take a class, or catch a show at this arts hub and historic theater. Open noon to 5 p.m. Tues, Wed, Fri, and Sat, noon to 8 p.m. Thurs.

Peterson Art Furniture. 28 NE 4th St.; (507) 332-2158; http://petersonartfurniture.com. This brick warehouse that once held a thriving furniture company in the early 1900s now houses 3 stories of antiques, including vintage furniture and lamps, books, and architectural salvage such as doors, hardware, ornate trim, and marble. Open noon to 4 p.m. Tues through Thurs and 10 a.m. to 4 p.m. Fri and Sat.

River Bend Nature Center. 1000 Rustad Rd.; (507) 332-7151; www.rbnc.org. This 750-acre blend of woods, prairie, and pond wraps around the surprisingly windy Straight River. It's a favorite place to see the seasons change with 10 miles of hiking and biking and 5 miles of cross-country skiing. Families can enjoy nature displays in the interpretative center, open 8 a.m. to 5 p.m. Mon through Fri and 8 a.m. to 4 p.m. Sat.

Sakatah Singing Hills State Trail. Trailhead near MN 60 and CR 21; (507) 334-4381; www.dnr.state.mn.us. You can access this 39-mile state trail near the chamber office and pedal by Wells and Cannon Lakes. Sakatah Lake State Park lies about 17 miles away. In the winter, the trail's used for snowmobiling.

where to eat

The Cheese Cave. 318 Central Ave. North; (507) 334-3988; www.cheesecave.net. If you love salads and gourmet sandwiches, this is the place to get them with fresh feta, smoked gouda, and Amablú gorgonzola and St. Pete's select blue cheese. This is also an outlet store for the Amablu and St. Pete's cheeses, which are aged in sandstone caves. You can get a variety of imported cheeses here as well, order wine and cheese pairings, enjoy their fresh-made cheese curds, and shop a variety of gourmet pastas, crackers, olives, and jams and jellies. They also offer monthly cooking classes. Open at 10 a.m. Tues through Sat. $.

Lyon's Meats. 101 NW 4th St.; (507) 334-9399; www.lyonsmeatsmn.com. While this is primarily a meat shop that has been in operation since 1959, it also serves hickory barbecue pork sandwiches, grinder hot beefs, and almond chicken salad sandwiches from 11 a.m. to 2 p.m. Tues through Sat. They've teamed up with St. Paul's Summit Brewing Company to make beer brats, which you can buy to grill at home. Open at 9 a.m. Mon through Sat, closing at 6 p.m. weekdays and 4 p.m. Sat. $.

Sweet Spot Candies. 209 Central Ave.; (507) 334-0600; www.sweetspotcandies.net. If you have kids in tow, take them on a trip down memory lane with nostalgic candies, homemade waffle cones and ice cream, big bear paws, kettle corn, and fudges such as malted milk ball or vanilla fudge pizza. You can even get tie-shaped fudge or sign up for the fudge-of-the-month club. $.

where to stay

Dancing Winds Farmstay Retreat. 6863 CR 12, Kenyon; (507) 789-6606; www.dancing winds.com. Fourteen miles east of Faribault, this 1856 Norwegian farmstead is a working goat farm that has welcomed guests to enjoy the countryside for more than 20 years. You can learn about the goats, cheesemaking, and make a breakfast with fresh local produce in the guesthouse. $$.

Sakatah Lake State Park. 50499 Sakatah Lake State Park Rd.; Waterville; (507) 362-4438; www.dnr.mn.state.us. About 17 miles west of Faribault, this park is popular for 62 drive-in campsites, 5 more remote bike-in sites, 1 camper cabin, and canoeing and fishing on this widening of the Cannon River. $.

owatonna, mn

In addition to Owatonna's orphanage museum, Owatonna (population 23,000) offers another gem: the National Farmer's Bank. It's attractive with its brick exterior, terra-cotta green trim, and arched windows, but that's just a hint of the opulence inside. It's considered one of Minnesota's architectural masterpieces.

getting there

Grab I-35 at Faribault and drive about 16 miles south to Owatonna.

where to go

Cabela's. 3900 Cabela Dr.; (507) 451-4545; www.cabelas.com. You can argue this is a megabox store, but its 150,000-square-foot showroom is the most-visited destination in Owatonna (and Minnesota's first Cabela's). Visitors can join in workshops, browse museum-like wildlife displays, troll for outdoor merchandise, and dine on ostrich, buffalo, and wild game at the cafe. Open daily.

National Farmer's Bank (now Wells Fargo). 101 N. Cedar Ave.; (507) 451-5670; www.owatonna.org. This bank has been called a jewel box, a symphony of color, and one of the best examples of Prairie School architecture. Louis Sullivan, creator of the skyscraper, designed this bank, which was finished in 1908. Light filters in through huge stained-glass windows, glitters across gold leaf, 2.25-ton cast-iron chandeliers with intricate scrolls and oak leaf designs, and warms the palette of greens, browns, and ambers throughout the building. Visitors can admire the bank from its lobby or walk up to the balcony for a closer look at detailing and a beautiful mural depicting farmers in the field. Open 8:30 a.m. to 5 p.m. Mon through Fri and 8 a.m. to noon on Sat. Free.

State School Orphanage Museum. 540 W. Hills Circle; (507) 774-7369; www.orphanagemuseum.com. Once close to 300 acres, this former state orphanage with 16 historic cottages and other buildings is now home to city offices, an art center, and this museum, which touchingly gives a voice to the 10,635 children who lived here between 1886 and 1945 after being orphaned, abandoned, or neglected. The museum includes pictures, artifacts, and personal stories, and Cottage 11 was recently restored to look as it did when boys lived here around the 1930s. You can get a 50-cent map of the grounds or listen to narrations at 4 audio stations. There's also a memorial and a cemetery. Open 8 a.m. to 5 p.m. Mon through Fri and 1 to 5 p.m. Sat and Sun (access the museum through the art center on weekends). Donations welcome.

where to eat

Costa's Candies and Restaurant. 112 N. Cedar Ave.; (507) 451-9050; www.costas-candies .com. You can get a homey breakfast or lunch—think pancakes, burgers, milk shakes, and Coke floats—plus cafe staples with Grecian flare at this 1919 downtown landmark. They serve Greek salads, a Grecian Delight egg scramble, and gyros, but are best known for their candies. Look for handmade caramels, toffees, nut clusters, truffles, and gooey chocolate-covered cream candies. Open 7:30 a.m. to 3 p.m. Mon through Sat. Candy counter stays open until 6 p.m. weekdays and 4 p.m. Sat. $.

southwest

day trip 01

southwest

follow the minnesota river valley:
jordan, mn; belle plaine, mn;
henderson, mn; st. peter, mn

Southwest of the Twin Cities, US 169 heads into the wide valley of the Minnesota River. It's a favorite destination in September and October with its tall bluffs filled in by fall colors and big signs beckoning visitors with a bounty of apples.

Do more than pull over for a peck or a pie and you can enjoy the history of these towns where the Minnesota River was a highway for the area's Native Americans and pioneers arriving with high hopes. When the starving Dakota rose up against the failed promises of the Traverse de Sioux treaty, the US-Dakota War broke out. While that war was overshadowed by the nation's Civil War, it remains one of Minnesota's darkest chapters and America's bloodiest battles.

Unlike the wide forge-ahead Mississippi River, the Minnesota bends and twists like yarn held taut and suddenly released. It snags and twists through the woods and floodplains that fill each spring. Follow the river on side roads and byways that amble by farms and small towns, wooded ravines and quiet bends. Keep your eyes open for deer and eagles along the water's edge.

jordan, mn

This city of about 8,000 offers a nice reprieve from strip malls and big-box retailers on the outer ring of the Twin Cities. It retains its historic character with brick-and-sandstone buildings and homes tucked into steep hills.

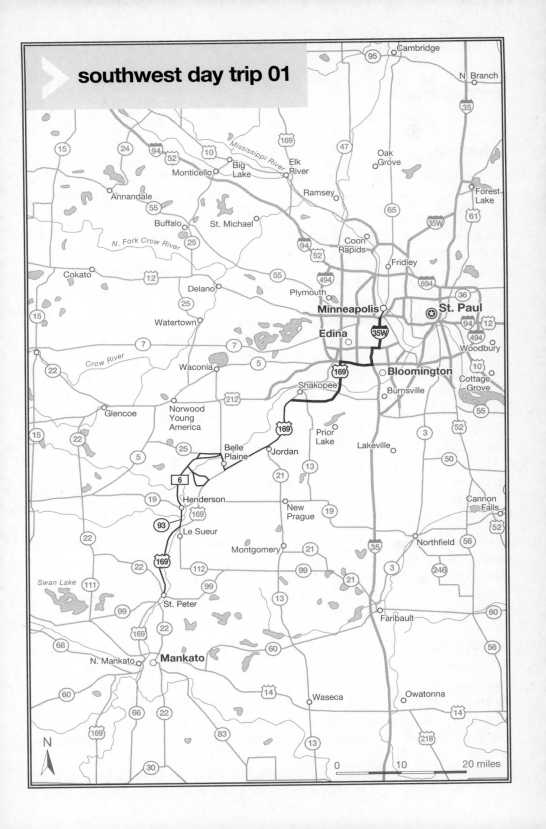

getting there

Follow US 169 south out of the Twin Cities from I-35, about 35 miles to Jordan.

where to go

Jordan Chamber of Commerce. 315 Broadway St.; (952) 492-2355; www.jordan chamber.org. You can download a walking tour by clicking the tourism tab at www.jordan .govoffice.com.

Jim's Apple Farm. 17365 Johnson Memorial Dr. (US 169). If you love novelty sodas, quirky candy, hot sauces, and gag gifts, give yourself plenty of time to explore this screaming yellow roadside barn. Take a Christmas list and be prepared to laugh at everything from electric blue Brainwash soda to bacon-flavored toothpaste, wasabi lip balm, and mints that supposedly taste like corn dogs. It's the dizzying array of sodas that stands out the most with close to 200 flavors from across the country, including Minnesota's own Spring Grove sodas and Killebrew root beer. You can, of course, get fresh apples, pies, pastries, pumpkins, jams and jellies, and imported dry goods, too. They don't take credit cards or have a website or even a phone number for inquiries. Open 9 a.m. to 7 p.m. July through Thanksgiving.

Minnesota Harvest. 8251 Old Highway 169 Blvd. at Apple Lover's Lane; (952) 492-2785; www.minnesotaharvest.net. This has ranked among Minnesota's most beloved fall destinations for generations. It was slowly reviving in 2011 after being closed in 2005 with bakery and cider equipment sold off. You can still enjoy tractor rides among its 283 hilltop acres and u-pick choices among its 25,000 apple trees, including Honeycrisp, Honeygold, Haralson, Fireside, Connell red and Cortland. Vendors offer waffles with cinnamon-laced apples, roasted sweet corn, pulled pork sandwiches, and apple brats on the weekends.

Wagner Apple Farm. 18020 Xanadu Ave.; (952) 492-2367. The giant red apple grabs the attention of US 169 road-trippers and lures them in for seasonal local produce including Honeycrisp apples, Haralsons, Cortlands, and outside tables piled high with bright orange pumpkins. Inside you'll find their own honey from nearby hives, apple pies, apple butter, jams and jellies, and gourmet popcorn.

where to eat

Carasim Coffee & Collectibles. 231 Broadway St. South; (952) 492-5553. The big band music playing inside this cute cafe fits perfectly. You can browse for antiques in the side rooms or have a seat in a booth for soups such as chicken tortilla, strawberry-rhubarb pie (in season), salads, sandwiches, bars, muffins, truffles, coffee drinks, and chai. On Friday nights, you might find live music upstairs in The Hub of Jordan. Open Wed through Sun. $.

Feed Mill Restaurant. 200 Water St.; (952) 492-3646. While this century-old former feed mill looks a bit ho-hum on the outside, step inside for lovely views of a wooded Minnesota River tributary from the restaurant's generous windows. It's a peaceful view for enjoying American classics such as hefty morning omelets, hot beefs, and Czech soup that taps the area's ethnic heritage. Closed Mon. Open 6 a.m. to 8 p.m. Fri and Sat and for breakfast and lunch Sun, Tues, Wed, and Thurs. $$.

where to stay

Minnesota River State Recreation Area. 19825 Park Blvd.; (952) 492-6400; www.dnr .state.mn.us. There are 25 rustic sites at the Quarry Campground (no running water or flush toilets) in the Lawrence unit south of Jordan. A handful of the sites are along the water and make it easy to forget you're anywhere near a metropolitan area. $.

Nicolin Inn B&B. 221 Broadway St. South; (800) 683-3360; www.nicolinmansion.com. This 5-room B&B sits in the heart of downtown with a shady side garden. Rooms all have their own feel from the rich colors and stately look of the Nicolin room to the Mertz room's Art Deco reds, blacks, and zebra stripes. Breakfasts may include Scotch eggs, frittatas, crepes, quiches, and an array of creative scones such as chocolate ginger. $$$.

belle plaine, mn

Everybody knows Emma Krumbee's in Belle Plaine. At the intersection of US 169 and CR 3, it rules as one of the state's biggest apple-related attractions with several thousand visitors flooding into their fields for the annual—and comically creative—scarecrow festival. You can, for example, see pumpkins decorated as Nativity animals or Clifford the Big Red Dog going after a Lady Gaga scarecrow with a meat dress. Emma Krumbee's has expanded into a restaurant franchise that's popped up in two more Minnesota locations and two in Wisconsin.

getting there

Follow US 169 south of Jordan about 8 miles to Belle Plaine.

where to go

Emma Krumbee's Orchard. 311 Enterprise Dr. East; (952) 873-3006; www.emmakrum bees.com. Fall is peak season with 6,000 apple trees, u-pick apples, and extra games and activities, such as feeding the resident goats or climbing a mountain of straw. The orchard and general store are open year-round for shopping and seasonal goods from spring flowers and summer produce to Christmas trees. When weather cooperates, they also have u-pick hydroponic strawberries, which don't require any kneeling to harvest. You can get casual meals, such as pulled pork sandwiches or apple brats from the General Store, along with pastries, breads, caramel apples, pie, turnovers, and cider doughnuts. Admission to the Scarecrow Festival: $5/person.

where to eat

Emma Krumbee's Restaurant & Bakery. 351 Enterprise Dr. East; (952) 873-4334; www .emmakrumbees.com. Go nostalgic here: grab one of the aqua vinyl seats in the main section and order up diner classics, such as chicken dumpling soup, hot beef or pork over homemade mashed potatoes with gravy, or a classic burger with a malt or shake. Leave room for dessert or take it to go from the bakery. $.

henderson, mn

Henderson's pretty downtown—only a few blocks long—shows up almost unexpectedly and ambles uphill into the wooded bluffs. It's one of Minnesota's oldest towns, but still has just over 900 residents. If you adore small towns and nostalgia, visit on a summer Tuesday night when classic cars rumble along Main Street.

getting there

Head into downtown Belle Plaine to cross the Minnesota River and grab the Minnesota River Valley Scenic Byway. It curves and ambles for about 10 miles into Henderson. Along the way, watch for Jessenland, the state's earliest Irish settlement, marked with a country church and hillside cemetery.

where to go

Ney Nature Center. 28003 Nature Center Ln.; (507) 248-3474; www.neycenter.org. This 446-acre former homestead east of Henderson is now threaded with trails that follow former oxcart and stagecoach routes, loop around ponds, through Big Woods remnants and natural prairie, and past historic farm buildings. There are also great overlooks for viewing the Minnesota River Valley. It's open for winter skiing, too.

where to eat

Toody's. 417 Main St.; (507) 248-3326. Tiny but welcoming, this soda fountain serves up ice cream and hot coffee and a daily lunch special such as goulash. The storefront also contains a pharmacy and art center, displaying local paintings, pottery, and photography. $.

where to stay

Henderson House B&B. 104 N. 8th St.; (507) 248-3356; www.hendersonhousemnbb .com. This sturdy brick home perches above downtown Henderson and the river valley.

It features rustic plank floors, vintage textiles and accessories, and sepia-toned portraits that evoke Minnesota's earliest decades, roughly 1860s to the 1880s. In the backyard, a relocated 1850s log cabin has been restored for folk classes such as maple syruping, snowshoe making, rug-hooking, and chair caning. The backyard chicken house is also expected to be back in action and providing fresh eggs for breakfast. Ask for a room facing the valley to see the moon and sun rise. $$.

st. peter, mn

St. Peter was a gathering place long before settlers started moving into Minnesota. It was here at the Traverse des Sioux crossing that tribes, traders, oxcarts, and explorers would ford a shallow part of the Minnesota River. It connected the Big Woods to the east to the prairies in the west.

This also is where one of Minnesota's most momentous documents—the 1851 Traverse des Sioux Treaty—was signed with the Dakota. It opened up 24 million acres for white settlement. The city of St. Peter was founded two years later. It was even considered a candidate for the state capital, which explains the extra wide main street. While that didn't pan out, it's still impressive to drive through downtown.

There are 40 St. Peter buildings on the National Historic Register. Brick and sturdy, they rise beautifully against a blue fall sky. Gustavus Adolphus College, built in 1862 on the bluff above downtown, keeps the city youthful and thoughtful and tied to its Lutheran Swedish roots. Among the key events is an annual Nobel Conference that brings together global leaders in science to discuss ethics and cutting-edge issues from genetics and the energy crisis to the impact of globalization.

getting there

You can get there the speedy way down US 169 or take the Minnesota Valley Scenic Byway from Henderson to Le Sueur (land of the Green Giant), across an iron bridge and past St. Peter's symbolic pearly gates.

where to go

Linnaeus Arboretum. 800 College Ave.; (507) 933-6181; http://gustavus.edu. Named for a Swedish botanist, this 125-acre arboretum includes a dozen formal gardens such as a white garden, a Swedish garden, and a rose garden. Two miles of trails wind through its restored natural areas that represent Minnesota's various biomes: tallgrass prairie, wetlands, coniferous forest, and deciduous woods. There are also a Melva Lind Interpretive Center and an 1866 cabin that was built by Swedish settlers in the nearby community of Norseland. Visitors can take a self-guided arboretum tour with 21 interpretive stops or check for guided tours on the events calendar. It's open for skiing in the winter.

Seven Mile Creek Park. Six miles south of St. Peter on US 169; (507) 931-1760; www .dnr.state.mn.us. You can park near the Minnesota River and a boat landing, then take a tunnel under the highway and into the ravines carved by Seven Mile Creek. There are 8 miles of trails in this 628-acre park. They wind past the creek's clear pools stocked with brown trout each spring. You can also see exposed sections of Jordan sandstone, which is older than the creamy yellow Kasota sandstone mined on the other side of the Minnesota River.

Swedish Kontur. 310 S. Minnesota St.; (888) 836-6631; www.swedishkonturimports .com. If you want to fit in with St. Peter's Swedish heritage or stay stylishly warm in the middle of winter, you can find a large selection of Scandinavian sweaters here, along with dinnerware, table linens, cookbooks, silver jewelry, folk art decor, and gifts.

Treaty Site History Center. 1851 N. Minnesota Ave.; (507) 934-2160; www.nchsmn.org. A public television documentary explains the events leading up to the US-Dakota War of 1862. The effect and tragedies of it reverberated up and down the Minnesota Valley. It led to the largest hanging in US history as 38 Dakota warriors were killed. The rest of the nation was forced out of state to reservations in the Dakotas.

In addition to Native American and pioneer artifacts and stories, the museum site includes trails leading to the river, interpretive signs about the oxcart trails converging here, and examples of native prairie plantings. Admission $4, adults; $2, students. A $6 combo pass lets you into St. Peter's Cox House for tours, too.

W.W. Mayo House. 118 N. Main St., Le Sueur; (507) 665-3250; www.mnhs.org/places/ sites/wwmh. Twelve miles north of St. Peter costumed guides offer tours of this 1859 home built by Dr. W.W. Mayo. He had his first medical practice upstairs before he and his sons went on to found the Mayo Clinic in Rochester. It later became the home of the Cosgroves who founded the Green Giant Company. Open for three or four days a week Apr through Oct; call for details. Admission: $4, adults; $3, seniors; $2, children 6–17.

where to eat

Cedars Grille. 408 S. 3rd St.; (507) 934-3314; www.cedarsgrille.com. You can have a seat on the warm-weather patio or inside the restored Konsbruck Hotel for American fare and Middle Eastern specialties such as grilled kebabs, herbed pork tenderloin, crab cakes, and a Mediterranean combination platter. Dessert may include raspberry mango cheesecake, berry layer cake, baklava, or a decadent chocolate cake. If you just want a drink, there's a beautiful bar in the front lobby. $$.

St. Peter Food Co-op & Deli. 228 Mulberry St.; (507) 934-4880; www.stpeterfood.coop. You can grab cold sandwiches and salads for warm-weather picnics or dine at the hot bar at this impressively large co-op. You can get hot sandwiches, do a build-your-own burrito, or try out specials such as chicken and andouille gumbo and savory vegetarian soups. Open 7 a.m. to 9 p.m. daily. $.

Whiskey River. 34166 MN 99; (507) 931-5600; www.riversp.com. This bustling restaurant sits just across the Minnesota River from St. Peter. It doesn't overlook the water, but it does have great views of backyard gardens packed with feeders to attract songbirds and hummingbirds. Its menu includes chicken dumpling or beer cheese soup, smoked beef brisket, parmesan-crusted chicken, a melon salad with salmon, and their version of a Waldorf salad with homemade bacon dressing. There's a rich caramel pecan fudge cake among the desserts. $$.

where to stay

Konsbruck Hotel. 408 S. 3rd St.; (507) 934-3314; www.cedarsgrille.com. A block off St. Peter's main street, the historic Konsbruck Hotel stands sturdy and welcoming with 5 swank and spacious rooms above the Cedars Grille. Each has its own character with exposed brick walls plus colorful and luxurious decor, bedding bathrobes, and spacious bathrooms. A few have balconies and fireplaces near soaking tubs, and all have access to a cozy central gathering room. $$.

Riverside Municipal Campground. (507) 931-1550; www.ci.st-peter.mn.us/recreation. There are 11 campsites along an oxbow of the river in this 120-acre park that includes a playground, picnic areas, and access to hiking, biking, and ski trails. There is a 2-acre fishing pond for children, but no swimming is allowed there or in the river. Reservations are first-come, first-served only, and campers must register at the police department at 207 S. Front St. $.

worth more time

If you keep driving another 20 miles, you'll reach **Minneopa State Park** southwest of Mankato (54497 Gadwall Rd.; 507-389-5464; www.dnr.state.mn.us). Southern Minnesota's largest waterfall flows across sandstone ledges and drops into a lush, wooded gorge. It's especially popular in the spring and after storms when the falls are the most dramatic and in September and October when colorful maple and basswood leaves drift across the surface of the creek. You also don't need a Stairmaster after heading down the WPA-built steps into the shady sandstone gorge and back up again. In the winter, the falls freeze into funky formations.

The falls are along a tributary away from the Minnesota River, but the park covers 1,145 acres and offers 61 campsites along a bluff overlooking the Minnesota. There is also one camper cabin. On the opposite side of the river—along scenic Judson Bottom Road—you can stop at Minnemishinona Falls, a gentle flow that drops 45 feet into a gorge below a footbridge. The county park is at 40923 Judson Bottom Rd.; (507) 931-1760.

day trip 02

southwest

a taste of germany:
new ulm, mn

new ulm, mn

Outside New Ulm's visitor center, oompah-pah polka pipes into the street. A few blocks down, the Glockenspiel draws a crowd three times a day to hear its bells play and watch figurines of pioneers, Germans, and an Indian twirl beneath the clock tower.

New Ulm, population 13,500, wears its German heritage proudly. It was settled as a utopian town, with businesses and homes built into the hillsides overlooking the Minnesota River Valley. It features some of Minnesota's most ornate and distinctive buildings and some of its best festivals.

If you want the absolute best view, make your way to the top. Drive uphill on Center Street, then climb 99 steps up "Hermann the German." You might be huffing and puffing, but it's worth the breathtaking view of both the valley and the picturesque steeples and town below.

You can reward yourself with a beer (or root beer). New Ulm's Schell's Brewery has been making it for more than 150 years, so this is one of the oldest family-run brewers in the nation. *Prost!*

getting there

Take US 169 southwest out of the Twin Cities until you reach St. Peter. Take a right onto MN 99 and follow it southwest to US 14. Go west on 14 until it reaches New Ulm. It's a 95-mile drive from the Twin Cities.

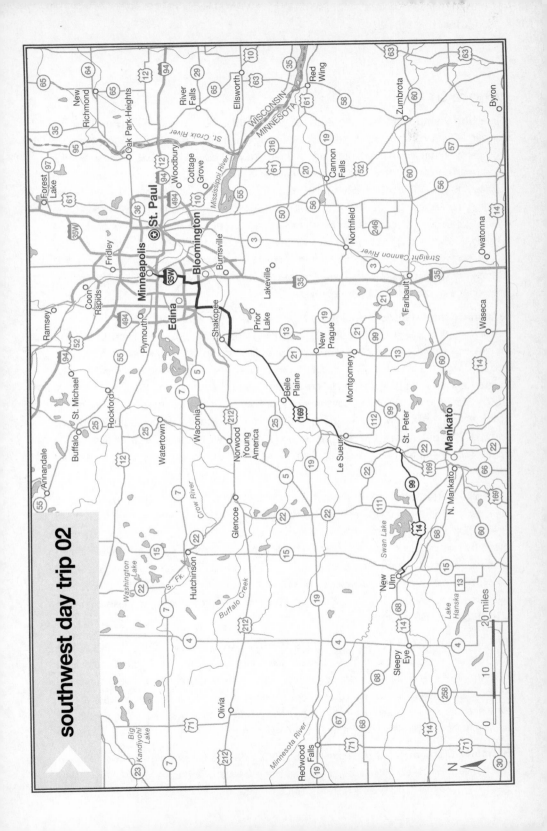

southwest day trip 02

where to go

New Ulm Visitor Center. 1 Minnesota St.; (507) 233-4300; www.newulm.com. This visitor center isn't hard to find in the heart of downtown. If you need an extra clue, listen for oompah-pah music piped into the street. You'll get great advice here, and you can borrow iPods with one of the state's best downtown walking tours, which uses historic buildings to highlight key events from the city's past, including its founding as a utopian German settlement in the 1850s, the US-Dakota War of 1862 when it almost burned to the ground, the heyday of beer production, and how Bohemian artists left their mark. The podcasts have photos, music, and good narration for stories you might otherwise miss, such as hearing about the town's women who hid from the uprising in a basement with a powder keg they planned to ignite rather than be taken captive. You also can download the podcast on your own device or buy a $5 CD with a driving tour.

Brown County Historical Society. 2 N. Broadway; (507) 233-2616; www.browncounty historymnusa.org. New Ulm's most ornate building (and former post office) houses 3 floors of historical exhibits about New Ulm's history, agricultural roots, and artistic legacies. The top floor, which feels like a giant attic, includes a birchbark canoe, buggy, Native American regalia, buffalo robe, uniforms, paintings, and other artifacts from the US-Dakota War of 1862. Starving after unfulfilled government promises, a Dakota skirmish sparked attacks upon white settlers. New Ulm residents created barricades and held off attackers but lost most of their buildings, and Dakota tribes were pushed west to remote reservations. The museum is one of the better places to learn about one of the darkest chapters in Minnesota history.

Flandrau State Park. 1300 Summit Ave.; (507) 233-9800; www.dnr.state.mn.us. It takes four days to fill the only man-made, sand-bottom pool in the state park system. It's a unique place to cool off with clear well water, views of the Cottonwood River, and a historic stone bathhouse. Book early for camping spots here—especially if you want one of the two camper cabins. It's one of the best parks for young families. Visitors can take 8 miles of hiking trails that wind through woods, prairie, and along the river or try them in the winter with cross-country skis. The staff stokes up a nice fire in its stone warming house. Entrance fee: $5/day; skis: $10; snowshoes: $6.

Glockenspiel. 327 N. Minnesota St.; (888) 463-9856; www.newulm.com. A Native American, pioneers, a polka band, and a barrel maker are among the dozen figurines that twirl from this 45-foot-tall chiming clock at noon, 3, and 5 p.m. At Christmas, some figurines are replaced with a Nativity scene. You can see another German icon, a heritage tree, at 101 S. Minnesota St. The sculpture includes town events on each branch, including a riverboat and the railroad, the New Ulm Battery, and a beer wagon.

Hermann Monument. 14 Monument St.; (888) 463-9856; www.newulm.com. For an impressive view of the Minnesota Valley, climb the 99 steps and up a short ladder to the

river of history

New Ulm lies along one of the prettiest and most poignant sections of the 287-mile Minnesota Valley Scenic Byway. This is the most concentrated area for learning about the US-Dakota War, which marks its 150th anniversary in 2012.

In addition to exhibits at the Brown County Museum and New Ulm's downtown walking tour, there are other noteworthy sites that tell stories from Minnesota's challenging early years of statehood.

Fort Ridgely State Park and Historic Site. *72158 CR 30, Fairfax; (507) 426-7840; www.dnr.state.mn.us. The visitor center 20 miles from New Ulm tells how white settlers fled here to safety and how the fort—thinly guarded during the Civil War—fended off the 1862 attacks. You can golf the family-friendly 9-hole course tucked among the fort ruins or camp here. $5 state park admission required.*

Harkin General Store. *66250 CR 21, New Ulm. Costumed interpreters introduce visitors to the goods early pioneers would need for their homesteads, from nails and buckets to coffee grinders and bonnets. This was one of the area's earliest settlements along the Minnesota River, but it faded away after the arrival of trains in 1873 replaced the river for transporting goods to farming communities.*

Land of Memories Park. *At Amos Owen Lane off US 169, Mankato; www.mahkatowacipi.org. In the spirit of reconciliation, the Dakota hosts a public powwow the third full weekend in September. It honors the 38 Dakota warriors who died during the largest mass hanging in US history. The Mahkato Pow-Wow website includes more background on the US-Dakota War, plus etiquette tips for attending pow-wows. Land of Memories Park with its large stone bison at the entrance welcomes campers and offers a canoe launch on the river throughout the warm months.*

top of the 102-foot-tall monument affectionately dubbed "Hermann the German." It honors Hermann, who defended Germanic tribes against a Roman imperial army in AD 9. These days, Hermann's a national symbol of the contributions German-Americans have made. There's a small museum in the monument's lower level, as well. Admission: $1.75. Free for kids 5 and under.

Minnesota Music Hall of Fame. 21 N. Broadway; (507) 354-7305; www.mnmusichalloffame.org. Minnesota's music legends such as Bob Dylan, Bobby Vee, Judy Garland, and Prince are all recognized in this museum, but polka is king. The majority of the displays pay homage to homegrown old-time bands influenced by their European roots. It can be a fun walk down memory lane for visitors who remember the heyday of Minnesota's ballrooms and polka legends such as Whoopee John. Admission: $3.

The Sausage Shop. 301 N. Broadway; (507) 354-3300; www.thesausageshop.com. It's not a true German town without a meat market. Browse the cases here for landjagers, a firm pork and beef sausage; mild, tender weisswurst; Nurnberger brats with hints of ginger and lemon; plus old-fashioned wieners, bacon, summer sausage, smoked ham, jellied beef, and dried beef.

Schell's Brewing Co. 1860 Schell Rd.; (507) 354-5528; www.schellsbrewery.com. Riding up a winding, wooded road, you wouldn't expect a brewery at the end of it. Then again, that's part of the charm. You can take a tour to see the huge copper kettle and loud bottling machines and taste some of the brews, but it's the wooded setting, beautiful gardens, and historic Schell's mansion that will likely stick with you. There are even peacocks that stroll the estate and take visitors by surprise as they preen in the sun or let out a call.

This is the nation's second-oldest family-run brewery, surviving Prohibition by selling soda (they still make their own root beer and Buddy's line of pop) and making it through the 1970s by selling off trees to make payroll. You'll get all the details during the $3 tours (kids under 12 are free). Tours include a walk through its museum and samples of beers such as Firebrick, a Vienna-style amber lager, the Pilsner, and seasonal brews such as Maifest, a blond double bock, or Zommerfest, a honey ale. It's free to roam the grounds, the museum, and shop in its extensive store—a great place to get vintage Schell's or Grain Belt souvenirs. Schell's brews 16 of its own beers plus all the former Grain Belt recipes and close to 60 contract brews. Afternoon tours daily Memorial Day through Labor Day. They do sell out, so reservations are a good idea. Call for off-season details.

Wanda Gag House. 226 N. Washington; (507) 359-2632; www.wandagaghouse.org. Even if you never read the children's book *Millions of Cats* (in print since 1928), this tour of Wanda Gag's childhood home sparks an appreciation for her career as an author and lithographer. It also offers a colorful glimpse into the struggles and triumphs of free-thinking, unconventional Bohemian artists, including her father and sister, in the early 1900s. Open May through Oct 10 a.m. to 4 p.m. Sat and 11 a.m. to 2 p.m. Sun. Also open for Christmas displays in December. Call for details.

Weeds and Reeds. 500 N. Broadway; (507) 359-1147. This cute turreted 1926 brick gas station provides an unusual, fun setting for an attractive hodgepodge of antiques (vintage 7-Up signs to gum racks) and modern housewares, decor, and gifts, such as eco-cleaners, retro linens, and tomato-shaped teapots. If you visit the first weekend of the month April through December, an antiques flea market spills out the front door.

where to shop

It can feel like Christmas year-round with New Ulm's large selection of German imports—especially holiday ornaments, nutcrackers, and fine chocolates.

Domeier's German Store. 1020 S. Minnesota; (507) 354-4231. The shelves and aisles are tightly packed in this shop tucked into a residential neighborhood. You'll find glassware and steins, clocks ticking away on pillars and walls, gummi candies and chocolates, glittering glass-blown ornaments, spaetzle and dumpling mixes, and European condiments and seasonings. Don't forget to look up. Postcards are plastered across the ceiling.

GutenTag Haus. 127 N. Minnesota; (507) 233-4287; www.gutentaghaus.com. A wall of tick-tocking cuckoo clocks welcomes visitors into this main street store where ethnic pride shows on T-shirts and cookbooks, wool hats and crystal-cut vases. Most enchanting, though, is the back of the store where it feels like Christmas even if you're wearing flip-flops and smell like suntan lotion. Blown-glass ornaments sparkle while carved wooden ornaments from Santas and snowmen "smokers" line the shelves. Many come from Germany's Ore Mountain region, which is known for creating nutcrackers, Schwibbogen (intricately carved candle arches), and windmill pyramids that twirl with the heat of a candle.

Lambrecht's Gifts. 119 N. Minnesota; (507) 233-4350; www.lambrechtsgifts.com. This 2-story downtown shop carries fashionable women's clothing, floral arrangements, home decor, and an adorable toy room, but you also can find hundreds of Christmas items spread throughout holiday-themed rooms including one with a snow village. They even sell heirloom-worthy ornament sets designed for a bride and groom.

where to eat

George's Fine Steaks and Spirits. 301 N. Minnesota St.; (507) 354-7440; www.georgessteaks.biz. This classic downtown steakhouse opens for dinner with New York steak and T-bones, stuffed portobello mushrooms, kebabs, lamb chops, and appetizers such as tuna shooters (cubed and broiled ahi tuna with wasabi and fries). You can order prime rib on Friday and Saturday. Opens 4 p.m. Mon through Sun. $$.

The Grand Kabaret. 210 N. Minnesota St.; (507) 359-9222; www.thegrandnewulm.com. New Ulm's 150-year-old Grand Hotel comes to life from 6 p.m. to midnight each Friday and Saturday with the Grand Kabaret live entertainment and a simple menu. Waitstaff in black T-shirts printed with lederhosen serve wine flights, hot tea, and cold beer (including Schell's Deer Brand beer with olives—a "German martini"). You can munch your way through cheese-and-fruit platters, a local cheddar and sausage plate, olive bowls, organic hummus and vegetables, soups such as Mexican chicken or carrot ginger, and desserts like key lime bars, pound cake with fresh berries, and cookies. The hotel's second floor will eventually be a center for arts and culture. $$.

Lola's Larkspur Market. 16 N. Minnesota; (507) 359-2500; www.lolaslarkspurmarket .com. This spacious yet cozy brick-walled restaurant downtown displays local artwork and a great array of pastries and desserts, soups, sandwiches, and specials that embrace both comfort food and gourmet dining. Try caramel pull-aparts or oatmeal brûlée for breakfast, puff-pastry chicken potpie or pasta for lunch, or dinners such as a springtime serving of tender halibut with sauteed morel mushrooms with sweet pea and parmesan risotto. Look for free live music on Friday and Saturday nights. $$.

Morgan Creek Vineyards. 23707 478th Ave.; (507) 947-3547; www.morgancreekvine yards.com. "Winedown for the Weekend" on Friday nights when the owners pull crispy pizza from a brick oven, pour wine, serve appetizers, and offer live jazz on the patio outside the winery dug into the hillside of a pretty valley about 8 miles southeast of New Ulm. When cooler weather rolls in, the best seats are around the bonfire. They've been making 14 differ-ent wines since 2003 with Minnesota-developed, winter-hardy varieties. Marquette grapes, with a pinot noir heritage, are used for Puck's Pride, a dry red wine aged in oak. The sweeter Frontenac grapes are used for port and rose while Frontenac Gris's flavor of strawberries and honey go into their Sweet E dessert wine. Open Fri through Sun May through Dec. $$.

Veigel's Kaiserhoff. 221 N. Minnesota; (507) 359-2071. New Ulm's most venerable res-taurant reflects its heritage by serving schnitzel, smoked chops, and sausage—and having murals of castles painted on the walls—but it's best known for its tangy sweet ribs with a creamy mayonnaise-enhanced barbecue sauce. The 70-plus-year-old restaurant has a throwback feel, but it can be endearing—especially if you sit at one of 8 booths with little free jukeboxes. The music is dominated by Doris Day, Glenn Miller, Frank Sinatra, and a few polka bands (of course). $$.

where to stay

Bingham Hall B&B. 500 S. German St.; (507) 354-6766; www.bingham-hall.com. Look for a lot of extras with the 4 spacious, stylish rooms in this historic home: chocolates, light snacks, wine or beverages, a library of DVDs to watch, down comforters, and chenille robes. The Elijah room even includes a full-body massage chair. Start the day with filling breakfasts such as raspberry stuffed french toast. $$$.

Deutsche Strasse B&B. 404 S. German St.; (507) 354-2005; www.deutschestrasse.com. Guests at this sturdy 1884 home facing the Minnesota River Valley can enjoy breakfasts such as their unique coffee roast, homemade granola, banana custard with strawberry puree, Bavarian omelet or "crazy German quiche," and a flour-free Black Forest Bundt cake. Each of the 5 rooms carries a hint of Germany, whether it's a framed photo of Neuschwanstein, Black Forest murals, or a cuckoo clock. $$–$$$.

west

day trip 01

west

mysteries & water skis:
spicer, mn; new london, mn

If you want to avoid the flood of traffic heading "up north" each weekend, go west.
The Little Crow Lakes region anchored by New London and Spicer offers an old-fashioned lake getaway with great beaches, camping, mom-and-pop resorts, and a weekly waterskiing show.

This is the kind of time-warp place where a kid can bike up to the ice-cream stand, ask for the "usual," and know he'll get it. These towns east of Willmar are each barely over 1,000 residents and surrounded by even smaller farming communities.

This western section of the state has always been heavily agricultural with a Nordic heritage. You can still find white country churches with pioneer cemeteries and Swedish meatball dinners advertised on the bulletin boards.

If you're good at following maps, venture onto the 245-mile Glacial Lakes Scenic Byway and try not to get lost. Chances are you will, but that, too, can be part of the adventure.

spicer, mn

This town has long been a favorite summer destination thanks to Green Lake, the largest in the area at 5,000 acres. The town's founder built a summer cottage here, but it was so large and distinctive with its English manor style and turret that locals started calling it the Spicer Castle. The name stuck, and it's now one of Minnesota's historic inns.

If you visit in the winter when Glacial Lakes State Trail opens to snowmobilers and the lake fills with fish houses, you might also catch sight of Spicer's Ice Castle on Green Lake.

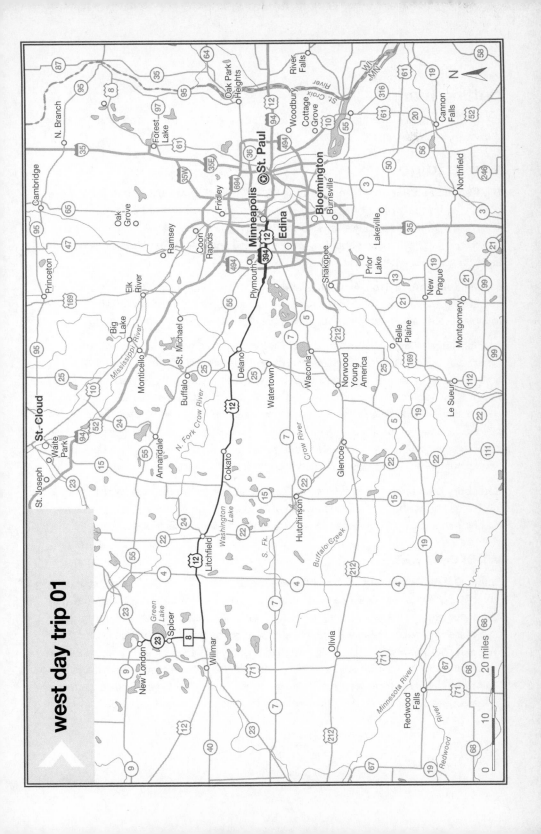

west day trip 01

getting there

Follow US 12 west out of the Twin Cities about 50 miles. Go north on Kandiyohi CR 8 for 7 miles to reach Spicer.

where to go

Big Kahuna Fun Park. 190 Progress Way; (320) 796-2445; www.spicerfun.com. If you've got kids in tow, this place brings together minigolf, go-karts, bumper boats, and games. There's a Powerwheels course for kids too young for go-karts. Open 11 a.m. to 9 p.m. daily Memorial Day through Labor Day. Call for spring and fall weekend hours. Prices start at $4.50 per person per activity.

Glacial Lakes State Trail. www.dnr.state.mn.us. This 22-mile paved trail follows the former Burlington Northern route to link New London and Spicer to Willmar with a connection to Sibley State Park. In the winter, parts of it are open to snowmobiling.

Glacial Ridge Winery. 15455 Old Mill Rd.; (320) 796-9463; www.glacialridgewinery.com. Open year-round, this winery features almost two dozen kinds of wine, many made using northern hardy grapes such as Frontenac, La Crescent, Edelweiss, Prairie Star, and St. Pepin. They also have a rhubarb wine and one that uses five varieties of apples from the on-site Johnny Appleseed Orchard. The orchard has 850 trees and 12 varieties of apples that are for sale, along with pumpkins and pies throughout the fall. Special events include free Thursday night concerts mid-May through mid-September, Friday night soup suppers throughout the winter, and weekly winery tours at 2 p.m. Saturday.

Saulsbury Beach. 151 Lake Ave. North, on Green Lake; www.spicermn.com. This is the favorite gathering spot and considered one of Minnesota's great beaches. Lifeguards help supervise the action. You also can bike around the 12-mile perimeter of the lake.

where to eat

Spicer Castle Restaurant. 11600 Indian Beach Rd.; (320) 796-5870; www.spicercastle .com. This gracious old home opens to the public for dinner Tuesday through Saturday with casual burgers and sandwiches or entrees such as walleye with wild rice and mushrooms, crab-stuffed halibut, three-cheese ravioli, and pork chops with bourbon barbecue sauce. Friday and Saturday nights are 3- or 5-course Murder Mystery Dinners, an interactive 2-hour party that involves guests in solving a crime set in a 1920s speakeasy or Scottish castle. During the summer, there also are 2.5-hour dinner cruises on Green Lake aboard the 23-passenger *Spicer Castle Belle.* The restaurant serves brunch on Sunday. $$$.

where to stay

Bug-Bee Hive Resort. 29659 Queen Bee Ln., Paynesville; (320) 243-4448; www.bugbee hiveresort.com. Fourteen miles northeast of New London, this resort has a variety of suites and cottages with up to 6 rooms along Lake Koronis with a beach, water toys, playground, boat rentals, summer kids' programs, family activities, and an indoor pool. $$$.

Dickerson's Lake Florida Resort. 13194 2nd St. Northeast; www.dickersonsresort .com. Thirteen cabins—almost all right along the water—make it easy to hop in a boat, splash in the water, or build sand castles on 674-acre spring-fed Lake Florida. Cabins range from 1 to 5 bedrooms and include kitchens and use of kayaks, hydrobikes, row-boats, and bicycles. $$.

Spicer Castle Inn. 11600 Indian Beach Rd.; (320) 796-5870; www.spicercastle.com. Each of the 8 rooms in this 1895 English-style mansion is unique with a variety of amenities such as fireplaces, claw-foot tubs, and access to the lakeside deck. Eunice's Room features wood wainscoting, 14 windows, and a suspended bed that swings. There also are 2 rooms in the estate's former Honey House, 2 rooms in the Garden House, and 2 historic cabins that can be rented. $$.

new london, mn

With a pretty millpond as its centerpiece, New London's Main Street offers a refreshing assortment of shops and local artists. Most are open Monday through Saturday. You can find a full listing at www.shoppingnewlondon.com.

The town's big-ticket outing is the Friday night waterskiing shows. The Little Crow Ski Team has been performing for three decades, earning two national championships and 16 regional championships along the way. It's a unique outing for families and nice way to kick off a summer weekend.

getting there

From Spicer, travel north 6 miles on MN 23/9. Follow MN 9 to the left when the two high-ways split to enter downtown New London.

where to go

Heritage Falls Market. 42 Main St.; (320) 354-3291. This shop pays homage to Minneso-ta's ethnic groups with cuckoo clocks from Germany, Norwegian sweaters, Swedish linens and pewter, nostalgic toys, and gifts such as jumbo truffles, fragrant lotions, and candles.

Kaleidoscope. 26 Main St. South; (320) 295-0767; http://kaleidoscopeanartistsgallery .com. Close to a dozen artists sell their work here, including pottery, baskets, fiber arts, photographs, and paintings in oil, pastels, and watercolors often inspired by the local area.

Little Crow Ski Team. 311 2nd Ave. Southeast; www.littlecrow.com. Settle into the bleachers along the Crow River to see the acrobatic athletes build four-tiered pyramids, soar across jumps, and inspire applause while zipping across the water at Neer Park. Shows start at 7:30 p.m. in June and July and 7 p.m. in August. Be sure to double-check the schedule. The team sometimes hits the road for competitions or may offer additional home shows. Reserved seating: $8. Regular admission: $5, adults; $3, kids. If the bleachers fill up, you can grab a spot on the hill to watch.

Mill Pond Mercantile. 24 Main St. North; www.millpondmercantile.com. The biggest shop in town is this collection of candles, garden art, framed prints and decorations, gourmet foods, and table settings. Leave time to explore the other specialty and gallery shops in New London.

Sibley State Park. 800 Sibley Park Rd.; (320) 354-2055; www.dnr.state.mn.us. This state park makes the most of its location with a popular beach on Lake Andrew, an interpretive center featuring the area's wildlife and fauna, and 18 miles of trails. The top trail—quite literally—is the one to Mount Tom. The hill, a long-ago lookout and spiritual place for the Dakota, features a historic stone tower where you can look across its 2,510 acres. Other trails head through the woods and along ponds. In the winter, visitors can cross-country ski or snowshoe. The park includes 132 campsites, half of which are near the beach and convenient for families with young children. There also are 4 camper cabins.

where to eat

The Deep Freeze. (320) 354-0093. Two blocks from the Glacial Lakes State Trail you can get summer favorites such as sundaes, malts, freezes, hot dogs, barbecue sandwiches, chips, and ice-cream cones swirled with flavors like cotton candy, bubble gum, and mocha cappuccino. Closed Nov through Mar. $.

northwest

day trip 01

northwest

city of granite & gardens:
st. cloud, mn

st. cloud, mn

It's hard to decide which is more impressive: the saturated colors, fragrant roses, and graceful fountains of Clemens Gardens or the shady Munsinger Gardens beneath a canopy of pines and nestled along a serene stretch of the Mississippi River.

While different in character, these two gardens cover several city blocks and rank among Minnesota's best free attractions. Across the river from Munsinger Gardens, a cupola and the historic buildings of St. Cloud State University line the embankment. A short walk away, the Mississippi thunders over a dam, then gently flows among the Beaver Islands, a peaceful place to paddle.

St. Cloud, population 80,000, is also known as The Granite City. Locally quarried granite was used to build its imposing 1860s state prison, elegant downtown buildings, benches and pathways in the gardens, and for buildings and monuments throughout the US.

The best place to appreciate this rocky past? Hands-down Quarry Park & Nature Preserve. This 600-plus-acre county park encompasses more than 30 water-filled quarries where you can fish for trout, dive in on hot summer days, or find a serene place to picnic or take a stroll through woods and prairie. Need more adventure? It's also popular for mountain biking, cliff jumping, scuba diving, and rock climbing.

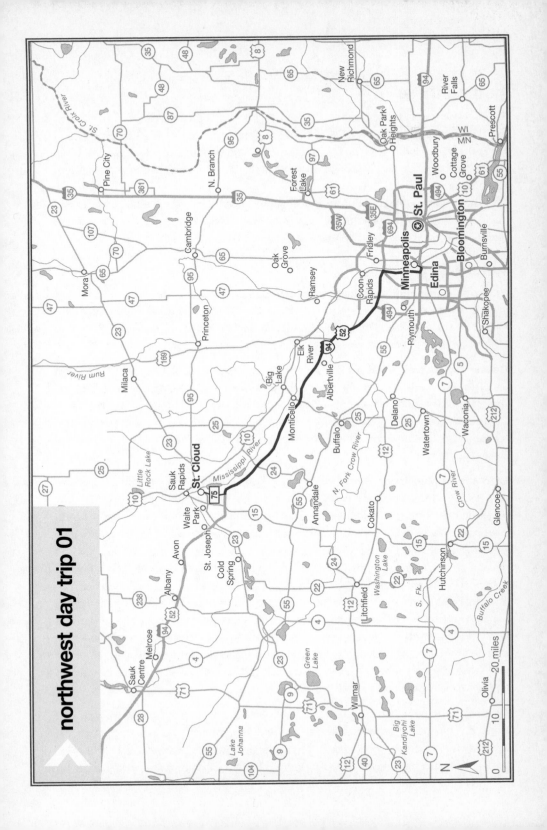

northwest day trip 01

getting there

Take I-94 northwest to St. Cloud. It's about 70 miles from the Twin Cities.

There are three main exits. Exit at CR 75 to get downtown or MN 23 to reach Quarry Hill Park. You also can take US 10 and enter St. Cloud on the east side at MN 23. Waite Park is technically its own city on the west side of St. Cloud, but they blur together like Twin Cities suburbs.

Worth noting: Amtrak's Empire Builder stops in St. Cloud, but the hours are tough. You'd arrive at midnight amid St. Cloud's scrap yards and have to board at 5:30 a.m. to return to the Twin Cities—and that's assuming it's on time.

where to go

St. Cloud Convention and Visitors Bureau. 525 US 10 South, Ste. 1; (320) 251-4170; www.granitecountry.com. Free guided tours of St. Cloud's historic sites can be down-loaded at www.ci.stcloud.mn.us/Planning/Downtown or look for "Preserving St. Cloud History" on iTunes. It covers downtown, Barden Park, and the Highbanks neighborhood.

Beaver Island Trail. West bank of the Mississippi; (320) 255-7216; www.ci.stcloud.mn .us. This 3-mile trail starts at the River's Edge Convention Center downtown and heads downriver past historic homes, St. Cloud State University, and through a wooded tunnel of trees. It's the most popular place in the city to in-line skate, jog, walk, bike, and push strollers. Park downtown or at the trailhead south of St. Cloud State's Halenbeck Hall and football stadium.

Clemens & Munsinger Gardens. Michigan Avenue and Kilian Boulevard (Clemens) and Riverside Drive Southeast and 13th Street South (Munsinger); (320) 258-0381; www .munsingerclemens.com. Munsinger Gardens were planted about 90 years ago with hosta-lined paths that meander and curve past swaths of lush begonias and coleus, granite urns overflowing with sweet potato vines, a gazebo, vintage log tourist cabin, wishing well and stream, and an historic ox-head fountain that's a nod to the area's location along oxcart trade routes. A path leads up the hillside to Clemens Gardens, another world with full sun-shine, geometric designs, an impressive iron treillage, and elegant fountains. The 6 themed gardens, which were planted in the 1990s, include a rose garden and a white garden that was modeled after Sissinghurst Castle in Kent, England. You can park along the streets or drive to a lot beneath the University Bridge. It connects to sprawling and wooded Riverside Park where there's a splash pad, playground, disc golf course, and viewing area for the dam and Beaver Islands. Open sunrise to sunset. Free, but donations are welcome.

Outdoor Endeavors. Halenbeck Hall, 720 4th Ave. South; (320) 308-3772; www.stcloud state.edu/campusrec/outdoorendeavors. You can rent canoes and kayaks through the university for a leisurely paddle down the Mississippi River to Clearwater about 15 miles away, then catch their shuttle back to campus. There are also a few rustic campsites on the Beaver Islands. It's a peaceful outing with the honk of geese, twitter of songbirds, trill of toads and frogs, or even the sight of deer leaping between the islands. Outdoor Endeavors can offer tips on the best channels to follow since a few can be shallow. It takes about 3 hours to do the trip. Call for current times and to make a reservation. Prices run about $35 with a shuttle.

Outdoor Endeavors also rents canoes and paddleboats for $8/hour at Lake George, a man-made lake in the heart of St. Cloud with nice views of St. Mary's Cathedral and downtown.

Pioneer Place on Fifth. 22 5th Ave. South; (320) 203-1233; www.ppfive.com. This imposing granite-pillared building offers a modern, intimate venue for performances such as musician Mason Jennings, "Deer Camp" theatrical comedies, or bands that open the floor so the audience can enjoy South American dancing.

You can choose from more than 250 wines, mojitos, and other drinks at The Veranda (www.verandalounge.com), a wine bar with seating indoors or on the granite veranda overlooking historic 5th Avenue. The Veranda hosts live music with jazz on Monday and acoustic music on Saturday and Sunday.

Quarry Park & Nature Preserve. 1802 CR 137, Waite Park; (320) 255-6172; www.co .stearns.mn.us. Melrose Deep 7 quarry ranks as the hottest way to cool off with chilling spring-fed water. Other highlights include the chance to see massive retired quarry equipment, climb a beautiful overlook, tackle a challenging mountain bike technical trail, walk a floating bridge across the wetlands, and see unusual wildflowers such as prickly pear cactus. Autumn is one of the best times to visit with the quarries acting as glassy mirrors reflecting the woods' fall colors. During the winter, there's an illuminated trail for cross-country skiers. Daily parking pass: $4.

Stearns History Museum. 235 S. 33rd Ave.; (320) 253-8424; www.stearns-museum.org. As one of the state's best history museums, it takes visitors into a virtual quarry, shows off the Pan automobile, and offers special exhibits such as a T. Rex named Sue, miniature circuses, and a comparison of late 1800s German immigration to the experience of Hmong and Vietnamese immigrants in the 1970s. Admission: $4, adults.

where to shop

You can find just about every chain and big-box store packed along Division Street through St. Cloud. Stick to the historic downtown (www.stclouddowntown.com) for the best concentration of unique shops. Many of the buildings feature unique granite accents and plaques with historic information. Most close on Sunday, and it's wise to call for seasonal hours.

Books Revisited. 607 W. St. Germain; (320) 257-3120; www.booksrevisited.com. This is the kind of store where you can get happily lost for hours, shuffling across wooden floors and into a maze of more than 100,000 used books, from exotic cookbooks and children's classics to rare first editions or massive sports encyclopedias.

Bumbledee's. 711 W. St. Germain St.; (320) 257-3387; www.bumbledee.com. This eclectic, playful hodgepodge of antiques and art fits right in with the building's pressed-tin ceilings and cream-colored St. Cloud brick walls. The inventory constantly changes and might include a painting of Dorothy's red slippers, curvy art glass vases, cowboy boots, vintage fishing lures, furniture, and retro kitchenwares. If you need a break, there's a love seat and coffeepot in the archway that connects Bumbledee's with Northern Brights.

Marishka's. 811 W. St. Germain; (320) 217-8538; http://marishkashoppe.com. Whether you want to decorate the house with new antiques or adorn yourself with scarves or jewelry, this shop blends a little of everything in its rooms. Look for shoulder bags, funky shirts and hats, sparkly rings, vintage glass jars, reclaimed sinks, and garden decor.

Northern Brights. 707 W. St. Germain; (320) 654-1814; www.northernbrights.com. For purse and wallet fanatics, this shop is one of the most Technicolor places to find a new one. Owner Paige LaDue Henry creates three different lines of purses made in St. Cloud and sold nationwide. One features glitzy threads and bangles encased in plastic, another features handmade fabric bags, and the Morphology line pulls together unique assortments of fabric and wool flowers. The shop also has other bags, vibrant clothing and accessories, scarves, and beaded jewelry.

Paramount Arts Gallery & Gifts. 913 W. St. Germain; (320) 257-3120; www.paramount arts.org. The vertical marquee blazes brightly on this 1921 theater, which has been restored to its original grandeur. Inside, more than 50 artists from a radius of 70 miles sell their paintings, hand-felted hats, pottery, purses made from neckties, handblown glass tumblers, pens encased in rare woods, stained glass sculpture for the garden, and jewelry at this gallery. Ask to peek into the theater or check out what's playing for the evening or weekend.

where to eat

Anton's Fish and Whiskey. 2001 Frontage Rd. North; (320) 253-3611; www.antons restaurant.com. On St. Cloud's far western edge, this used to be far enough out of town that it ran as a Prohibition speakeasy and distributor of Stearns County's infamous Minnesota 13 moonshine. It's expanded many times, but still has some original log walls and a focus on seafood, steaks, and giant popovers with honey butter. You can dine inside or out, but make a reservation if you want a seat overlooking the Sauk River or in one of the booths designed like a covered wagon. Open for lunch and dinner Mon through Sat and dinner on Sun. $$.

Bravo Burritos. 66 33rd Ave. South; (320) 252-5441; www.bravoburritos.com. Don't let the strip mall location put you off. This St. Cloud favorite has been cooking tender, savory meats for fist-size burritos for more than 30 years—long before the Chipotle chain was born. Our favorite is the combo burritos with three meats, such as zippy cubes of beef Colorado, spiced chorizo, carnitas pulled pork, pork verde stewed with tomatillos, chocolate-brown chicken mole, and tangy chicken verde. $.

Café Renaissance. 2140 Frontage Rd. North, Waite Park; (320) 253-9300; www.cafe renaissance.com. The warm colors, arches, and white pillars clue you in to the Mediterranean flavor of this restaurant on the west end. Look for spanakopita, moussaka, shish kebabs, Moroccan chicken, braised veal shank, and Greek samplers. Gluten-free items offered. $$.

Granite City Food & Brewery. 3945 2nd St. South; (320) 203-9000; www.gcfb.net. This popular chain with American fare, their own line of beer, and Sunday brunch is worth mentioning since this is the original location. A long-ago entrance arch to St. Cloud welcomed visitors to "the Granite City." $$.

House of Pizza. 19 5th Ave. South; (320) 252-9300; http://houseofpizzamn.com. If you love your pizza with a classic thin crust, savory sausage, and dense cheese, this restaurant has been serving them up since the 1940s. You can also head next door to the legendary Red Carpet with a rooftop martini bar. $$.

Jules Bistro. 921 W. St. Germain St.; (320) 252-7125; www.julesbistrostcloud.com. This small but classy cafe sits conveniently next to the Paramount Theatre and Arts District, serving appetizers such as bruschetta with creamy goat cheese and a sweet dried fruit tapenade, plus sandwiches such as house tuna salad on olive cheddar bread; a caprese grill with fresh mozzarella, tomato, and pesto on honey white bread; and a grilled avocado portobello Reuben. Look for every variation of chili here, along with wood-fired pizzas and evening specials such shrimp with angel hair pasta. $$.

Mexican Village. 509 W. St. Germain St.; (320) 252-7134; www.mexicanvillagestcloud .com. You'll find the usual lineup of Mexican food bracketed by free chips and salsa and jumbo margaritas, but the atmosphere's fun with a water fountain, tucked-away booths, bright colors, and murals that make it popular with young families. $.

Star of India. 2812 W. Division St.; (320) 281-3388; www.starofindiamn.com. St. Cloud is full of buffets, especially at lunch, but this one stands out for its freshness and the chance for newcomers to Indian cuisine to easily sample a range of flavors from tandoori chicken, zippy beef curry, and fragrant masala dishes to vegetable pakora, puddings, and their warm slabs of naan. $$.

Val's Rapid Serv. Lincoln Avenue. If you're a sucker for icons of days gone by, don't miss this tiny 50-year-old institution 2 blocks from US 10. You order and pay for your burgers, toppings, malts, etc., with automated machines in a tiny lobby, then wait for a deliciously grease-splotched bag with a mountain of great fries. $.

White Horse Restaurant & Bar. 809 W. St. Germain St.; (320) 257-7775; www.white horsemn.com. The menu changes frequently, but it's always globally diverse and creative with items such as crab bisque, Senegalese peanut soup, Thai steak salad, Indian vegetarian curry, misoyaki salmon, and jaegerschnitzel. $$.

where to stay

Heritage House B&B. 402 6th Ave. South; (320) 656-5818; www.heritagehousebbmn .com. This elegant brick 1904 Queen Anne Victorian sits in St. Cloud's historic district not far from the St. Cloud State University campus and downtown. Four guest rooms are named for the area's English, Swedish, French, and German heritage. The English suite includes a soaking tub built into the home's tower. Guests can use the pool table and game room, plus the reading room and a movie library. $$.

Riverside Guest Haus. 912 Riverside Dr. Southeast; (320) 252-2134; www.riversideguest haus.com. This 1937 home sits tucked among the gracious houses along the Mississippi across from St. Cloud State University. It's within walking distance of Clemens and Munsinger Gardens, and does a lot of its own landscaping. Guests can choose from the Garden room with a private second-story patio filled with flowers or the River room facing the Mississippi River. Breakfast is served on the three-season porch or in the kitchen nook. $$–$$$.

Victorian Oaks B&B. 409 9th Ave. South; (320) 202-1404; www.vicoaks.com. With its French Second Empire mansard roof, widow's walk, and wrought-iron railing on the roof, this 1891 Victorian looks like a well-kept haunted house. It's all elegance inside. The candlelit breakfast might include scrambled eggs with feta, bacon, and asparagus; eggs Benedict served with flaming cheese; or the same french toast recipe used on the Northern Pacific Railroad during its heyday. There are 3 guest rooms, including the Lake George Suite with a second-story balcony overlooking St. Cloud's man-made lake. It's an easy stroll to Lake George or to downtown. $$.

day trip 02

northwest

saints, scribes & lake wobegon:
st. joseph-collegeville, mn;
avon-albany, mn; freeport, mn;
sauk centre, mn

If you're a fan of Garrison Keillor's *Prairie Home Companion* every Saturday on National Public Radio, you already have an image of central Minnesota along the I-94 corridor. These are the small towns that collectively inspired Lake Wobegon where "All the women are strong, all the men are good looking, and all the children are above average."

You've also heard plenty of skits and songs that poke endearing fun at Lutheran church basement suppers, mystery hot dish, and things like lime Jell-O marshmallow cottage cheese surprise.

Well, here's a little secret: The Lutherans with Scandinavian descent were added to fictional Lake Wobegon for a dose of ethnic diversity, Minnesota-style. The heritage of St. Cloud and surrounding Stearns County are so strongly German Catholic that even into the 1970s it was considered among the top Catholic counties in the nation—right up there with New Orleans, LA, and New Ulm, MN.

The Benedictine monks and nuns who settled here in the later 1800s built the College of St. Benedict in St. Joseph and St. John's University in Collegeville. Both are known for their dedication to the arts, with St. John's drawing international acclaim for its astonishing hand-scribed St. John's Bible project.

Get off the beaten path enough, and you may catch a German lilt in the patter of older locals playing a hand of Schafkopf (sheep's head, a German card game) in a small-town tavern. Or you might pass backyards where an inverted bathtub creates a mini-shrine to the Virgin Mary.

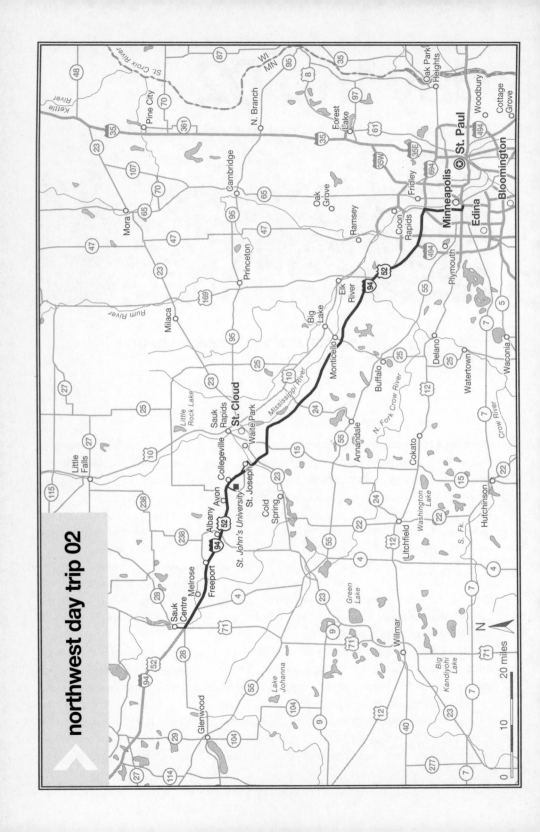

northwest day trip 02

The best way to soak up the rural small-town vibe is by bike, following the 46-mile Lake Wobegon Trail from St. Joseph to Osakis. It appropriately intersects with Sauk Centre, the city that inspired *Main Street,* by another famed Minnesota author: Nobel Prize–winning Sinclair Lewis.

st. joseph-collegeville, mn

St. John's University and Abbey for men and the College of St. Benedict and Monastery for women work together and collectively anchor these two small towns on the western edge of St. Cloud. St. John's commissioned a global team of experts to painstakingly illustrate and write out the Bible by hand—the first such project in 500 years. A video at the university explains how they create the intricate, vibrant illustrations on vellum using feather quills, hand-ground minerals for color, and gold leaf to richly illuminate the pages.

Completed passages have been featured in the Smithsonian, at the Minneapolis Institute of Arts, and alongside the Dead Sea Scrolls. Illustrations include monarchs, dragonflies, birds, and celestial heavens—sights that can be seen on St. John's 2,700-acre rural campus. A wooded path winds around St. John's Lake Sagatagan to the picturesque Stella Maris chapel, or you can wander through large swaths of prairie. Both are good places to meditate on the beauty of art and nature and the lines that blur between the two.

getting there

Follow I-94 about 72 miles to Stearns CR 2, the St. Joseph exit. Collegeville is 3 miles to the northwest. You'll go through one of I-94's prettiest and most wooded passages in Minnesota as you drive under the pedestrian and biking bridge that connects the campuses.

where to go

Art and Heritage Place. St. Benedict's Monastery, 104 Chapel Ln., St. Joseph; (320) 363-7113; www.sbm.osb.org. Some of the best shopping and artwork can be found in this combination museum, gallery, and gift shop. The sisters sell delicate handpainted scarves, handmade cards, jewelry, pottery, and candy and cracked wheat bread mixes from the monastery kitchens. Open 10 a.m. to 4 p.m. Tues through Fri and 1 to 3:30 p.m. Sat and Sun.

Collegeville Orchards. 15517 Fruit Farm Rd., St. Joseph; (320) 356-7609; www.college villeorchardsmn.com. Near the St. John's campus, these orchards draw families for the 20 varieties of apples, pumpkins, harvest crafts, honey and jams, and a petting zoo with alpacas, rabbits, potbelly pigs, goats, miniature horses, and ducklings.

The Grande Depot. 8318 MN 23, St. Cloud; (888) 257-5510; www.thegranddepot.com. This 1912 Soo Line Depot was relocated from Eden Valley to this spot along the interstate where it houses two upscale stores one exit south of St. Joseph. Accentric offers seasonal and home decor, fragrant bath and body products, and gourmet foods such as sauces, dressings, jams, and jellies. Cork and Cask is the place to grab wine or beer, imported cheeses, and crackers for a picnic. Open 9 a.m. to 7 p.m. daily.

Hill Museum and Manuscript Library. 31802 CR 159, Collegeville; (320) 363-3514; www .hmml.org. The main attraction here is the St. John's Bible (www.stjohnsbible.org), but it's also home to the world's largest collection of images from ancient manuscripts—more than 115,000 of them from Europe, Ethiopia, the Middle East, and India. Open 8 a.m. to 4:30 p.m. Mon through Fri and noon to 4 p.m. on Sat starting the first weekend in May through mid-Dec. Free.

Lake Wobegon Trail. 605 1st Ave. Northeast, St. Joseph; (320) 255-6172; http://lake wobegontrail.com. This 46-mile trail begins here and heads north to Avon, Albany, Freeport, Melrose, Sauk Centre, West Union, and Osakis. Each town has trailheads with shelters. Most have water and restrooms or are near a local city hall or cafe. You can take a spur trail to Holdingford and connect to the Soo Line Recreation Trail or to the Central Lakes Trail in Osakis. If you want to sweeten a ride, there's an annual Caramel Roll Ride the second weekend in June.

St. John's Arboretum. Collegeville; (320) 363-3163; www.csbsju.edu/Arboretum. Get oriented at the prairie kiosk on the way onto campus. Trails loop across native prairie, through maple and basswood forest, and across wetland boardwalks that are part of the 2,830-acre arboretum. Natural history lectures are offered fall through spring, along with special events such as the maple syrup festival, spring birding, and a moonlight winter hike to call for owls.

St. Joseph's Farmer's Market. Four blocks north of County Highway 75 on CR 2; (320) 363-7723; www.stjosephfarmersmarket.org. Look for the St. Joseph water tower to find this community hot spot Friday evenings from mid-May through mid-October. Organic vendors within a 30-mile radius sell heirloom vegetables, organic eggs, free-range chicken and lamb, wild rice, apples, artisan cheeses, plants, cold-pressed sunflower oil, baked goods and soaps. Musicians often liven up the scene, and the Lake Wobegon Trail begins from this spot. Open 3 to 6:30 p.m.

where to eat

Kay's Kitchen. 303 College Ave., St. Joseph; (320) 557-0030; www.kayskitchen.us. As homey as its classic neon sign with an ice-cream cone, this has been a gathering place since 1972. Eggs, caramel rolls, and hash browns give way to burgers and pulled pork sandwiches, hamburger steak, pie, and apple strudel during the course of the day. Open daily breakfast through dinner. $$.

where to stay

Abbey Guest House. 31802 CR 159, Collegeville; (320) 363-2573; www.abbeyguest house.org. There are 29 modest rooms in this guesthouse run by the Benedictine monks of Saint John's Abbey. Most face the lake or the Abbey Church and were designed to be part of a quiet getaway. Meals can be included. $.

The Pillar Inn. 419 Main St., Cold Spring; (320) 685-3828; www.thepillarinn.com. About 15 minutes from St. Joseph, this B&B in one of Cold Spring's grander homes has three guest rooms, including one with a Casablanca theme featuring tropical Art Deco decor. Breakfast main courses may include their fruit-filled puff pancakes, sausage crepes, or wild rice quiche. Packages are offered for horseback riding, birding, and massage. $$–$$$.

avon-albany, mn

The Lake Wobegon Trail from Avon to Albany is the easiest point-to-point stretch since the cities are only 6 miles apart with less than 5,000 residents combined. That makes it all the more impressive to know about 10,000 people showed up for a July 4, 2009, live broadcast in Avon to celebrate *Prairie Home Companion*'s 35th anniversary.

The streets are a tad quieter on a typical day. Catch the 10-mile spur to the pretty covered bridge in Holdingford and you can hear the cows mooing.

getting there

The Avon exit of I-94 is 5 miles from the Collegeville exit. Albany is the next exit after Avon.

where to go

Albany Golf Club. 500 Church Ave., Albany; (320) 845-2505; www.albanygc.com. This 18-hole par 72 course looks as inviting as a classic main street with its rolling greens, mature trees, and the historic church steeple in the background. $30/weekends.

Aunt Annie's Quilts and Silks. 109 Avon Ave. South, Avon; (320) 356-1061; www.aunt anniesquilts.com. Look for the vibrant mural, and you'll find this longtime shop that's filled with Asian silks, exotic batiks, African prints, hand-dyed wool and silk cord, and anything else textile artists and quilters would crave. They also sell silk paints and inks and artwork, such as gelatin prints, that use fabric as a medium. Closed Sun and Mon.

where to eat

Fisher's Club. 425 Stratford St. West, Avon; (320) 356-7372; www.fishersclub.com. Favorite items at this lakeside restaurant: Rainy Lake walleye breaded and deep-fried, walleye tacos, homemade pies such as rhubarb, strawberry shortcake, and local Cold

Spring Brewery beers. George Fisher was a major league baseball star and opened the club in 1932. Garrison Keillor became a co-owner in 2005. You can dine outside on the deck overlooking the swimming beach on Lower Spunk Lake. Open late-Apr through Oct. $$.

where to stay

El Rancho Manana Campground. 27302 Ranch Rd., Richmond; (320) 597-2740; www .camperm.com. There are 120 sites at this popular campground, recreation area, and riding stables about 9 miles south of Avon on Long Lake. The 1,208-acre property includes horse trails, family programs, a playground, biking trails, boats, canoes, and hydrobikes for fun along the beach. $.

freeport, mn

This town of about 630 residents sits in the heart of farm country, but you'll see a lot more than cows thanks to the Hemker Park Zoo.

getting there

Head 6.6 miles northwest of Albany on I-94 and exit at CR 11.

where to go

Hemker Park Zoo. 26715 CR 39; (320) 836-2426; www.hemkerzoo.com. This family-run zoo opened to the public in 1994. It offers an impressive array of animals from around the world, including penguins, lemurs, zebra, spider monkeys, wildebeest, a camel, macaws, flamingos, and cranes. Guided tours are offered at 10 a.m. and 1 p.m. Open May 1 to October 31. Admission: $7.25, adults; $6.25, seniors; $5.25, kids 1–12.

where to eat

Charlie's Café. 115 Main St. East; www.charliescafe.com. Come for homey breakfasts, hot roast beef sandwiches, and the Wednesday night German dinners with smoked chops, hocks, pot roast, and wiener schnitzel. If you can only grab one thing, get a "40-acre caramel roll" or a slice of pie. They make meringue look like a work of art. Their bestseller? Sour cream raisin pie. $.

sauk centre, mn

Sauk Centre, population 4,300, is best known as the hometown of Sinclair Lewis, author and first American to win the Nobel Prize for literature. He lived here from 1889 to 1903, working the night shift at the local Palmer House Hotel and writing. He won a Pulitzer for *Main Street,* but it was later withdrawn due to its critical portrayal of small-town America.

You can still stay or dine at the historic 20-room Palmer House, but it's not walking in Lewis's footsteps that draw visitors to lodge here as much as it is its national recognition for numerous ghosts.

getting there

Exit at US 71 off I-94 about 15 miles northwest of Albany.

where to go

Sinclair Lewis Boyhood Home. 810 Sinclair Lewis Ave.; (320) 352-5201; www.visitsauk centre.com. Guides give tours of where Lewis lived with his family from 1889 to 1903 and showed early signs of creativity, mischief, and a deep need for adventure. His father was the town doctor, and you can see how those experiences as well as the literature readings his stepmother hosted were worked into the plots of his books. He wrote 22 novels, 6 of which were set in Minnesota. He's considered one of America's greatest authors—particularly during the 1920s—but his sharp social commentary didn't sit well with his hometown. Nonetheless, when he died in Rome in 1951, his ashes were flown back to central Minnesota. Tours run June through Sept. Admission: $5, adults; $3.50, students; $2, children 6–12.

Sinclair Lewis Interpretive Center. 1220 S. Main St.; (320) 352-5201; www.visitsauk centre.com. Doubling as the convention and visitors' bureau, this interpretive center includes many Sinclair Lewis artifacts, including his college diploma, early editions of his books, his writing desk, and Nobel Prize.

Pride of Main Street Dairy. 214 Main St. South; (320) 351-8300; www.prideofmainstreet .com. One of the state's few remaining dairies sells hormone-free organic milk; rich, creamy chocolate milk; kefir, a drinkable yogurt-like drink; and ice cream.

where to stay

The Palmer House Hotel & Restaurant. 500 Sinclair Ave.; (320) 351-9100; www.the palmerhousehotel.com. Even if you're not spending the night, you can soak up the atmosphere at this century-old main street hotel with original tin ceilings and stained glass. They serve meals from 7 a.m. to 9 p.m. daily. There are also 2-hour history tours the second Sunday of the month for $20/person. If you spend the night, be prepared for things that go bump in the night. The site's original hotel built in 1863 burned down around 1900, but it apparently left a few spirits behind. Guests have reported doors slamming, the sound of knocking, abrupt temperature changes, the voices of children, and lights going on and off—especially in rooms 11 or 17. $.

day trip 03

northwest

land of vikings & lakes:
alexandria, mn

alexandria, mn

All hail Big Ole. This Minnesota Viking has nothing to do with football. But he does stand 28 feet tall in the middle of downtown with the bold claim on his shield: "Alexandria: Birthplace of America."

He's one of Minnesota's best-known characters when it comes to roadside attractions and funny photo ops (where else can you look up a giant man's skirt?). But he also represents one of the state's greatest mysteries: Does the Kensington Runestone found in 1898 prove Vikings were here in 1362—long before Christopher Columbus?

You can draw your own conclusions at the local museum or ignore the brouhaha and beeline for the lakes. More than a dozen of them ring Alexandria. No wonder Alexandria has the easy breezy feel of a vacation town with a dash of Nordic flair.

getting there

Follow I-94 about 135 miles to Alexandria. It takes about 2 hours and 15 minutes to get here. Give yourself extra time if you're heading north on a Friday or returning on a Sunday when there's cabin traffic.

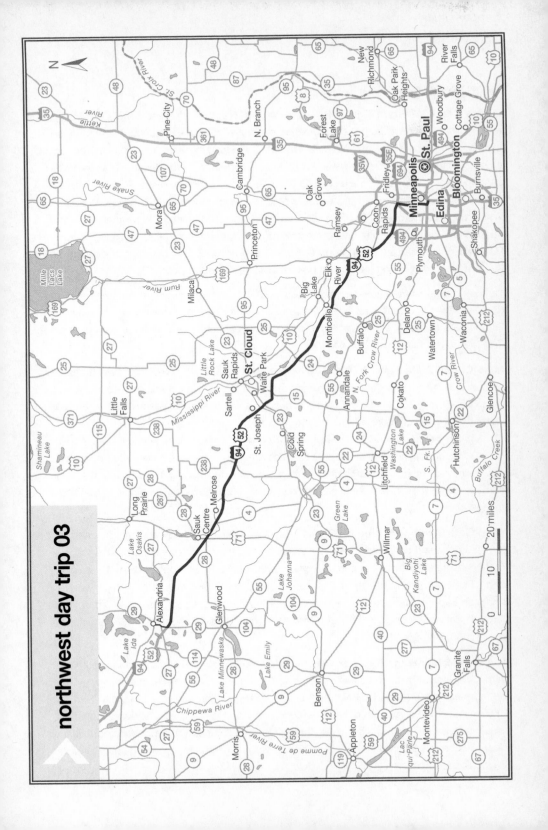

northwest day trip 03

where to go

Carlos Creek Winery. 6693 CR 34; (320) 846-5443; www.carloscreekwinery.com. Huge and sprawling, this winery boasts a Siberian elm maze, 8,000 apple trees, frequent enter- tainment, and 2-person surrey bikes ($10 to rent) for touring the vineyard. Winter visitors can cross-country ski along their trails and even have the chance to dogsled in the winter ($30/ person). Year-round tastings are complimentary for their long list of wines. Among them are Celebrate, a sparkling wine with the taste of Honeycrisp apples, Hot Dish Red, Wobegon White, and You Betcha Blush. They also have a peach chardonnay and several apple and fruit blends. Visit on Sat afternoons for year-round live music or Fri through Sun Memorial Day through Labor Day. Open noon to 6 p.m., staying open an hour later or opening an hour earlier on weekends and during peak season Apr through Dec.

Central Lakes Trail. 206 N. Broadway; (320) 763-3161; www.dnr.state.mn.us. This 55-mile paved bike trail runs along a former Burlington Northern railroad route between Fergus Falls to the west and Osakis to the east, where it connects to the Lake Wobegon Trail that runs south toward St. Cloud.

Lake Carlos State Park. 2601 CR 38 Northeast, Carlos; (320) 852-7200; www.dnr.state .mn.us. Campers can get close to the northern shore of Lake Carlos with many of these 121 campsites. The 1,230-acre state park is also popular for its shallow beach and crystal-clear water that's ideal for young swimmers and toddlers.

Winter visitors can ski 5 miles of rolling terrain or snowmobile along 9 miles of park trails before connecting to the 500-mile Douglas Area Trail Association network. Snowshoes can be rented, along with GPS units (they're free) for geocaching in warm months. Four camper cabins also available. Fees: $5, daily park pass; $16–$24, campsites; $45–$55, camper cabins.

Minnesota Maritime Museum. 205 3rd Ave. West; (320) 759-1114; www.mnlakesmaritime .org. You can find historic displays on resorts and fishing at this museum, but the focus is on Minnesota's boat manufacturers, including Alexandria Boat Works, Larson Boatworks, and Chris-Craft. It's a great place to admire the skillfully built curves of vintage wooden boats and appreciate how they've evolved over the decades. Open 10 a.m. to 5 p.m. Mon through Sat and noon to 4 p.m. Sun May 15 through Oct 15. Admission: $6, adults; $5, seniors; $3, kids ages 5–17.

Runestone Museum. 206 Broadway St.; (320) 763-3160; www.runestonemuseum.org. While the Runestone anchors this museum with Viking lore, you'll also find extensive wildlife and pioneer-era displays and Native American artwork. You can tour buildings from the 1800s—including a replicated Fort Alexandria and a one-room schoolhouse behind the museum. Open 10 a.m. to 4 p.m. Mon through Sat year-round, with expanded hours during peak season. It's also open 11 a.m. to 4 p.m. Sun in the summer. Admission: $6, adults; $5, seniors; $3, children.

Theatre L'Homme Dieu. 1875 CR 120 Northeast; (320) 846-3150; www.tlhd.org. This beloved theater has presented a strong lineup of summer productions—often comedies and light fare—since 1961. You can settle in for everything from *Triple Espresso* to a Patsy Cline tribute.

where to eat

Bug-a-Boo Bay. 2800 N. Nokomis; (320) 846-1122; www.bugaboobay.com. This Lake L'Homme Dieu restaurant draws a crowd with its Caribbean colors, flavor, and festive flare. The menu features items such as jerk chicken, grilled mahimahi, seafood gumbo, steak Oscar with crab and asparagus, and firecracker pasta. You can arrive by boat or vehicle, sit inside or outside, and often catch live music. Open daily for lunch, dinner, and Sunday brunch during the summer. Closed for weekday lunches and all day Monday in the off-season. $$–$$$.

Depot Express. 104 Broadway St.; (320) 763-7712; www.depot-express.com. You can get three meals a day in this historic Burlington Northern depot with a patio overlooking Lake Agnes and a location right along the Central Lakes Trail. Among their signature items are a wild rice crunch salad (with crispy chicken), strawberry salad, a crab bucket, beer-battered walleye, specialty pizzas, a sweet caramel apple pizza, popovers with honey butter, and ice-cream drinks. Open 8 a.m. to 1 a.m. $$–$$$.

Eddy's Interlachen Inn. 4960 CR 42 Northeast; (320) 846-1051; www.interlacheninn .com. Located near the thin strip of land separating Lake L'Homme Dieu and Lake Carlos, this restaurant serves homey meals such as meatloaf, along with green-olive cheeseburgers with homemade potato chips, salmon Oscar served over baked barley and pasta L'Homme Dieu with chicken, Italian sausage, and sun-dried tomatoes in a cream sauce. $$–$$$.

Sixth Avenue Wine and Ale. 115 6th Ave. East; (320) 759-2277; www.sixthavenuewine andale.com. Linger over wine with an assortment of meats, olives, artisan cheeses, spiced nuts, fruit, and french bread. Entrees include roast pork with apple and cranberry chutney, crab-stuffed sole, and shrimp pizza and pastas. Dip into a chocolate fondue pot or the chocolate blossom, dark chocolate ganache and toasted walnuts wrapped in puff pastry and drizzled with caramel. Open 4 to 10 p.m. Tues and Wed, 4 to 11:30 p.m. Thurs through Sat. $$.

Terrace Mill Company Restaurant. 27165 Old Mill Pond Rd., Terrace; (320) 278-2233; www.terracemill.org. A scenic road trip 12 miles south of Alexandria takes you to this popular summer restaurant overlooking a pretty pond. The 1903 storefront is filled with unique wood sculptures by Orlando Haugland and features an idyllic porch for surprisingly diverse lunch offerings. Look for Greek and chicken salads, lasagna and linguini with meatballs, Moroccan meatballs, ponsit (the national dish of the Philippines) and pastitsio, a Greek dish with layers of pasta, cheese, meat, and a white cream sauce. Afterward, you can tour one of the few survivors from Minnesota's heyday as the world's milling capital. You can see some of the mill's original equipment and work from local artists. There's also a keystone arch bridge and a Heritage Cabin with a rosemaling and other Norwegian folk art. The mill's terraced lawn is set up nicely for the late-September Fall Festival and Fiddler's Contest. Open 10 a.m. to 2 p.m. for Sunday brunch and from 11 a.m. to 2 p.m. for lunch and 5 to 9 p.m. Wed through Sat Mother's Day through Halloween. $$.

where to stay

Arrowwood Resort & Conference Center. 2100 Arrowwood Ln. Northwest; (320) 762-1124; www.arrowwoodresort.com. This ranks among Minnesota's largest resorts with 200 guest rooms along the shore of Lake Darling in hotel-style rooms, suites, apartments, and newly built log townhomes. The 450-acre resort also is home to Minnesota's first big indoor water park, a spacious indoor pool, beach and boats, trail rides, a golf course, and tennis and basketball courts. There are snowmobiles, sleigh rides, and a skating pond for winter visits. All rooms have microwaves and minifridges. $$$–$$$$.

Cedar Rose Inn Bed and Breakfast. 422 7th Ave. West; (320) 762-8430; www.cedar roseinn.com. There are 4 rooms in this 1903 gabled Tudor mansion, nicely situated within a block of Lake Winona and 3 blocks from downtown. Once considered part of Alexandria's well-to-do "silk-stocking district," it still feels gracious and luxurious with stained-glass windows, vintage furnishings, and fancy chandeliers. Breakfast includes egg bakes, pancakes or french toast, and extras such as caramel rolls. $$.

Peters Sunset Beach Resort. 20000 S. Lakeshore Dr., Glenwood; (320) 634-4501; www .petersresort.com. This classic family resort has welcomed folks to the shores of Lake Minnewaska (the state's 13th largest lake) since 1915. It's about 20 miles south of Alexandria and includes 24 rooms and suites, plus 10 luxury townhomes, and a variety of cottages—some large enough for reunions. Amenities include a beach packed with water toys, basketball and tennis courts, a playground, saunas, and packages for their Pezhekee Golf Course. Meal packages are also available with food served in the historic dining room. Open May through Oct. $$$.

appendix a: regional information

north

day trip 01

Little Falls Convention and Visitors Bureau. 606 SE 1st St., Little Falls, MN; (320) 616-4959; www.littlefallsmn.com.

day trip 02

Brainerd Lakes Area Welcome Center. 7393 MN 371 South, Brainerd, MN; (800) 450-2838; www.explorebrainerdlakes.com.

day trip 03

Nisswa Chamber of Commerce. 25336 Smiley Rd. (Nisswa Square), Nisswa, MN; (800) 950-9610; www.nisswa.com.

Pequot Lakes Welcome Center. Trailside Park (along MN 371), Pequot Lakes, MN; (218) 568-8911; www.visitbrainerdlakes.com.

day trip 04

Cuyuna Lakes Chamber of Commerce. 221 4th St., Ironton, MN; (218) 546-8131; www.cuyunalakes.com.

Mille Lacs Area Tourism Council. 630 W. Main St., Isle (on the southeast corner of Mille Lacs Lake), MN; (888) 350-2692; www.millelacs.com.

day trip 05

Cloquet Area Chamber of Commerce. 225 Sunnyside Dr., Cloquet, MN; (800) 554-4350; www.visitcloquet.com.

Hinckley Convention & Visitors Bureau. 109 Tobies Mill, Hinckley, MN; (800) 952-4282; www.hinckleymn.com.

Moose Lake Chamber of Commerce. 4524 S. Arrowhead Ln., Moose Lake, MN; (218) 485-4145; www.mooselakechamber.com.

Sandstone Area Chamber of Commerce. Sandstone, MN; (320) 245-2271; www.sand stonechamber.com.

day trip 06

Duluth Convention & Visitors Bureau. 21 W. Superior St., Duluth, MN; (800) 438-5884; www.visitduluth.com.

northeast

day trip 01

Falls Chamber of Commerce. 106 S. Washington St., St. Croix Falls, WI; (715) 483-3580; www.fallschamber.org.

day trip 02

Cable Area Chamber of Commerce. 13380 County Hwy. M, Cable, WI; (800) 533-7454; www.cable4fun.com.

Hayward Lakes Visitors and Convention Bureau. 101 W. 1st St., Hayward, WI; (715) 634-4801; www.haywardlakes.com.

east

day trip 01

Stillwater/Oak Park Heights Convention and Visitors Bureau. 201 S. Main St., Stillwater, MN; (651) 439-4001; www.discoverstillwater.com.

day trip 02

Chippewa Falls Visitor Center. 10 S. Bridge St., Chippewa Falls, WI; (888) 723-0024; www.visitchippewafallswi.com.

Eau Claire Area Convention and Visitors Bureau. 4319 Jeffers Rd., Eau Claire, WI; (888) 523-3866; www.visiteauclaire.com.

Greater Menomonie Area Chamber of Commerce & Visitor Center. 342 E. Main St., Menomonie, WI; (715) 235-9087; www.menomoniechamber.org.

southeast

day trip 01

Alma Chamber of Commerce. (608) 685-4442; www.almawisconsin.com.

Pepin Visitor Information Center. (800) 442-3011; www.pepinwisconsin.com.

Stockholm Merchants Association. (715) 442-2266; www.stockholmwisconsin.com.

day trip 02

Red Wing Visitors and Convention Bureau. 420 Levee St., Red Wing, MN; (800) 498-3444; www.redwing.org.

day trip 03

Lake City Tourism Bureau. (877) 525-3248; www.lakecitymn.org.

Wabasha-Kellogg Area Chamber of Commerce. (800) 565-4158; www.wabashamn.org.

day trip 04

Visit Winona Visitor Center. 924 Huff St., Winona, MN; (800) 657-4972; www.visitwinona.com.

day trip 05

Lanesboro Area Chamber of Commerce. 100 Milwaukee Rd., Lanesboro, MN; (507) 467-2696; www.lanesboro.com.

south

day trip 01

Rochester Convention and Visitors Bureau. 111 S. Broadway, Ste. 301, Rochester, MN; (507) 288-4331; www.rochestercvb.org.

day trip 02

Northfield Convention and Visitors Bureau. 205 3rd St. West, Northfield, MN; (800) 658-2548; www.visitingnorthfield.com.

day trip 03

Faribault Chamber of Commerce. 530 Wilson Ave., Faribault, MN; (507) 334-4381; www .visitfaribault.com.

Owatonna Area Chamber of Commerce and Tourism. 320 Hoffman Dr., Owatonna, MN; (507) 451-7970; www.owatonna.org.

southwest

day trip 01

Jordan Chamber of Commerce. 315 Broadway St., Jordan, MN; (952) 492-2355; www .jordanchamber.org.

St. Peter Tourism and Visitors Bureau. 101 S. Front St., St. Peter, MN; (507) 934-3400; www.stpeterchamber.org/convention-and-visitors-bureau.

day trip 02

New Ulm Visitor Center. 1 Minnesota St., New Ulm, MN; (507) 233-4300; www.newulm .com.

west

day trip 01

Spicer Commercial Club. (320) 796-8066; www.spicermn.com.

Willmar Lakes Area Convention & Visitors Bureau. (800) 845-8747; www.willmarlakes area.com

northwest

day trip 01

St. Cloud Convention and Visitors Bureau. 525 US 10 South, Ste. 1, St. Cloud, MN; (320) 251-4170; www.granitecountry.com.

day trip 02

Sauk Centre Convention and Visitors Bureau. I-94 and US 71, Sauk Centre, MN; (320) 352-5201; www.visitsaukcentre.com.

St. Cloud Convention and Visitors Bureau. 525 US 10 South, Ste. 1, St. Cloud, MN; (320) 251-4170; www.granitecountry.com.

day trip 03

Alexandria Lakes Area Chamber of Commerce. 206 Broadway, Alexandria, MN; (320) 763-3161; www.alexandriamn.org.

appendix b: festivals & celebrations

Sometimes events are so big, they become part of a town's identity. Think Grandma's Marathon on the North Shore; Bavarian Blast in New Ulm, MN; or the Birkebeiner in Cable, WI. These are the events that bring people from around the state and around the world. You can celebrate everything from bald eagles and rhubarb to Shakespeare and the defeat of outlaws. This list is by no means complete, but it's a good seasonal sampling to get you started.

For more details and additional festivals, go to www.exploreminnesota.com or www.travelwisconsin.com.

january

Brainerd Jaycees $150,000 Ice-Fishing Extravaganza. Brainerd, MN; www.icefishing.org. About 7,000 participants come from several states away to grab one or more of the 10,000 holes drilled into Hole in the Day Bay on Gull Lake. Winners can drive home a new truck, ATV, or score ice-fishing gear and other big prizes that make this one of the world's largest charitable ice-fishing contests.

John Beargrease Sled Dog Marathon. Duluth, MN; (218) 722-7631; www.beargrease.com. This famed race includes a 390-Mile Marathon and a 150-Mile Mid-Distance Race that run along the North Shore of Lake Superior. Onlookers can join the Cutest Puppy Contest, Opening Ceremonies, and meet mushers in Duluth before it kicks off. Winners can qualify for the Iditarod.

february

American Birkebeiner. Cable, WI; (715) 634-5025; www.birkie.com. More than 9,000 cross-country skiers from around the world meet in Wisconsin's north woods to race more than 50 kilometers (32 miles) from the Telemark Resort near Cable to the finish line in downtown Hayward. The "Birkie" is part of the Worldloppet, a circuit of 15 Nordic ski races held on four continents. It's the largest cross-country ski marathon in the nation.

Eelpout Festival. Walker, MN; (320) 259-6010; www.eelpoutfestival.com. Usually the third weekend in February, this event is Minnesota's twist on spring break with plenty of ice antics, a bit of bawdiness, a polar plunge into Leech Lake, sled dog rides, an on-ice auto race, and competitions for the best ice-house encampment and best catch of eelpout.

Grumpy Old Men Festival. Wabasha, MN; (651) 565-4158, www.wabashamn.org. The town that inspired *Grumpy Old Men* celebrates winter with an ice-shack contest, Frisbee games, golf tournaments on snow, bird watching, and a spaghetti dinner and dance.

march

Soar with the Eagles. Wabasha, MN; (651) 565-4158, www.wabashamn.org. Wabasha's National Eagle Center brings in speakers, special activities, and river tours on weekends throughout March. It is the best time of the year to see eagles soaring, catching fish, nesting, screaming, and chattering. Be sure to not miss this unforgettable experience. There are themed weekends, a variety of speakers, displays, a raffle, and river tours.

april

Bluff Country Studio Art Tour. Southeastern Minnesota; (507) 452-0735; www.bluffcountry studioarttour.com. More than two dozen artist studios and galleries stay open for this 3-day event the last weekend of the month in the Lanesboro, Harmony, and Winona areas. Artwork includes paintings, pottery, jewelry, weaving, quilting, beads, wood carving, and multimedia projects.

may

Kettle River Paddle Festival. Sandstone, MN; www.kettleriverpaddlefest.com. With spring waters rushing, this festival includes the Kettle River Run with a kayak, canoe, and raft race, a whitewater rodeo, paddling films, and fireworks in downtown Sandstone.

100-Mile Garage Sale. Lake Pepin; (612) 309-3995; www.mississippi-river.org. You can mix a scenic road trip with bargain hunting the first weekend in May when 15 Mississippi River towns host citywide garage sales. They range from Red Wing south to Winona on the Minnesota side and across to Wisconsin from Fountain City to Prescott.

Stand Still Parade. Whalan, MN; (507) 467-2696; www.standstillparade.org. The town may be too small for a moving parade, but this lighthearted version draws a crowd for floats, heritage foods, and vendors to this quaint town on the Root River Valley Trail and Bluff Country Scenic Byway.

june

Grandma's Marathon. Duluth, MN; (218) 727-0947; www.grandmasmarathon.com. Usually the second weekend in June, the Grandma's Marathon route from Duluth up the North Shore ranks as the 13th largest marathon in the country and one of its largest multi-race festivals. The 2011 races drew more than 17,000 participants from 49 states and 42 different countries, along with 50,000 race fans and 5,000 volunteers.

Granite City Days. St. Cloud, MN; (320) 251-4170; www.granitecitydays.com. This 4-day event kicks off with a concert and art show and includes a downtown parade, community block party, canoe paddle down the Sauk River, music, and an outdoor expo at Lake George.

Great River Shakespeare Festival. Winona, MN; (507) 474-7900; www.grsf.org. Starting in late June and running for about 6 weeks, this festival includes professional productions of Shakespeare's plays. They change year to year and usually include a mix of tragedy and more lighthearted productions performed at Winona State University.

Rhubarb Festival. Lanesboro, MN; (507) 467-2696; www.rhubarbfestival.org. The first Saturday in June belongs to the sweet-tart plant that made this the Rhubarb Capital of Minnesota. Events at Sylvan Park include rhubarb golf, a rhubarb stalk throw, and cooking contests with soups, chutneys, sauces, jams, and chili.

Rochesterfest. Rochester, MN; (507) 285-8769; www.rochesterfest.com. This weeklong citywide celebration includes dances, concerts, plays and musicals, special tours of Mayowood, a kennel club carnival, Frisbee dogs in action, a treasure hunt, a grand parade, and a moonlight launch of hot air balloons.

Stamman Scandinavian Festival. Nisswa, MN; (218) 963-2620; www.nisswastamman.org. The Pioneer Village comes to life with 3 stages filled with Swedish, Finnish, Danish, and Norwegian music, dancing, and singing. About 150 folk musicians participate.

july

Agate Days. Moose Lake, MN; (218) 485-4145; www.mooselake-mn.com. You'll find traditional elements of a celebration such as music, a car show, and an art show, but there's also a gem and mineral show throughout the weekend and a hunt for agates in downtown.

Bavarian Blast. New Ulm, MN; (507) 359-2222; www.bavarianblast.com. Grab the lederhosen for New Ulm's biggest German celebration of the year. This mid-July weekend includes a grand parade, sauerkraut-eating contest, plus musicians from Germany, regional musicians, beer tents, craft shows, and children's games. Look for appearances by the town's gnomes and Narren, characters that wear traditional carved wooden masks.

Bean Hole Days. Pequot Lakes, MN; www.pequotlakes.com. More than 3,000 people line up for free bowls of the town's prized beans, which are cooked in giant cast-iron pots underground for 18 hours at Trailside Park. The tradition (and secret recipe) goes back more than 70 years and anchors a weekend of events that include a coronation, music, and a hunt for a hidden paddle.

Fourth Fest. Duluth, MN; (800) 438-5884; www.visitduluth.com. This daylong music and food fest at Bayfront Park ends with a lot of bang. About 40,000 pounds of pyrotechnics explode and shower across Duluth Harbor, synchronized to music.

Honor the Earth Pow-wow. Hayward, WI; (715) 634-8662; www.haywardareachamber .com. The largest powwow in North America takes place the third weekend in July and brings in 10,000 people from tribes across the country, Canada, and beyond. The gathering honors Mother Earth and the Creator with traditional drumming, dancing, and singing, plus crafts and food, a coronation, and a traditional arts cooking contest.

Lumberjack World Olympics. Hayward, WI; (715) 634-2484; www.lumberjackworld championships.com. Lumberjacks and lumberjills from the US, Canada, Australia, and New Zealand compete and show off their strength, agility, and speed with events such as sawing, log rolling, and pole climbing.

august

Bayfront Blues Festival. Duluth, MN; (715) 394-6831; www.bayfrontblues.com. One of the largest outdoor music festivals in the Midwest brings together 30 national performances on 2 concert stages with Lake Superior in the background. Additional weekend events include a Moonlight Mardi Gras Cruise and live blues at nearly 20 Duluth nightclubs.

Grand Celebration Powwow. Hinckley, MN; www.millelacsojibwe.org. More than 1,200 dancers, drummers, and singers from nearly every tribe in the US and Canada come for this traditional powwow. Spectators can learn about the tribes' traditions through performers, the foods, and artwork on display.

Lucas Oil NHRA Nationals. Brainerd, MN; (218) 824-7223; www.brainerdraceway.com. More than 100,000 fans pack the stands at Brainerd International Raceway for Minnesota's biggest car-racing event. The full-throttle rumble of engines can be heard from miles away.

september

Carlos Creek Winery Grape Stomp. Alexandria, MN; (320) 846-5443; www.carloscreek winery.com. Huge and sprawling, this winery hosts one of the state's biggest events with its annual September Grape Stomp with multiple live bands, artists, and even an *I Love*

Lucy look-alike contest. The dress division in the Grape Stomp contest could be one of Minnesota's most creative ways to trash a wedding dress or at least give it a new color.

Chequamegon Fat Tire Festival. Cable, WI; (715) 798-3594; www.cheqfattire.com. This weekend of mountain biking events is anchored by a 40-mile race with about 1,850 competitors, with another 900 riders in The Short & Fat, a 16-mile race through the forest.

Defeat of Jesse James Days. Northfield, MN; (507) 645-5604; www.djjd.org. About 150,000 people come to this event the weekend after Labor Day to see townspeople reenact the James Gang's notorious 1876 bank raid. There's also a PRCA rodeo, old-time tractor pull, midway, parade, and arts and crafts show.

Little Falls Arts & Crafts Fair. Little Falls, MN; (320) 632-5155; www.littlefallsmnchamber .com. More than 600 juried arts and craft exhibitors sell pottery, paintings, jewelry, clothing, rugs, furniture, and more at Minnesota's most legendary art show the weekend after Labor Day.

Rock Bend Folk Art Festival. St. Peter, MN; www.rockbend.org. Thousands of people gather along the Minnesota River each September for this free 2-day festival. There are 2 stages going all weekend with a variety of music, along with family activities at Minnesota Square Park.

october

Harvest Fest and Giant Pumpkin Weigh-Off. Stillwater, MN; (651) 351-1717; http:// discoverstillwater.com. The biggest pumpkins in the Midwest are brought to the shores of the St. Croix River for a weigh-off. The world record of 1,810.5 lbs. was set here in 2010. The event includes vendors, a street dance, a pumpkin drop, carving demonstrations, chili feed, beer and wine tasting, gondola and trolley rides, and even a regatta for folks game enough to paddle a carved out pumpkin down the river.

Irvin Haunted Ship. Duluth, MN; (218) 722-5573; www.decc.org. This retired ore ship offers an extra dose of eerie and puts a different spin on a typical walk through a Halloween haunted house. The event runs throughout the month until Halloween.

South Central Minnesota Studio Art Tour. www.studioarttour.com. Close to two dozen studios open their doors and display paintings, sculpture, pottery, textiles, stained glass, and jewelry created by close to four dozen artists from Northfield, Faribault, and Cannon Falls.

november

Bentleyville. Duluth, MN; (218) 740-3535; www.bentleyvilleusa.org. The free Bentleyville Tour of Lights Thanksgiving through Christmas transforms Bayfront Park into an illuminated wonderland with a castle, replicas of the lift bridge and ore boats, and lights that synchronize with music. Bonfires are kept blazing for warmth and roasting marshmallows.

Polar Express. Duluth, MN; (218) 722-1273; www.northshorescenicrailroad.org. Kids can have their own Polar Express experience Friday through Sunday from the day after Thanksgiving through the weekend before Christmas. The event starts at Fitger's hotel and shopping complex with a campfire, hot chocolate, cookies, Santa, and reindeer before boarding the vintage steam train to The Depot decorated like the North Pole. Each child gets a souvenir bell.

december

Christmas Candlelight House Tour. Winona, MN; (507) 454-2723; www.winonahistory.org. Several historic homes welcome visitors to admire their craftsmanship and wander through rooms extensively decorated for the holidays.

Ice Festival. Sandstone, MN; www.sandstoneicefest.com. This event in Robinson Park includes ice climbing, winter camping, skijoring, snowshoeing, cross-country skiing, and dog sledding.

Lucia Dagen. Scandia, MN; (651) 433-5053; www.gammelgardenmuseum.org. Lucia with her wreath of candles appears for this traditional Lucia Day service in the Gammelgården Museum's historic Gammel Krykan, the oldest surviving Lutheran sanctuary in Minnesota. The Swedish celebration includes a Swedish breakfast buffet and Lucia program by Svenskarnasdag Choir in the community center across the street.

>> index

INSIDERS' GUIDE®

The acclaimed travel series that has sold more than 2 million copies!

Discover: Your Travel Destination.
Your Home. Your Home-to-Be.

Albuquerque

Anchorage &
  Southcentral
  Alaska

Atlanta

Austin

Baltimore

Baton Rouge

Boulder & Rocky Mountain
  National Park

Branson & the Ozark
  Mountains

California's Wine Country

Cape Cod & the Islands

Charleston

Charlotte

Chicago

Cincinnati

Civil War Sites in
  the Eastern Theater

Civil War Sites in the South

Colorado's Mountains

Dallas & Fort Worth

Denver

El Paso

Florida Keys & Key West

Gettysburg

Glacier National Park

Great Smoky Mountains

Greater Fort Lauderdale

Greater Tampa Bay Area

Hampton Roads

Houston

Hudson River Valley

Indianapolis

Jacksonville

Kansas City

Long Island

Louisville

Madison

Maine Coast

Memphis

Myrtle Beach &
  the Grand Strand

Nashville

New Orleans

New York City

North Carolina's
  Mountains

North Carolina's
  Outer Banks

North Carolina's
  Piedmont Triad

Oklahoma City

Orange County, CA

Oregon Coast

Palm Beach County

Palm Springs

Philadelphia &
  Pennsylvania Dutch
  Country

Phoenix

Portland, Maine

Portland, Oregon

Raleigh, Durham &
  Chapel Hill

Richmond, VA

Reno and Lake Tahoe

St. Louis

San Antonio

Santa Fe

Savannah & Hilton Head

Seattle

Shreveport

South Dakota's
  Black Hills Badlands

Southwest Florida

Tucson

Tulsa

Twin Cities

Washington, D.C.

Williamsburg & Virginia's
  Historic Triangle

Yellowstone
  & Grand Teton

Yosemite

**To order call 800-243-0495
or visit www.Insiders.com**

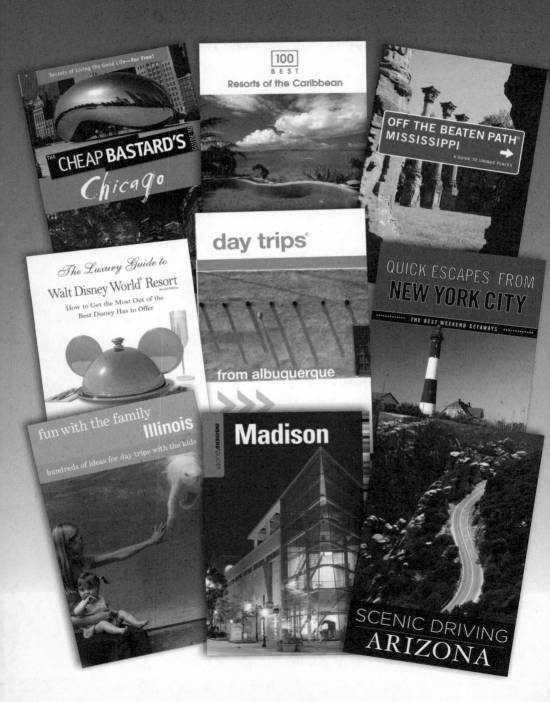